Eckhard Lisec

Turkish Armed Forces From Early History to Modern Times

PELEUS
STUDIEN ZUR GESCHICHTE GRIECHENLANDS UND ZYPERNS

HERAUSGEGEBEN VON HEINZ A. RICHTER

BAND 98

HARRASSOWITZ VERLAG AG WIESBADEN
IN KOMMISSION

VORMALS VERLAG FRANZ RUTZEN
WWW.RUTZEN-VERLAG.DE

Eckhard Lisec

TURKISH ARMED FORCES

From Early History to Modern Times

2020

HARRASSOWITZ Verlag • Wiesbaden
IN KOMMISSION

PELEUS
Studien zur Geschichte Griechenlands und Zyperns
Herausgegeben von Heinz A. Richter
Band 98

Bibliografische Information der Deutschen Nationalbibliothek
Die Deutsche Nationalbibliothek verzeichnet diese Publikation in der Deutschen Nationalbibliografie; detaillierte bibliografische Daten sind im Internet über http://dnb.d-nb.de abrufbar.

Bibliographic information published by the Deutsche Nationalbibliothek
The Deutsche Nationalbibliothek lists this publication in the Deutsche Nationalbibliografie; detailed bibliographic data are available in the internet at http://dnb.d-nb.de

Umschlagvignetten:
Umschlagbild: 2 Fotos von Mustafa Kemal Atatürk
Gegenüber Titelblatt: Innenbild einer Schale des Peithinosmalers, Berlin, Pergamonmuseum (CVA Berlin 2, Taf. 61).

Printed in Germany on fade resistant and archival quality paper (PH 7 neutral).
Gesamtherstellung: Beltz Druckpartner, Bad Langensalza

VERLAG FRANZ PHILIPP RUTZEN
D - 83324 Ruhpolding, Am Zellerberg 21
Tel. 08663/883386, Fax 08663/883389, e-mail: franz-rutzen@t-online.de
In Kommission bei Harrassowitz Verlag • Wiesbaden, www.harrassowitz-verlag.de

ISSN 1868-1476
ISBN 978-3-447-11438-7

CONTENT

FOREWORD

My actual field of research is Greek and Cypriot contemporary history, but since both states are located in a region whose historical developments have an impact on them, I also had to deal with the developments there. The results were studies on the Balkan wars, the First World War (Gallipoli and Macedonia) and the armed conflict with the Ottoman Empire in the Greek-Turkish war. Especially the first studies also dealt with the military in the Ottoman Empire. However, these representations were strictly limited to the time period in which the events took place.

In my search for specialists for the Ottoman Armed Forces I came across the retired Brigadegeneral Eckhard Lisec quite early, who proved to be extremely competent in answering my questions. This was hardly surprising, since he had spent several years as a department head in the NATO Corps Staff in Istanbul and knew the Turkish armed forces very well. During his stay in Turkey, he was interested in the history of the Ottoman Empire and the Turkish Republic. He also learned the Turkish language and deepened this knowledge as a guest auditor at the University of Bonn.

In 2018, the result of his many years of study was available in the form of a book about the Turkish army from its early beginnings to the present. This study closed a gap and in its precise detailed knowledge went far beyond what I knew about the Turkish armed forces.

The study first dealt with the period from antiquity to the conquest of Constantinople in 1453. The second part was devoted to the development of the Ottoman Empire This part is highly interesting, especially those parts that trace the end of the Ottoman Empire. The third part contained a description from the proclamation of the Republic to the present.

While working on my studies, Lisec's account was always a valuable addition to my studies from the Greek and Cypriot point of view. I got the impression that Lisec's study should be made available to a wider readership and should also be brought to the attention of Greece and Cyprus. Due to the language barrier, this could only happen if his study was also published in English.

I felt that Lisec's excellent study fitted into the PELEUS series I edited, as it contained a lot of necessary additional information also about this research area, which was not accessible elsewhere. I therefore suggested Lisec to revise his study on the Turkish Army and translate it into English. He was very enthusiastic about the idea and went to work. We kept in contact and I informed him about the necessary procedures.

Now Lisec's study is available and has been published as volume 98 of the PELEUS series. His study is the only one of its kind in historical research on this subject in a generally accessible language, i.e. English. I can only hope that it will find the necessary interest. As editor of the PELEUS series, I am proud to include this volume in the series.

Heinz A. Richter

INTRODUCTION

Recent events in Turkey have raised the question not only for Turkey but also for the Turkish army "Quo Vadis" ?[1]

Anyone who wants to understand the tradition of the army, in this case the armed forces [2], the thinking and intentions of its Kemalist-style general staff [3], must first delve deep into the history of the pre-Ottoman, Ottoman and Turkish armed forces. The answers to the recurring questions over the centuries are revealing:

- What is the army's mission?
- What is the relationship between the army and politics?
- What is the relationship between the army and religion?
- Can the army keep up with the necessary innovations?

While today the General Staff and the older officer corps - as in other armies - have a largely conservative orientation, this does not apply equally to the younger ones, especially conscripts. Ultimately, they also form part of the supporters of the President of the Republic Recep Erdoğan; Without them, the election victories of the ruling party AKP [4] would have been unthinkable. Influences from the UN, NATO or the EU, from other states, especially in the context of foreign missions, have been added to the Turkish army's leadership and subordinate corps, their corps spirit. The Ergenekon [5] trials showed that even the homogeneity in the general/admiral ranks became fragile, with people burdening each other, active as well as retired, which sometimes led to considerable prison sentences. The extent to which the Fethulla Gülen movement, the re-emergence of Islam and the attempted coup d'état in 2016 have also left their mark on the army will have to be left to future analysis.

It becomes clear that the Turkish army - like the Ottoman army - cannot be regarded as homogeneous. A successful classic coup since 2002, the year the AKP took power, against large parts of the population was hard to imagine. This has also proved true and will probably remain so unless there is a clear change in the political situation, caused e.g. by a tangible economic crisis.

The author does not presume, as an outside observer, to completely feel the heart and soul of the proud Turkish army, to be able to fully understand its thinking, even though he had been a member of four NATO Staffs (in Germany, Belgium, Turkey). Findings from German comrades who e.g. completed a Turkish training course, served temporarily as an exchange officer in the Turkish army, had insight as defence attaché or only had private/official dealings with Turkish soldiers complete the picture. In addition, there are numerous reports by German officers, especially from the First World War, who evaluated the sometimes difficult relationship between the two cultures. Here the range on both sides extends from rejection to adaptation or even admiration. The adapted German soldier was at that time in his homeland with a negative undertone as *"vertürkt"* (too Turkish), while on the other hand the Turcophile German Marshal von der Goltz is still highly appreciated by historically oriented Turks.

---

1 Latin: "Where are you going?" According to the Gospel of John 13:36, Simon Peter asked Jesus, "Lord, where are you going?" This is said to have taken place in the 1st century on the Via Appia in Rome.

2 Turkish abbreviatin: TSK - *Türk Silahlı Kuvvetleri.*

3 Turkish: *Genel Kurmay Başkanı.*

4 *Adalet ve Kalkınma Partısı* - Party of Justice and Progress.

5 Here: A series of trials in the years 2007 - 2016 against hundreds of active/retired soldiers and civilians, which largely ended in acquittals. (see below).

The author also does not presume to know the history of the Turkish military completely, even though he has done extensive literature studies, including Turkish texts. The bibliography at the end of the book is therefore only a small excerpt and does not list the many hundreds of relevant INTERNET files from the Turkish influenced VIKIPEDI or WIKIPEDIA.tr. Most of them are mentioned in the footnotes. A more or less objective picture results only from the exploitation of all information, including personal experiences.

It should not be the purpose of this book to describe even approximately the complete Turkish military history, e.g. the many battles over the centuries. Although they also provide answers to the above questions, they mostly confirm largely timeless military findings, as formulated by Clausewitz [6] (1780 - 1831), for example. However, certain phases of history are more revealing when they shed light on the relationship between the army and its environment. They are more likely to allow conclusions to be drawn about the future role of the army in a modern democracy.

This book is a revised translated version of the author's book "Die Türkische Armee" which was published in 2018,[7]

My special thanks go to Prof. Dr. Heinz Richter for his comprehensive and extremely knowledgeable support in the preparation of this book, both in terms of content and organization. It was his suggestion to make the contents more accessible to the English-speaking world by publishing in the PELEUS series edited by him.

6 Cf. Clausewitz „Vom Kriege".

7 Eckhard Lisec, *Die türkische Armee*. Von Mete Han (209 v. Chr). über Atatürk zur Gegenwart (Berlin: Miles Verlag, 2018) - ISBN 978-3-945861-68-4.

EARLY HISTORY UNTIL THE FALL OF CONSTANTINOPLE

The Origins of the Army before the Foundation of the Ottoman Empire 1299

"Kara Kuvvetleri kuruluş tarihi olarak, Büyük Hun Imperatoru Mete Han'ın tahta çikiş tarihi olan M.Ö. 209 yılı esas alınmıştır." "The main foundation date for the army is believed to be the accession to the throne of the Great Hun Ruler Mete Han in 209 BC."[8]

It is expressed in the coat of arms of the Turkish army (Fig. 1), not in the coat of arms of the armed forces. At that time there was only the army, i.e. the landforces. However, it is explained to both the army and the armed forces that the date of foundation is to be understood symbolically (*sembolik*). [9]

The army is the first and still most important branch of the Turkish armed forces. Its coat of arms is a composition of different elements. Standing in the crossed blades is Mustafa Kemal Atatürk, the founder of the modern Turkish army. Thus the coat of arms could have originated only in the 20th century. The star in the crescent moon has also been added to the Ottoman flag clearly after 1453. The 4 stars could represent the number of two land masses in Europe and Asia and two seas (Black Sea, Marmara Sea) in accordance with the Ottoman inscription on the 1st gate of the Topkapı Palace, built by Mehmet II the Conqueror:

"*Ruler of the two continents, prince of the two seas*".

One could also follow a somewhat mystical representation of Babinger.[10] On a commemorative coin of 1480, three conquered ladies (empires) are standing on a chariot, in front of them Mehmed the Conqueror, inscribed with *"Gretie, Thapesynt, Asie",* translated into our language thus *"parts of the Balkans with parts of Greece, the empire of Trapezunt and Anatolia".* The 4th star (empire) would therefore be an "empty throne chair", represented on the side wall, which the conqueror reaches for. What does it mean? Even the premonition of the later conquest of the Mameluk Empire in 1517? However, the 4 stars also appear in the coat of arms of the navy with the date 1081, even before the foundation of the Ottoman Empire .[11] But possibly the 4 stars only denote "the Army" as the highest command level below the level of the general staff, although even before 1923 during the 1st World War army groups already were formed.

Under the coat of arms the 16 stars symbolize the 16 Turkish predecessor states or empires of the present Turkish Republic *(16 Türk devlet).* However, it is difficult to trace the exact historical events as basis for a national historical hypothesis, as the first written documents only became available in the 14th century, apart from some earlier stone inscriptions in Old Turkish. An equestrian people naturally feeds on oral tradition.

The M.Ö. means *"Milâttan Önce",* i.e. before the birth (of Christ). At the time 209 - 174 B.C. a ruler of the Xiongnu in today's Mongolia and the border area to the Altai Mountains

---

8 Translation of an excerpt from the Turkish General Staff homepage by the author.

9 Until now, the Turkish Chief of General Staff must have led the army before his appointment, even if only for two days.

10 Babinger "Mehmed the Conqueror and his Time".

11 Mantran *"Osmanlı İmparatorluğu tarihi"* p. 178. The author of chapter 5 Bacque-Grammont speaks here of the state/area of the Mamelukes as the 3rd continent, *"üç kıta",* but if the above-mentioned counting method is continued, it will be the fourth. Authors use various fuzzy terms and speak on the one hand of continents and seas, on the other hand of empires.

was in power with the name Mete or Mao Tun or Maodun. Turkish military historiography therefore assumes that the Xiongnu were identical with the Huns, which is disputed by some modern researchers. [1] These Huns become part of the tradition. It is a fact that Mete carried out an army reform, which then, with a tightly-knit equestrian population, severely put the Han Chinese under pressure. This was not only because of their superior horse breeding, but also because of their equestrian and archery skills, including the production of composite bows. Also the invention of the stirrup has probably influenced their art of riding significant.[2]

Under Mete the Turkish term *Ordu*, [3] i.e. the army, is said to have originated, as well as the army structure according to the 10-er system, [4] which Turkey has maintained in the naming of its lower ranks. Genetic and language studies also indicate that Turks and Chinese have some things in common. Even the term "*Turk*" seems to be a Chinese term for a clan from the 6th century: *Tu-kue or Tujué.*

So the Turks obviously have no fear of contact with the Huns, even if the Huns were still used in the 1st World War to insult the Germans by the British: "The Huns". However, this was due to the infamous Hun speech of Kaiser Wilhelm II, who on 27.07.1900 farewelled the German expedition corps to China to suppress the Boxer Rebellion. He referred to the legendary Hun king Etzel [5] and demanded "no pardon".

It is significant that the Turkish army sees its roots long before the emergence of Islam around 622 AD, [6] although according to many Turkish scientists their ancestors possibly already followed monotheism. [7] As is well known, Mustafa Kemal Atatürk commissioned intensive historical and linguistic studies, which should also have proven the leading function of the Turkish language and the complete historical proof of the successful development and expansion of the Turkish people, the Turkish historical thesis. [8] In the end, both approaches could not be proven.

The date of origin 209 B.C., long before the emergence of Islam, at least underpins Atatürk's principle of Laicism *(Laiklik)*, the separation of religion and state, [9] which should also

---

1 E.g. by Schmaucher, Stickler or Scharlipp, because there is no verifiable continuous connection between the Altaic Huns from this time and the European ones in the 4th - 5th century, including the famous ruler Attila. https://tr.wikipedia.org. - *Türk tarihi.*

2 Scharlipp „Die frühen Türken in Zentralasien" p.6.

3 According to Schmauder the term "*ordu*" is assigned to the Avars, who in the 8th century called their circular palace complex with tents and wooden buildings a "ring". In "The Huns" p. 22.

4 So *Onbaşı* - the leader of 10, a non-commissioned officer's rank, or *Yüzbaşı* - the leader of 100, an officer's rank, or *Bınbaşı or Bimbaşı* - the leader of 1,000, a regimental commander.

5 The legendary figure of Etzel probably goes back to the historical Hun king Attila, who ruled in the area of today's Hungary in the 5th century and remained famous for his merciless warfare.

6 The year of the Hijra, the move of Mohammed from Mecca to Medina and the beginning of the Islamic calendar.

7 Other scholars, however, tend to support the thesis of natural religions/shamanism and totemism. Scharlipp, Wolfgang Ekkehard "The Early Turks in Central Asia" p. 56.

8 Known as Sun Language - Theory. *(Güneş Dil Teorisi).* The early Turkish of prehistoric man is the origin of all languages. This Turkish State Doctrine (1936 - 1938), was buried after the death of Atatürk, but still had consequences for the language reforms, which have not been completed in Turkey until today. According to the abstruse theory, Arabic and Persian words did not have to be erased, as they were anyway due to "Proturkish". It remains unclear whether Atatürk himself believed in the theory or pursued a special purpose. Both theories were probably intended to prove a certain superiority of the Turkish people, which is reminiscent of claims of other peoples as well to be the "Chosen People".

9 In the opinion of many, the Anglo-Saxon term "secularism" rather than the term "laicism", coined by France, would probably be more appropriate for Turkey.

apply to the army. However, this extremely important point will have to be returned to several times in other contexts.

The Turkish military history jumps then, probably for lack of concrete intermediate proofs, to the 11th century with the spectacular victory of the Turkish Seljuks at Manzikert or Malazgirt 1071 north of the Van Lake against the numerically superior Byzantines under the Emperor/Basileus Romanos IV (see map1). Before that the Seljuke Alp Arslan had already defeated the Christian Armenians with their capital Ani/*Anı*. Here, the western world suddenly became aware that a Turkish power had established itself in Eastern Anatolia and that the Byzantine Empire was in decline. The term "Turchia" first appeared in Western literature during the crusade of Barbarossa in 1190.

As for all great empires, including the Ottoman empire discussed below, the problem of pacification of the groups on the borders far from the capital Byzantium or later Constantinople or later İstanbul arose at some time, politically or militarily. The means to achieve this were enormous and could only result from a strong economic power. Added to this was the pressure to expand into opposing territories.

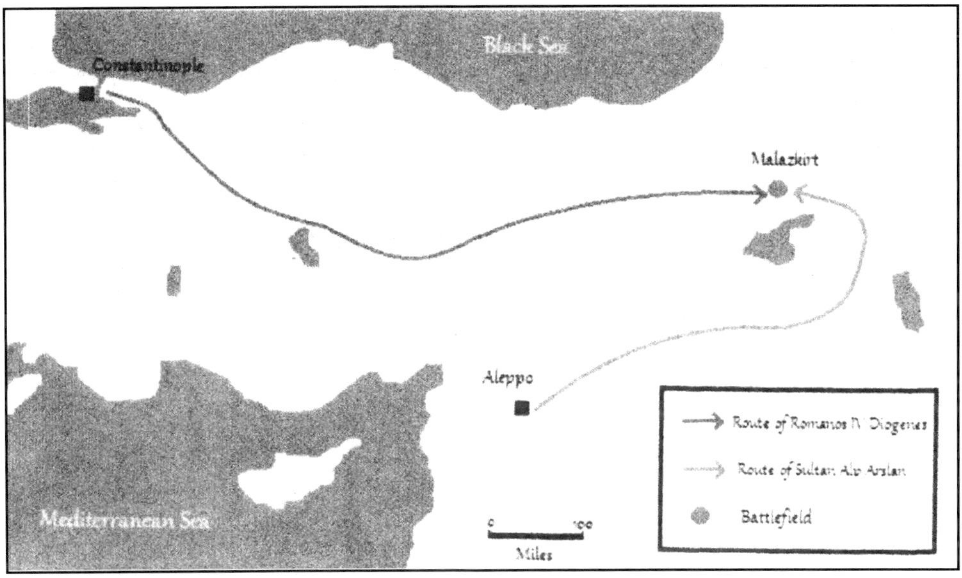

Map 1 The Battle of Manzikert/Malazgirt 1071

The Seljuks, in turn, were defeated by the Mongols[1] in 1243 in the Battle of the Koese Dağ east of Sivas, which led to their decline and the formation of the Ottoman Empire around 1299, initially in western Anatolia. After the conquest of Baghdad in 1258, the Mongols withdrew again from about 1336, also weakened by fights against the Mamelukes.[2]

From the ninth century onwards, these Turkish mercenaries, known for their military prowers as bodyguards or as corset-staff in the troops, entered into various rulers' services, in-

1 Also called İlhane or İlkhane. They founded a state with the capital Tabriz (1256 - 1336).

2 In contrast to mercenaries who served for a limited time, the Mamelukes had to serve for life, thus rather had the status of "bought slave soldiers". Arab. "mamluk" -"taken possession of".

cluding those of the Abbasids. Later, Mameluken-generals became independent and founded their own sultanates, from India to North Africa. In Egypt they replaced the Ismailitic/Shiite Fatimids.[1]

Around 1250 Aybak,[2] a powerful Mameluk ruler, establised a sultanate on the Nile. Since the Mamelukes had supposedly taken in a survivor of the Abbasids.[3] they would have taken over the caliphate as well. The heyday of İslam among the Abbasids, however, was over for the time being.

In 1517, the Ottoman Sultan Selim I defeated the Mamelukes near Cairo and, after a short period of persecution, took them into his own service. Now he ruled over the holy places in Mecca and Medina, which is why he took over the spiritual caliphate in addition to the secular sultanate. The caliphate was to remain in the Ottoman Empire until 1924.

As Sultan and Caliph, who as a non-related of Mohammed at least saw himself as his successor or even as "Allah's shadow on earth," [4] the ruler now united secular and religious power, as did the founder of the religion from the beginning. This central idea of a "God state" naturally contradicts the basic idea of democracy, the "rule of the people". However, the concentration of power gave the ruler - at least apparently - unrestricted freedom of action, which, however, was controlled: Theologically by the thereafter established *Şeyh - ül İslam*, who was allowed to exhibit *Fetva's* [5] works as an expert on Islam; secular laws were issued by the court. The military executed also a controlling function. A similar status was enjoyed by the Byzantine emperors, where the military as well exercised a controlling function, and even the Roman emperors, who were put on the shield by the military.

In the time of the Seljuk Alp Arslan the 2nd service, the navy, developed. The coat of arms[6] (Fig. 2) refers to the foundation year 1081. The aim was to secure the coasts of the Black Sea and the Mediterranean, later to become the naval power in the Mediterranean. Çaka Bey is considered to be the founder, who created the necessary infrastructure in Izmir and had ships built there.

The chronicle of the naval leadership reports that as early as 1090 Çaka Bey near the island of Chios/ Sakız [7] had already put the Byzantines to flight with 17 rowing boats and 33 sailors.

"Bizans Donanması ağır kayıplarla geri çekilmek zorunda kalmıştır". ("After heavy losses the Byzantine fleet was forced to retreat". Translation by the author).

In the 14th century, the Aegean Sea was not only the home of the Byzantines, but also of the Genoese. [8] However, a clear strengthening of the navy, also in terms of armament, only occurred in the Ottoman Empire under the conqueror Mehmet II (1451 - 1481).

---

1 So-called Shiite Seven, who ruled there in the period 909-1171. In contrast to the Shiite 12, they only relied on seven Imams.

2 Turkish: "The one looking at the moon". Also called Aybeg. He reigned 1250-1257.

3 Baghdad, the capital of the Abbasids, was destroyed by the Mongols in 1258, the ruling family allegedly not completely exterminated.

4 The dispute over the status of the caliph had long been a source of concern to the Muslim world, especially the Abbasids. It ended for Turkey with a decision by Atatürk, which exact name the last Ottoman caliph was allowed to bear until 1924.

5 In Arabic fatwa, the legal advice of a Muslim mufti.

6 https://www.dzkk.tsk.tr/icerik *(Türk Deniz Kuvvetleri Komutanlığı Tarihçesi).*

7 West of Izmir.

8 The Republic of Genoa was a naval power in the Mediterranean from the 13th century to 1797, with possessions in Constantinople (Pera, Galata), Trabzon and the Crimea, among others. The Republic and naval power of Venice competed with Genoa until 1797, which also maintained a settlement in Constantinople and trade routes to the Black Sea.

In the meantime, the Turkic tribes in Anatolia had also converted to the Muslim, mostly Sunni-Hanifite faith. This faith was probably, in spite of long and great religious struggles in both great monotheistic religions, already at that time much more attractive than the Christian faith, which contained a picture of the Trinity that was difficult to be understood. [1] The subsequent spread of the Turkic tribes to the West was thus not only that of a secular power but also of Islam. The border peasants and the religious fighters operating at the front, the *Gazi*, were offered land and prosperity in the West, where they were at the same time to have a culturally stabilizing effect in the conquered territories.

The janissaries, cavalry, artillery and the conquest of Constantinople 1453

Around 1299 the Beğ/Emir [2] Osman I (Gazi), leader of a Turkish/Oghusian tribe, founded the Ottoman Empire from a regional principality *(Beylik)* with the first provisional capital Söğüt and declared his territorium independent. Before that he had successfully asserted himself

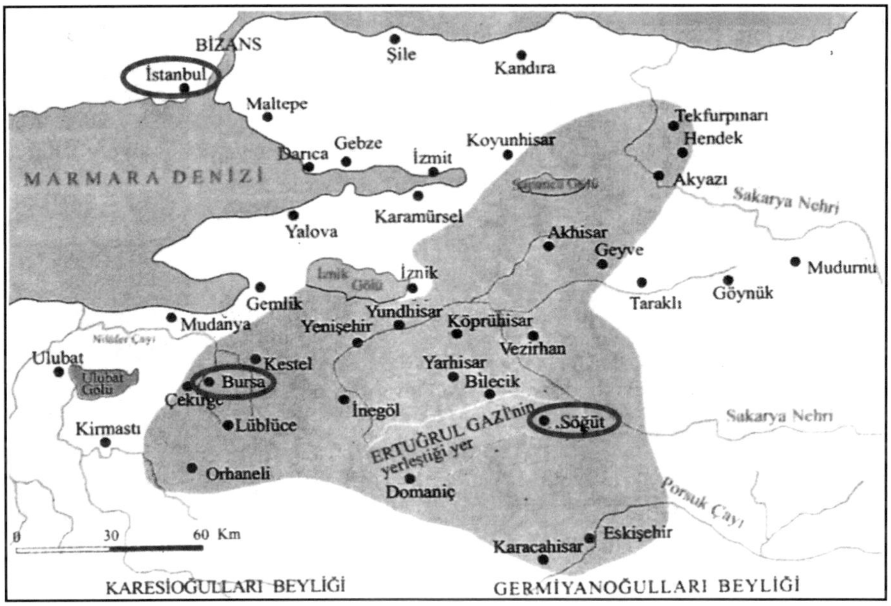

Map 2 The situation in 1326

against the Byzantines and neighbouring Turkish principalities. His son Orhan Gazi (1324 - 1362) moved the capital to Bursa in 1326 after ten years of successful siege. The map shows the geographical expansion around this time.

With the victory of Orhan over the Byzantines at Maltepe on the Kocaeli peninsula in 1329, even the conquest of Constantinople came within realistic reach. However, it was to last

1 See also the persecution of Salman Rushdie and his translators or publishers because of the book "Satanic Verses" (1988) in interpretation of Sura 53 verse 20.

2 Bayezit I (1389-1402) was the first to replace the term "Emir" with the term "Sultan". From 1517 the term "Caliph" was added.

until 1453, after parts of the Balkans had been taken into Ottoman possession about 100 years earlier.

Already in earlier battles, infantry had played an increasingly important role for the warring parties in Anatolia, in addition to cavalry. In the transition from moving battles to more static battles or even sieges of cities, the burden of the battle lay with the infantry, either accompanied by the cavalry or as an independent troop. Orhan awarded non hereditary fiefs to peasants, who in turn had to provide riders *(müsellem)* and foot soldiers (*yaya*) for military service.

Orhan's successor Murat I (1362 - 1389) continued the fiefdom system, whereby a fiefdom was called "*timar*" (Persian) or "*dirlik*" (Turkish), which meant "living". However, in addition to these provincial troops, he created central ones. This was the birth of the central cavalry and janissaries[1], the standing infantry of the Ottomans, the famous elite troops, characterized by an outstanding esprit de corps.[2] With a privileged direct subordination to the leader/sultan and regular payment by him, this quasi-palace troop was to remain incorruptible in contrast to the corruptible mercenary troops. However, later it also formed a "state within a state."[3] In its rise, its heyday and its decline, one can distinguish the three classical phases that apply to so many organizations. Until 1826, the year of its violent extermination[4], they were structured as follows:

First they recruited bachelors,[5] mostly Christians, trained them for many years in riding, archery, javelin throwing from horses, wrestling, races, in different languages, in Islam, and after the introduction of the first handguns in the 15th century also in shooting. Later, in the course of military developments, new training contents were added, combined with specialisations, e.g. for artillery or mining, sapper and pioneer work [6] for armour. The equipment used in combat included composite bows, crossbows, clubs, axes, *Yatağans,*[7] *Hançer*[8] and later rifles.

Even though the janissaries did not have the hard status of slaves[9], they came close to it. Therefore Muslims IAW the Qur'an were not allowed to become janissaries at first. From about 1369 on non-Muslim prisoners of war were forced to be conscripted in interpretation of the right of plunder also towards people according to the Qur'an 8,41.[10] While at first circum

1 *Yeniçeri* - new troops.

2 The Praetorian Guard (138 B.C. - 312 A.C.) of the Roman emperors was also already a standing troop for the direct protection of the ruler or general. Like the janissaries, they also influenced the succession to the throne. The Guard was disbanded by Constantine I after they had fought on the opposing side in the battle at the Milvian Bridge.

3 Pears "The Destruction of the Greek Empire and the Story of the Capture of Constantinople by the Turks p. 227.

4 *Vakayı hayriye* - in a sense the "charitable event" because the undisciplined janissaries had become a plague.

5 Azaben - (Arab.) bachelor, (Turkish.) *azap*. Term also for sailors.

6 Sappeurs e.g. for pioneer-technical position building, miners for tunnelling under walls like during the 2nd siege of Vienna. The different types of troops of the army were gradually created by diversifying the tasks.

7 Single-edged sabre. Mostly carried 2 weapons crossed over the chest.

8 Turk. Double-edged *scimitar*. Term from Arabic origin.

9 The keeping of a "kind of slave troops" was practiced earlier, as e.g. by the Abbasids, also the Seljuks. The prohibition of slavery for Muslims, which stems from Islam, also applied in principle to the Sultan's "recruited" harem ladies, for example. They were usually non-Muslims, but the Sultan was a Muslim. For the janissaries the term "*kul*" was used, which ranges between the term "servant" on the one hand and "slave" on the other. "*Kapı kulu*" was thus the troop at the "High Gate", the "*Bâb-ı Âli*", i.e. at court, the seat of government.

10 Qur'an 8,41 (after Paret): "*And you must know: If you make any booty, the fifth part of it belongs to God and to the messenger and to the relatives, the orphans, the poor and the one on the way...*". The fifth part, the so-

cision and forced conversion to Islam were not binding, because they were also not IAW the Qur'an 2,256, [1] the conception probably changed already towards the end of the 14th century.[2]

The janissaries had to lead a quasi-monastic life, similar to the Templars,[3] were not allowed to marry,[4] were stationed privately, later in barracks, were not allowed to own real estate. In accordance with the Qur'an, they were not allowed to drink wine or gamble. Prostitutes in the entourage were not tolerated.[5] They were only promoted during the war and were protected socially and later also by the medical service in case of injury or retirement. Their kitchen played a major role, and some of their rank was derived from the kitchen business.[6] During the war, pack animals were carried along for the janissaries, which facilitated the so important logistics. Very soon a civilian retinue was also carried along, the so-called "Orducu".[7] who like traders took over the tasks of logistic troops. A complete supply from the country in the conquered territories remained problematic, even though the campaigns were usually limited to the summer months. Even the later central cavalry did not find enough pasture land in the immediate vicinity of Istanbul. The size of an army with many mounts was therefore also subject to logistical limits.

The large soup kettle *(Kazan)* was a symbol of solidarity and protection. A janissary who was being punished could take refuge under the kettle. Conversely, drumming on the upturned cauldron[8] meant riot, later caused e.g. by lack of payment. The protective function of the cauldron can be compared to that of the stirrup of an enemy commander in different armies; in this case, touching the stirrup could even save lives. In peacetime, the janissaries, equipped only with a cudgel or scimitar, exercised a police function in the capital. The leader of the janissaries was called Ağa.[9].

The heyday of the janissaries was between the 15th and 16th century including the conquest of Constantinople in 1453. For the Sultan they always represented a power factor to be considered: "*Even Soliman the Great trembled before them, and they threatened many a sultan with the elevation of another member of the House of Osman.*"[10]

The success of the janissaries was also based on the *Devşirme* (Forced Recruitment) [11] of boys aged 8 - 20 years, demonstrably from 1438 in Thessaloniki/Selanik, from 1512 also in Anatolia. It covered an average of 2.5% of the Christian boys and took place irregularly every 4 - 12 years. In the year 1573 for example 8,000 were "read". Basically excluded were Roma/-Sinti, Romanians, Jews, Moldavians, Walachians, city dwellers, only widow children, married

---

called *pencik,* a word of Persian origin. In the translation of the Turkish *Diyanet,* the religious authority: *"...bilin ki ganimet olarak aldığınız herhangi bir şeyin beşte biri Allah'a, Resülüne, onun akrabalarına, yetimlere, yoksullara ve yolcuya aittir..."* Uyar & Erickson "A Military History of the Ottomans". p 18.

1 Qur'an 2,256 (after Paret): "*In religion there is no compulsion*". After Diyanet: *"Dinde zorlama yoktur".*

2 Uyar & Erickson "A Military History of the Ottomans" p.18. According to this, from 1379 on children were also recruited from Muslim families.

3 The Knights Templar were a spiritual order of chivalry in the period 1118 - 1312, directly answerable to the Pope. They were considered an elite unit during the crusades.

4 Until 1566.

5 Babinger "Mehmed the Conqueror and his time". p. 482.

6 For example "*çorbacı*" = the soup cook plus the rank of an officer as unit commander.

7 Uyar & Erickson "A Military History of the Ottomans" p .25.

8 *Kazan kaldırma* - Soup kettle upside down.

9 Commander of the Janissaries - *yeniçeri ağası.* He was equal in rank to a pasha and became a member of the Ottoman *Divan,* a kind of council of ministers. The term "*Ağa*" comes from the Mongolian with different meanings. In modern Turkish the term *ağabey* was shortened to *abi* and means older brother.

10 Yorga „Geschichte des Osmanischen Reiches", volume III p. 224.

11 Finished in 1683.

people, Anatolians and furthermore Muslims. Thus, the main areas of conquest were those in the Balkans since the middle of the 14th century. After the "harvest", the boys were mostly taken over into Muslim families and brought up there. Afterwards the aptitude of the children was determined and a selection was made for the various military or civil uses. For a large part, education and training was then continued in the training units of the janissaries.

Around 1453 the janissaries are said to have numbered only about 6,000 men[1] including the apprentices. They were organized into companies/*orta* of different sizes. Around 1809 the number of janissaries was already at least 50,000 men, in 1826 according to Wikipedia.tr [2]- even 140,000 (at least on paper). Janissaries were later also stationed at the periphery of the Ottoman Empire to secure the borders, not only of the respective capital: Bursa, Edirne,[3] Istanbul. Some provincial governors imitated the example of the capital, e.g. after 1517 in Aleppo or Damascus, also recruited "palace troops", janissaries and cavalry. However, these local janissaries/ (*yerli kulları*) were sometimes controlled by "imperial janissaries" sent from the capital. Rivalries that arose predictably led to skirmishes.[4]

During the campaigns, the palace troops accompanied their leader,[5] i.e. the sultan, and later, in his place, usually the grand vizier or a vizier, leaving behind a strong "stable guard" to protect the sultan. The trainees were then already employed in this guard. Janissaries were also used to accompany the annual *Hac*/pilgrimage to Mecca.

However, some, especially poor parents did not always see the boy harvest as a cruel early intervention in the families, but also as a chance for their children to have an attractive future. In the meantime, they were able to make a career in the civil palace service as so-called "white eunuchs",[6] but also to rise to top positions in the Ottoman administration due to their good education. The most famous Ottoman architect and master builder (*Mimar*) Sinan (1490 - 1588)[7] was also trained by the janissaries and previously held various military ranks.

After the conquest of Istanbul the strict rules were softened, which resulted in the gradual qualitative decline of the janissaries. Now born Muslims were also accepted from the Balkans,[8] and from about 1560 onwards also born Muslims from Anatolia. The prohibition of marriage,[9] alcohol, real estate ownership, living in barracks, and denial of other professions was lifted. This did not, however, affect their use as police or even fire brigade. In the final phase before their abolition in 1826, the janissaries dominated the flea market in Istanbul, there also as tax collectors, worked part-time or exclusively as oarsmen, landowners, etc. Their comrades in the recruitment offices were bribed. Many of them were only cartel-owners, often also sons of janissaries, who were happy to take advantage of the privileges of service.

Discipline was at its lowest point, mutinies were added, especially when the money was not paid or devalued. As early as 1444, there were the first demands for pay rises.[10] The janis-

1 Mantran "Osmanlı Imparatorluğu tarihi" p. 161.
2 Formerly Vikipedi.
3 Conquered 1361, then capital from 1367. After 1453 then Istanbul.
4 Nicolle "The Ottomans" p. 103/104.
5 Ibidem p. 103/104.
6 In the harem the "Black Eunuchs" served. Africa was in fact the region that provided the most eunuchs.
7 His most famous buildings are the Sülemaniye Mosque in Istanbul and the Selimiye Mosque in Edirne. A subject-related Istanbul University bears his name.
8 Jorga "History of the Ottoman Empire" Volume III p. 221.
9 Also the Catholic Church knows that the abolition of celibacy is problematic, not only for theological reasons. Married people, especially with children, will not be able to devote themselves exclusively to a purpose outside the family.
10 Babinger "Mehmet der Eroberer und seine Zeit" p.36.

saries influenced the dismissal or appointment of the sultans, assassinated Sultan Osman II in 1622 and revolted against the sultan and army renewer Selim III in 1807. Thus, slowly not only the anger of the people was aroused, but also that of Sultan Mahmut II (1808 - 1839). After a renewed uprising of the janissaries on 15.06.1826 the Sultan ordered their destruction.[1] This was carried out in the order of about 6,000 men by another part of the army, supported by artillery, starting at the meat market/*Et Meydanı*[2] in Istanbul; their barracks were located in the district of Aksaray. About 20,000 or so insurgents were arrested or killed, as they were easily recognisable by tattoos.[3] Survivors later earned their living in menial services, e.g. as stokers in Turkish baths (*Hamam*). The fame from the heyday of the janissaries survived, however. Today, after long interruptions, the Janissary music band is the only resurrected unit that is even allowed to wear beards,[4] performs at official events and displays a tourist attraction.

Although the Ottoman Sultan, from 1517 also Caliph, was Muslim - Sunni oriented, he allowed the janissaries to be religiously educated by the unorthodox, rather Shiite Bektaşı - Derviş order.[5] Haci Bektaş[6] lived as a mystic in the 13th century, i.e. before the janissary troops were formed. According to the actually anachronistic legend Hacı Bektaş is said to have wrapped his white sleeve around the head of a janissary and blessed the soldiers, which is why their headgear falling down into the neck shows the characteristic shape shown in the Fig. 4. According to another practical explanation, however, the headgear is said to have had a filling in the back, e.g. earth or sawdust, to soften a hostile blow to the neck. According to other claims, this form cap is said to have been an old Turkic tradition or to have been worn by Scythian archers.[7] Fig. 3 originates from the 6th century BC. The janissary shown in Fig. 4 is already wearing a modern rifle, so the earliest date is the 16th century.

The Bektaşı dervishes even went to war with the other soldiers, sometimes while singing, with a fur on their bare upper body and with bare feet. Their equipment was the halberd or double-axe, in peace their begging bowl and the cooking spoon.

The first pillar of the Ottoman army, however, remained the cavalry. It is necessary to distinguish between the palace cavalry in the capital and in the provinces, regular and irregular, paid and unpaid.

For the protection of the Sultan and the capital, 6 Muslim cavalry regiments *(altı bölük)* were established in addition to the janissaries. This cavalry units e.g. in 1473 comprised about 500 horsemen. They, however, were from the very beginning attached to the Sunni faith. Between both troops at the palace a certain rivalry developed, perhaps due to the different status, faith, salary and origin as well as the different way of fighting.[8]

---

1 Called "*Vaka-i Hayriye*", the "Charity Event". https://wikipedia.org. - *Vaka-i Hayriye.*

2 Often confused in literature with the hippodrome, the *At Meydanı*, even though the riots have been transferred there.

3 Klever "Sultans, Janissaries and Viziers". p. 229. Jorga "History of the Ottoman Empire". Volume V p. 316. The tattoo was a cross on the arm, according to Uyar & Erickson "A Military History of the Ottomans" p.39. Also a field mark or the symbol of the "Holy Cauldron"/"*Kazanı şerif*".

4 Beards are forbidden in the Turkish army, as allegedly not in accordance with laicism..

5 According to Wikipedia.tr. to a Sunni - Alevi (*sünni - alevi*) Islam.

6 Hacı Bektaş himself is probably not the founder of the order. The associated place of pilgrimage is Hacıbektaş in Central Anatolia.

7 According to another representation, this fashion is said to come from Italy. Neumann - Adrian, Michael et al. "Die Türkei" p.190. A janissary cap is still exhibited in Karlsruhe/Germany, which was captured by the felord Ludwig Wilhelm (1677 - 1707), called the "Türken Louis", during the Turkish wars. *Keçe* (turk.) - the neck protection made of felt. Also the forerunners of the janissaries, the infantry of the "*Yaya*", already wore white caps (*Ak börk*). Uyar & Erickson "A Military History of the Ottomans" p. 15.

8 These rivalries also exist in the armies of the present between branches of the armed forces and services. On

The mass of the cavalry was, however, from about 1376 onward held as militias in the provinces, provided by the above-mentioned *Timariotes*, whose fiefs were not hereditary. They were called up for the campaigns and were accompanied by foot soldiers (*Cebeli)*. In the 16th century the total number of *Timar-Sipahi* and *Cebeli* is said to have been about 100,000. The advantage of the non-hereditary feud was that no feudal nobility like that of the knights in the West could develop, the land was returned to the state again, finally by law in 1831.

The riders were called *Sipahi.*[1] Their decline until about 1800 had partly similar reasons as with the janissaries; in addition there was an uncontrolled mismanagement of the fiefdoms and the loss of importance of the cavalry.

Besides the regular cavalry there was the irregular, mostly unpaid cavalry. It was she who stormed ahead of the regular Ottoman army, prepared the way with great hardship and lived on booty. Part of its penetrating power was of course based on its psychological effect. The best known in the West were the *Akıncı*[2] , who to the horror of the defenders stormed ahead, prepared the way and operated with great harshness. Depending on the situation, they also acted on the flanks or in the rear, both of their own troops and of the enemy.

Fig. 5 shows two Akıncı riders in the battle of Mohacs in today's Hungary in 1526. You can see the weapons they fought with.

Traditionally, the Turkic peoples were skillful horsemen, even before the invention of the stirrup, and excellent archers. After a short attack they liked to practise tactically the feinted escape, fighting the pursuer in a so-called "Parthian shot", turning around and later in a crescent-shaped partial encirclement, in order to face and destroy him.[3]

The equipment of the cavalry was partly identical with that of the janissaries. The heavy cavalry, the *Sipahi*, protected their horses partly with saddlecloths, themselves with armoured shirts and metal hoods. The effectiveness of bow and arrow was also based on the penetrating power of the composite bow, also called reflex bow (*yayok*). Besides single shots, the enemy was sometimes fought with a simultaneous hail of arrows, which darkened the sky like a cloud and made evasion almost impossible.[4]

Already Sultan Orhan succeeded in cleverly exploiting Byzantine court disputes, their fratricidal wars and requests for help to extend his sphere of power to the Dardanelles at Gallipoli or Gelibolu. Following a renewed request for help from the Byzantine Basileus/Emperor to put down rebellions in the Balkans, Orhan crossed the Dardanelles in 1353 and settled in Rumelia.[5]

---

the one hand, they are serious in the official fight for importance and resources, but less serious in the form of personal banter.

1 The term was probably adopted via Algeria, a former Ottoman province as "Spahi" in French, as "Späher" in German. So the Sipahi were also "scouts" among other things. With the introduction of armoured troops in western armies in the 20th century, the forward (tank) reconnaissance units became the successors of the reconnaissance cavalry. The term "sipahi" was used in the Ottoman Empire both for the palace cavalry - also called "*Süvari*" - and for those in the provinces.

2 Turkish *"akın"* the blow, incursion, raid or attack. This light cavalry operated - depending on the situation - also laterally to the main thrust, in their own back or that of the enemy. Also known under the name "*Başı Bozuk*", the "distroyers in front". After their extensive dissolution in 1595, the basic idea continued e.g. in the form of individual sabotage troops behind the Greeks in the Turkish liberation struggle of 1919-1923.

3 https://de.wikipedia.org. - Parthian maneuver.

4 Yorga, Nicolae "History of the Ottoman Empire". Volume I. p.485. The next war was sometimes announced one year in advance, which only unnecessarily warned the enemy. p. 486.

5 The southern part of the Balkan Peninsula, which gradually came under Ottoman rule. Eastern Rumelia today corresponds to the European part of Turkey. Turk. designation "*Rum - eli*" = "Rumeli", i.e. land of Rum, the Romans.

In 1361 he occupied Edirne, which became the 2nd great Ottoman capital after Bursa. In 1389, his successor Murat I lost his life after winning the battle on the blackbird field against the Serbs.

His successor Bayezit I (Yıldırım) (1389 - 1402) had a castle built on the Anatolian side at the narrowest point of the Bosporus 1394 - 1397, *Anadolu Hisarı*, while he had besieged Constantinople since 1391. With the victory in the Battle of Nicopolis/Nicopol (Bulgaria) in 1396, the Sultan established the nimbus of invincibility and the actual beginning of the so-called "Turkish Wars". In this battle the light Ottoman cavalry (*Akıncı*) proved superior to the more immovable armoured riders of the crusaders in skilful cooperation with the janissaries. When retreating, the Ottomans let the enemy run into a field with pointed stakes, in order to smash him in return flanked by the Sipahi. The Ottomans' cry of terror was then underpinned by the victory at Varna in 1444, which was followed by further victories after isolated defeats in the west until 1529.

The next siege of Istanbul was to repeat itself, still unsuccessfully, in 1422 under Murat II. The city had, also thanks to its city walls, already repelled many sieges since its foundation in 330 AD and was to remain successful until 1453. Although the Ottomans had to accept military setbacks in the meantime, such as the one in 1402 against Timur-i Lenk/Tamerlan[1], and in other periods of weakness, such as in the civil war 1403-1413, they again armed themselves to go to Constantinople in 1452.

The Byzantine Empire was at that time only a morbid city-state, supplemented by the remote Pelopennes and some islands in the Aegean Sea (Map 3). The Basileus/ Emperor suffered under enormous financial difficulties, did not have a significant fleet[2] or even sufficient operational army. He depended on foreign troops, such as Catalan mercenaries, who became enemies if the Byzantines failed to pay, i.e. the Byzantines were hopelessly at the mercy of the oppressive superiority of the Ottomans. From the conquest of Constantinople in 1453, probably the most important battle of the Ottomans, we shall therefore not describe the course of the battle in detail, but rather mention some special features that should play a role in the sense of our above-mentioned questions about the army.[3]

It should be mentioned beforehand that, according to an old tradition, the Ottomans always offered the population a non-combat surrender with subsequent mercy (*Aman* - mercy) during sieges. According to Kreiser[4] this was in conformity with Sharia/*Şeriat law*, thus an Islamic tradition, probably also of the steppe peoples.

---

1 A relentless Mongolian emir and military leader.

2 In 1453, out of 26 ships on the Byzantine side, only 10 were Imperial, 10 more Venetian or Genoese. Commander of the Venetian fleet Alvise Diedo. Some ships, including Cretan supply ships, had fled as late as February 1453. Some ships had demanded payment from the emperor if they remained. The sailors of these ships were at least partly equipped with small arms.

3 E.g.from Runciman, Steven "Die Eroberung von Konstantinopel" or also from Norwich, John J. "Byzanz". The reports of contemporary Byzantine, Venetian, Genoese, Turkish or authors close to the Vatican, not listed in the bibliography, are contradictory, in need of interpretation, sometimes more like a glorifying court report, biased, emotional or only written down by hearsay. Figures should be particularly questioned. Some questions remain unanswered to this day, such as the period of looting and riots in the city or the exact fate of Basileus, Constantine XI, who was killed in the battle of the city.

4 Kreiser „Kleine Geschichte der Türkei“ p.96.

First of all some remarks on the Ottoman tactics of siege. (Map 4) It reveals planning[1], creativity and the will to fight, whereby these attributes are also to be attributed to the defender. Sultan Mehmet II knew that previous conquests had also failed because Constantinople had only been attacked from the land side. So the navy had to play an important role.

Map 3 The Byzantine Empire around 1450

With the crossing over the Bosporus and the construction of the castle or "storm exit position" "*Rumeli Hisari*" in only 6 months in 1452 on the European side opposite "*Anadolu Hisarı*" on the Anatolian side, the interruption of the supply traffic of the Byzantines, on land and at sea began. Devastations in the surrounding area made the supply of the city even more difficult.

By stationing the Ottoman fleet, mainly consisting of galleys[2], at the "Quay of the Double Columns"[3] in the area of Beşiktaş, the access to the Golden Horn should be prevented by

1 The term "plan" was only later literally taken over from Western languages into Turkish with the associated verb "*planlamak*" - to plan. As a devout Muslim one trusted with a certain fatalism in the rule of Allah, even unto death. In return, the author has gained experience of the excellent improvisation skills of the Turks, a special virtue.

2 Narrow, long, low warships with oars and sails, which in addition to the oarsmen also had considerably more fighters on board. The galleys were manoeuvrable, independent of wind, but not seaworthy. Allegedly they had guns on board as well. Critopulus, Michael "De rebus gestis Mechermetis". According to contradictory information, the Ottomans probably had about 145 ships on the spot after the transfer of ships from Gallipoli, i.e. 91 galleys and 55 pure sailors/supply ships. This resulted in a numerical maritime Ottoman superiority of about 6:1.

3 Diplokion, probably from the time of the Byzantin. Emperor Romanos I (870 - 948). Moltke still believed to have located this building.

sailors who wanted to come to the aid of Constantine XI [1](1448 - 1453) via the Dardanelles. However, this did not succeed in a naval battle on 20.04.1453 against 4 high-board, catapult-equipped sailors under the command of the Venetian Gabriele Trevisano, despite numerically

THE DEPLOYMENT OF THE OTTOMAN AND BYZANTINE TROOPS (ARMY AND NAVY) ON THE EVE OF THE 29.05.1453 IN CONSTANTINOPLE

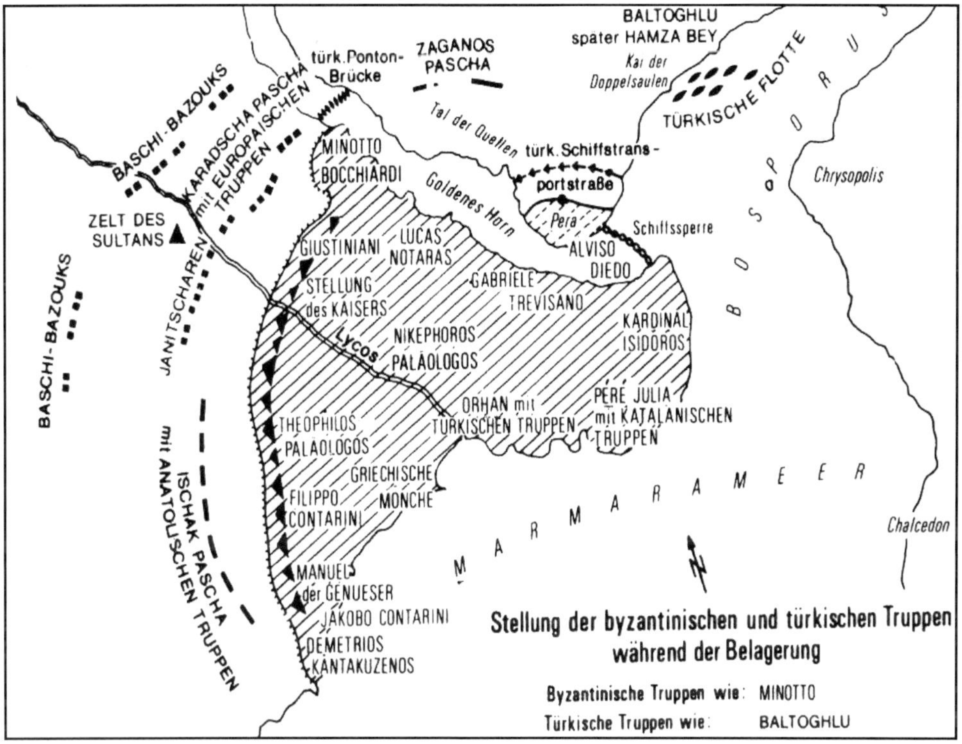

Map 4 *Representations of historical eyewitnesses, the Venetian governor in Constantinople Girolamo Minotto and the Turkish admiral Süleyman Baltoğlu in Runciman, Steven "Die Eroberung von Konstantinopel1453")*

oppressive Ottoman superiority in the Sea of Marmara off the Saray Point, so that the 4 ships were able to escape into the Golden Horn with minor losses after an almost fatal doldrums. Mehmet II punished his admiral Baltoğlu, allegedly a Bulgarian renegade, only with a bastonade[2] and had him replaced by the already experienced commander Hamza Bey[3].

The Byzantines in turn protected the entrance to the Golden Horn since September 1452, after a de facto declaration of war by the Sultan in June 1452, by a guarded floating barrier

1 Sometimes also called Constantine XII or XIII, as the counting method of Byzantine emperors is disputed.

2 Slashes on the sole of the foot.

3 He became the Captain/*Capudan Paşa*. The term "Admiral" is of Arabic origin and derived from *"amiral al - bahr*, " –"ruler of the sea", also called "*Amiral*" in Turkish.

chain, which had been fixed on the eastern side with the obvious help of the inhabitants of Pera/Galata.[1]

In order to reach the Golden Horn by ship nevertheless, the Sultan let about 72 light galleys on greased planks pass over land on 22.04.1453 after obviously already longer preparation under intentionally much spectacle, presumably through cleared forest and through the Maçka Valley past today's Taksim Square, to the great horror of the defenders.[2] The ships were stationed at Kasımpaşa on the north bank of the Golden Horn/*Haliç*, a counterattack by Byzantine ships on 28.04.1453 over the Golden Horn was repelled. On this occasion the Byzantines wanted to use the so-called "Greek Fire",[3] which could not be extinguished by water.

The Golden Horn now came increasingly under Ottoman control, partly due to the action of Ottoman artillery from the north bank, which also allowed the construction of a wooden pontoon bridge that connected to the Ottoman main army west of the land wall.

The main fight, however, took place at the land wall. The tent of the Sultan was built up opposite to the middle of the wall, approximately on the bank of the river Lycos, which flowed in a depression. Today it is no longer visible, as the Menderes Boulevard runs through the land wall there. On the defender's side opposite, the Emperor stayed; next to him, the Genoese Giovanni Giustiniani (Longo) as commander-in-chief of the land forces. The Emperor's army comprised only about 9,000 fighters, recruited from a population of 40,000 - 60,000, and consisted of Byzantines, Genoese, Venetians, Catalans and even Turks. The Sultan's army, on the other hand, comprised an estimated 100,000 fighters, regular and irregulars, cavalry and infantry, with a huge contingent of men and animals.

This results in a numerical ratio of about 10:1 in favour of the attacker. With the appropriate patience of the besieger, he had to win with fatigue tactics alone, no matter what tactical finesse the defender had come up with. After almost 1,5 months of fighting from 11.04. - 29.05.1453, the defender was simply exhausted and worn out, while the attacker threw three waves into the battle one after the other, the best, the janissaries, at the end. Added to this were two almost simultaneous tactical errors by the defender. On the one hand, the defender had forgotten to close a sally port, the Kerkoporta, near Tekfur Palace, and on the other hand, they had tried to rescue Giovanni Giustiniani, who was supposedly wounded by the shot from a field snake, by opening a gate of the inner wall. The psychological effect was devastating, as many defenders were now fleeing. The gaps could no longer be closed; the attacker overcame the already broken walls approximately in the course of the river Lycos. Mehmet II entered the city on 29.05.1453 through the (old) Edirne gate. It was a Tuesday, which is still considered a day of misfortune by the Greeks, who consider themselves the "heirs" of the Byzantines. Immediately after the breakthrough at the land wall, the navy also managed to enter the city from the Golden Horn. In the frenzy of looting, however, they almost forgot their

1 Pera - Greek "over there", because it is located opposite the old town. Today a district of Beyoğlu, just like Galata, today's Karaköy. The name remained famous because of the Galata Tower and the Galata Bridge. 1453 the most important Genoese trade colony, which had to submit to the Sultan on 03.06.1453 because of the collaboration with the Byzantines. Their fleet of 20 - 30 ships, however, behaved passively. The colony was Italian - catholic orientated and also accommodated many Jews.

2 Actions of a similar kind have occurred several times in history, e.g. in 1439 by the Venetians from the river Adige to Lake Garda, perhaps known to the Sultan. In the film by Werner Herzog, Klaus Kinsky played the leading role in a ship transport between two rivers in the South American jungle.

3 *Hygron Pyr*. Byzantine state secret regarding the exact chemical composition. This was not yet known to the Ottomans. The chemical warfare agent had already been successful against Arab sieges of Constantinople from the 7th century onwards. It was transported with crossbows or via pressurized copper pipes on the ship's bow or even by throwing -guns. The addition of saltpetre is said to have produced gunpowder from about 1225 onwards. The means of war can thus also be described as the forerunner of the later flamethrower.

military mission, partly abandoned their ships and thus did not prevent the escape of some besieged with their ships.

SCHEMATIC SKETCH OF THE LAND WALL

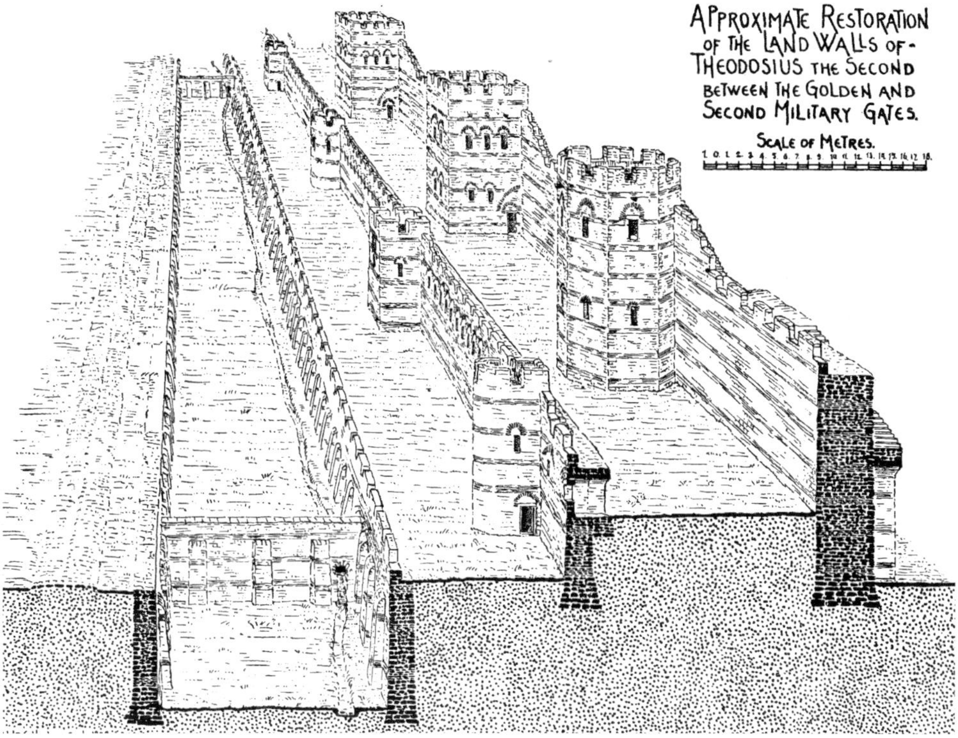

Map 5 Pears, Edwin „The Destruction of the Greek Empire and the Story of the Capture of Constantinople by the Turks". p. 241).

Some military peculiarities should be mentioned. The attacker used without much success a wooden siege tower[1] to overcome the 8m high outer wall, while the defender had entrenched himself between this wall and the 13m high inner wall, the so-called "Zwinger" (Kennel). Furthermore, the Ottomans, supported by Serbian miners and sappers, drove several tunnels against the walls, also without success. The mine warfare was probably still of conventional nature, i.e. with wood, fire and sword.[2] After Georgios Sphrantzes, Greek fire was probably used as counter mines. Explosive mines based on gunpowder were probably not yet available to either party. Mine fighting was to be repeated during the sieges of Vienna in 1529 and

1 Also already used by Murat II in 1422 before Constantinople.

2 During the siege of Vienna in 1529 there is already talk of mine explosions, obviously using black powder/explosives: *"Mines were exploded by Turkish sappers..."*. Lord Kinross "The Ottoman Centuries". p. 191.

1683, but without success for the attacker. In 1669, however, the tactic is said to have been successful in the fight against the Venetians on Crete.[1]

Artillery must be mentioned in particular. It was not - as is sometimes said - the main reason for the Ottoman success, but the almost continuous shelling of the Wall must have been psychologically damaging to the defenders, physically damaging to the Wall due to the large calibres, so that the Byzantines were constantly under repair.

The Fig. 6 shows one of the first artillery guns in Europe in the 14th century. It can be seen that the craftsmen probably came from the bell-foundry sector, the so-called "fire pot" was ignited with a fuse and shot an arrow. The black powder had obviously been developed about 100 years earlier. In Italy guns are said to have been used in Arco as early as 1322, in the Ottoman Empire in 1364 near Bursa, 1366 before Cairo, 1389 in Kosovo and also already during the siege of Constantinople in 1422. Artillery can therefore be seen as the successor to slingshots or catapults in siege technology. In the next stage of development, stones were also fired, followed by iron bullets. A Hungarian/Siebenbürger called Urban or Orban had built a giant gun in Edirne for the Sultan - the Basileus/Emperor allegedly could not afford it - with a bronze barrel of 8m length and 87 cm diameter, stone balls of about 500 kg, a range of about 1.5 km, a cadence of 7 rounds per day. It was transported with great effort to Constantinople until April 1453 and was used there with about 50 other cannons of the Sultan. Urban had allegedly built small cannons before for the Rumeli Hisarı to monitor the Bosporus. The cadence was so low because the barrel first had to cool down repeatedly and then has been greased. Urban may have been killed in a gun blast.

According to Michael Kritobulos, Mehmet II is also said to have given the demand for a steep-fire gun with the shape of the inclined Greek letter "gamma". It was built with the result of sinking a ship off Galata. This would have been the forerunner of a mortar or the later howitzers. Babinger confirms this.[2] After the conquest of Constantinople, a cannon foundry was built in Tophane around 1520.[3]

After Pears and Sphrantzes,[4] field snakes were also used in the battle. These were supported guns of smaller calibre with long barrel, from which arrows or balls made of stone or lead could be shot. A weapon which was mostly operated by 2 men and was used in Europe since the end of the 14th century.

In the 14th century, the development of the first handguns, whose 1st generation were called (stock) rifles,[5] ran almost parallel. Murat II is said to have used them before Constantinople in 1424; in 1453 the 2nd generation, the arquebuses (Fig. 7), were obviously already in use. At first they were heavy two-man guns, whose hooks absorbed the recoil and which were used especially as a laid-on rifle, thus favouring the defender behind a wall. One man aims, one man detonates. A further development was then the matchlock, which reduced the danger to the operators. Because of the low cadence, due to the inaccuracy of aiming and the short range, the arquebus was not really superior to the crossbow as a rifle that could still be ignited with a fuse wick. Arquebuses are said to have been used in 1444 in the battle during the last crusade near Varna, and in 1448 numerous German arquebuses were used by

1 Kreiser, Klaus „Der Osmanische Staat“ p.62.
2 Babinger, Franz „Mehmed der Eroberer und seine Zeit“. p. 94.
3 *Top* - Turkish. ball, *hane* - Turkish “ like arsenal”.
4 Pears „The destruction of the Greek Empire and the story of the capture of Constantinole by the Turks“. Sphrantzes “Die letzten Tage von Konstantinopel”.
5 Sometimes already called muskets by authors, although these were developed later, belonging to the 3rd generation of rifles. These errors resulted from the ignorance of new weapons and their designation in translations. For example, the crossbow was already called an arquebus.

Hungarians in Kosovo. According to Nicolle, in 1465 Ottoman ships are said to have been equipped with rifles (*tüfek*), which probably also meant arquebuses.[1] Already at this point it has to be stated that the equipment of the army with modern rifles should in future lag behind western standards by about 60-70 years, probably also a financial question. Thus, matchlock rifles/"*Fitilli muske*" were first introduced as in the Battle of Çaldiran[2] in 1514, but later the Damascus barrels made of special steel, which allowed a range of up to 300 m, were advantageous.[3]

As an interim assessment of our initial questions from the beginning the following can be stated for the period 1299 - 1453, even if the course of history has only been partially illuminated:

The Ottoman army's mission so far was conquest. It was supported by the above mentioned border peasants, the religious fighters/*Gazi*. With this, new resources could be secured again and again in order to finance the state expenditures and to keep the empire under control. The army went to war almost every summer, from which the agriculture suffered. Of course, this strategy could only be of limited duration, it should have entered a phase of consolidation at some point, i.e. fewer wars. In the 15th century the Ottoman Empire was on the verge of its greatest power.

The regular army of this multi-ethnic state was largely loyal behind the sovereign and his policies. The palace troops, especially the janissaries, as elite troops secured his personal protection and mostly the victory in a battle. The Timariotes provided the mass of the army with the cavalry and mostly ensured the numerical superiority.

The army was up to date in its armor and training. The navy was still at the beginning, which could be explained by a land power with late access to the sea.

The internal structure was sufficiently stable despite the variety of army components. The motivation of the soldiers to fight was, apart from the belief in the regular troops, given by salaries with social security as well as by the *Timar* system; in the irregular troops by looting.

Islam obviously had a great stabilizing influence on the army from the beginning over centuries, on the motivation of the soldier to fight, also to die as a martyr (*şehit*). Many passages in the Qur'an promise the orthodox believer/martyr eternal life in a paradisiacal environment after death, as well as victory through Allah's assistance in war.[4] However, the Qur'an does not cover the suicide of today's asymmetric warfare. Up to the Turkish war of liberation (1919 - 1923), battle cries resounded with reference to Allah. Later, the Holy Flag was also carried along (*sancak şerif*).[5]

Religion also played a major role on both sides in the conquest of Constantinople. However, only the practiced Islam on the Ottoman side will be mentioned here.

Already a *Hadis,* an alleged saying of the prophet, had annouced that the conquest of Constantinople was a religious duty and that the conqueror would receive great reward.

1 Nicolle,David „Die Osmanen" p. 91.

2 https://tr.wikipedia.org. - *Çaldıran Muharebesi*. The name is sometimes translated as "musket", but muskets were not available to the janissaries until about 1578. Uyar & Erickson "A Military History of the Ottomans" p. 50. The matchlock rifle was invented around 1475, so it could have been used here.

3 Kreiser „Der Osmanische Staat" p. 58/59.

4 Eternal life: 2,154. Paradisiacal conditions, great reward, happiness: 3.15 - 4.74 - 5.35 - 15.45 - 47.6 - 52.17 ff. - 78.31. Fight for Islam, victory and support of Allah: 3,160 - 9,40.

5 However, the Ottomans did not take it from Baghdad until 1595, which had been conquered against the Persians in 1534. It is said to date from the time of the 2nd caliph Omar (634-644), the son-in-law of Muhammad. Today it is kept in the Topkapı palace among other holy relics in Istanbul. As it was wrapped in a green cloth, this colour became that of Islam, while the red colour was the colour of worldly power for the Ottomans. See also the Turkish flag of today.

Constantinople was considered a "Golden Apple" since the 7th century, as was Vienna in the 16th century; Mehmet II was probably aware of this *Hadis*.

During the siege, Mehmet II sought advice from the Ulema[1] on whether and when to attack. When setting up for battle, he made sure that on his "right hand" were the predominantly Muslim Anatolians under İshak Paşa, on his left the "European" troops under Karaca Paşa, i.e. those from Thrace and the Balkans, who were probably still predominantly non-Muslim. This Ottoman tradition, which was mostly practiced, was based on the "day of judgment" after death mentioned in the Qur'an and the division of companions according to classes: *"And those of the right - what kind are they? 56, 27. "And Huris are at their service" 56, 35. "And those on the left - what kind are they?" 56, 41. "They are in scorching embers(?) and hot water" 56, 42. (according to Paret).*

Both commanders visited and motivated their troops by speeches on the day before the attack, on 28.05.1453, and gave them time for religious acts; on the Ottoman side according to Sphrantzes not only for ablutions and prayers, but surprisingly also for fasting. Mehmet II promised his soldiers the city as a reward in the holy war, in the narrower sense according to old tradition the permission for the three-day plundering,[2] because Constantine XI had not surrendered. The troops answered with the cry *"Allah is Allah and Mohammed is his prophet"!* Muslim comrades forgave each other before the possible imminent death, a good custom that would last until the 20th century.

Still on 29.05.1453 Mehhmet II visited the Hagia Sophia and converted the site into a mosque. Other churches followed. Only Atatürk revised this in 1935, when among other things the Hagia Sophia was declared a museum. Some Turkish Muslims today demand again the re-conversion into a mosque, as it has already been done with the Hagia Sophia's in İznik and Trabzon.

After the conquest, Mehmet II had the later so-called Eyüb district outside the Istanbul land wall declared the fourth Holy Place of Islam after Mecca, Medina and Jerusalem, but did not formally inform the Islamic world about it. After all, the caliphate was not won until 1517. However, other cities claimed this status even before that, such as Kairouan (in Tunisia) and Damascus. The reason for the declaration was as follows: The Sheikh Akşemseddin was allegedly commissioned by the Sultan to find the place where the Arab banner bearer and comrade-in-arms of the Prophet Mohammed, Ebu Eyyûb El-Ensari, had fallen outside the city during the 2nd (or 3rd) Arab siege of the city in 672 or 674. The place with his sword was "found" and a mosque was built there in 1458, as well as a gravesite. The place is still a central Muslim place of prayer today, especially for women; it houses a large burial ground south of the Golden Horn.

Akşemseddin is said to have performed the sword belting of Mehmet II at this place, an enthronement ceremony which was to be valid for all following sultans there. Later the Mevlevi Dervishes[3] carried out the belting of the sword. After the ceremony a new sultan triumphal procession followed via "*divan yolu*" (Divan street) to the palace in the city centre. According to Ottoman tradition, Mehmet II also had a coin minted, this time with the verbally horned inscription "*Islambol*", which means "full of Islam".

1 The religious scholars in Islam.

2 In the historical accounts it remains unclear whether Mehmet II let the looting or at least the destruction of the infrastructure end still in the evening of the 29.05.1453. In any case, riots against the population continued.

3 In the West also called "Dancing Dervishes". They are a Muslim brotherhood of Islamic mystics (*Sufi*), recently also with female members. They were founded in the 14th century by a son of the Persian mystic Rumi in Konya. His full name was Dschalal ad-Din ar-Rumi with the Persian surnames "Maulana" or the Turkish "*Mevlana*". This means "our master".

Thus, it is important to note that religion played a major role, practically an integral part, for the Ottoman army and its commander at that time.

For the administration of the city, Mehmet II appointed Karistiran Süleyman as governor, coming of course from the officer corps; he left him 1,500 janissaries to ensure public order. This again shows that the transition from the status of a soldier to a civilian or military/civilian office was also a fluid one, just as conversely regional military Turkish commanders, as in World War I, also assumed governor functions in personal union. For the janissaries this meant that they now had to perform police duties as well. Also here a smooth transition and already a forerunner of the Jandarma, a hermaphrodite between military on the one hand and police in the countryside on the other hand, to be founded later in the 19th century.

An indirect effect on the army and the general security situation was also the Sultan's liberal measures regarding non-Muslim religious communities, including non-Muslims in the army. Mehmet II appointed the monk Gennadios II Scholarios as Greek Orthodox Patriarch on 1453, as the office was orphaned. After 1458 follows the appointment of the Armenian Patriarch Hovakim and the appointment of the Grand Rabbi Mosche Kapsalı. These persons were later given powers of limited self-government of their tributary religious communities, which led to the Ottoman "*Millet*"system.[1]

In the overall picture, the conquest of Constantinople in 1453 was a world political event. It meant not only the downfall of the Eastern Roman Byzantine Empire, which had existed for more than 1,100 years, but also the strengthening of Russia by the Byzantines taking over the leading role for the Greek Orthodox Church. This was plus a strengthening of the Catholic religion and the Pope. Mehmet II, however, was able to prevent any further crusade intentions.[2] Islam remained on the advance, as the Ottomans had further expansion plans. The next major goal of the Ottoman Sultans was the second "Golden Apple", Vienna.

But Mehmed II did not fail to take defensive measures, e.g. to protect the Dardanelles from enemy fleets and the facilities there, including the headquarters of the "*Kaptan Paşa*". From 1456 he had two forts built at the narrow part of the Dardanelles, *Kilit ül Bahr* (Sea Castle) on the west bank and *Kale Sultaniye* (Sultan Castle) on the east bank. In 1658, a grand vizier had new forts built at the entrance to the Dardanelles with *Sed ül Bahir* (earth wall at the sea) on the west bank and *Kumkale* (sand castle) on the east bank, mainly against the Venetians. These forts and others also rendered valuable services against the Allies in the Battle of Çanakkale/Gallipoli from November 1914 to January 1916.

With the conquest of Constantinople in 1453, according to Turkish historical understanding, the founding phase (*kuruluş dönemi*) of the Ottoman Empire ends.

The years 1453-1566[3] are called the ascension phase (*Yükselme dönemi*), 1566-1683 the phase of standstill (*duraklama dönemi*), 1683-1792 the phase of regression (*gerileme dönemi*) and 1792-1922 the phase of dissolution (*dağılma dönemi*).[4]

---

1 It was a legal system on the basis of Islamic law. The Muslims saw themselves as the "ruling ethnic group", "*millet-i hakime*". In the 19th century further millets were added, which were finally dissolved in 1923. In Turkish, the term "*millet*" was later increasingly understood as "state" in the context of the emerging nationalism.

2 Generally the battle of Varna in 1444 is considered the end of the last crusade against the Ottomans / Muslims.

3 1566 as the year of death of Süleyman I.

4 https://tr.wikipedia.org - *Osmanlı Imparatorluğu gerileme dönemi.*

THE ARMY IN THE OTTOMAN EMPIRE

Further rise and fall until 1826

With the subsequent conquest of the small empire around Trapezunt/Trabzon in 1461 by an enclosure on land and water, the Greek/Byzantine Orthodox Church in Anatolia lost its last refuge. When in 1478 also the Crimean khanate[1], inhabited by Tatars, with the Crimea and the Sea of Azov came under control, the Ottoman fleet dominated the Black Sea.

Up to his death in 1481, Mehmet II achieved further successes with considerable conquests in the Balkans, in the Aegean Sea, against Venice by taking Morea/the Peloponnese.1479 he concluded an agreement with Venice. He promised the Pope not to attack Rome. In Otranto, Mehmet II temporarily set foot on Italian soil in 1480. The fleet, mainly consisting of galleys based on the Venetian model, had meanwhile taken a great upswing, also through the construction of shipyards.

One problem remained the obligation of rowers for the galleys. They were recruited in the majority of slaves ("galley slaves")[2], from volunteer mercenaries or sometimes from passengers who worked their sea voyage in this way. Galley slaves were e.g. barracked in the feared *Bagno* (ital. "bath") in the district Kasımpaşa in Istanbul in the war port there on the northern edge of the Golden Horn, which perhaps meant the Turkish bath/*Hamam* here, but in general usage in the West was also the term of a penal institution[3].

While under his successor Bayezit II there was a certain stagnation, his successor Selim I was able to occupy Egypt in 1517 through the successful fight against the Mamelukes and take over the caliphate, as already described. This also paved the way for a further expansion along the North African coast. Also parts of northern Mesopotamia with Mosul were conquered.

Before that, however, Selim I had to avert a danger to eastern Anatolia in two respects, which emanated from the Iranian Safavids[4]. In the Battle of Çaldiran nw. of the Van Lake in 1514, he defeated the Safavids, also with the help of superior artillery and "muskets"[5], conquered Tabriz and, in addition, curbed the Shiite[6] influence and separation efforts of Shiite-oriented parts of the population in the east. The Shah Ismail I had decreed for the Safavids the (12er) Shia as state religion and maintained elite soldiers, the so-called *Kızılbaş*/Red Heads.[7] The conflicts with the Safavids were to last until 1590, the year in which the Ottoman Empire bordered the Caspian Sea in the east and reached its greatest expansion there. In the south, Mesopotamia and the Arabian Peninsula including Yemen came under Ottoman control in the 16th century, even though it remained fragile until 1918. Baghdad and Basra were incorporated in 1534-1623, Baghdad then again in 1638-1917. In East Africa, parts of Ethiopia and Northern Sudan, the Ottomans were only able to establish themselves temporarily. The giant empire suffered increasingly from its expansion, unrest at its borders and the limitations of its resources.

---

1 https://de.wikipedia.org. - Khanate of Crimea.

2 Klever „Sultane, Janitscharen und Wesire“ p. 227.

3 https://de.wikipedia.org. - Bagno (penal institution).

4 The Safavids had emerged from a Sufi order that became Shiite. They ruled an empire 1484-1524 with the core area in today's Iran.

5 Schi'at - arab. the party of Ali ibn Abi Talib, the son-in-law of the Prophet.

6 Literally "red heads" because of their red headgear. The 12 tails were supposed to represent the 12 Shiite Imams. Later the term was also applied to the Alevis who were connected with the Bektaşı order. Disputes between these and the predominantly Sunni Ottomans and Turks reach up to the present.

7 https://en.wikipedia.org - Yemen.

With the enthronement of Süleyman I the Magnificent or the Lawgiver/*Kanuni* [1] (1520-1566), according to general opinion, the heyday of the Ottoman Empire began, which reached its greatest expansion in 1683, but on the other hand already in the 16th century showed first signs of decline. Important successes during this period were the conquests of Belgrade in 1521 and Buda/Alt-Ofen as well as Mohaç/Mohacs in Hungary. Once again the old tactics of the Ottoman equestrian people were successfully applied: Simulated retreat followed by an embrace of the enemy.

A first bitter setback, however, was the first siege of Vienna in 1529, from which it is correctly, briefly and succinctly stated in a Turkish textbook of the upper school.[2] "*Ancak Viyana'yı kuşatmak önceden planlanmadığı için gerekli hazırlıklar yapılmamıştı. Büyük topların getirilmemesi ve kış aylarinin gelmesı üzerine kuşatma kaldirildi ve ordu geri döndü.*" ("But the plans necessary for the siege of Vienna had not been made before. Because the big guns had not been carried along and the winter months came, the siege was broken off and the army was repatriated." Translation by the author).

Two important details should not remain unmentioned here. Carrying the heavy artillery was extremely difficult and time-consuming due to the poor road conditions in the Ottoman Empire. Therefore, when deciding to leave them behind, the time factor was obviously predominant.

It must also be noted that in the meantime an artillery corps had become the third pillar of the standing palace troops (*Kapı Kulu*). Murphey[3] lists this corps from 1527 onwards with a strength of about 2,000 men, growing to about 8,000 in 1670. But these figures also included the manufacturers and repairers of the weapons, the *Cebeci*, who outnumbered the operators. Even in modern armies it is important to keep the ratio of fighters to supporters small, the so-called "Tooth or Teeth to Tail Ratio", but on the other hand to have sufficient resources especially for logistics in the broad sense.

But back to the battle. It lasted only from 27.09.-16.10.1529. The army under the leadership of Sultan Süleyman I was about five times superior in numbers to that of the Holy Roman Empire (about 100,000 fighters against about 17,000-20,000),[4] was probably already weakened by previous campaigns, had - compared to about 72-100 guns of the defender - only about 300 light cannons, which were of lower calibre and therefore unsuitable for breaking through the city walls of Vienna. Carrying heavy artillery would otherwise have been a very difficult and time-consuming undertaking. The attacker had possibly not yet sufficiently equipped the Sipahi and Janissaries with arquebuses, in contrast to the defender. The Turks were undersupplied due to previous plundering of the region and remained unsuccessful in the deployment of the miners, as before in Constantinople. The defender had been able to locate the miners' activities by observing filled water vats. Countermeasures taken by the defender were counterblasting (called "squeezing"), clearing out or creating air shafts to reduce the blast effect.

Hummelberger[5] reports some more details. Rain and snow e.g. made it very difficult for the attacker to "mine" due to the high groundwater level, and the softened ground also affected the accuracy of the artillery.

---

1 The western epithet is "the magnificent", the Turkish "the lawmaker".

2 Lise Tarih 2 from 2005.

3 Murphey "Ottoman Warfare 1500-1700" p. 45.

4 According to Kreiser, Klaus, the share of the available central troops (*Kapı kulu*) consisting of janissaries, cavalry and artillery was about 15,000, "Der Osmanische Staat" p. 230. Including the cadets, this number was to grow to 70,300 men by 1670. according to Hummelberger, Walter: „*Kriegsvolk, so auf heutigen Tag alhie vorhanden…über 12.000 zu ross und fuss nit ist*" then still strengthened by about 5.000 men.

5 Hummelberger, Walter "Wiens erste Belagerung durch die Türken 1529".

According to Hummelberger, the defender had also committed major omissions. Due to lack of money, the 4.5 km long ring wall around Vienna was in bad condition, about 900 houses had been built beforehand, all of which had to be torn down to get a free field of fire and to deprive the attacker of cover. In addition, the defender had to sink his 28 "battleships" of the Danube flotilla because no personnel could be found. The moat, which could have been flooded, had been littered, so it had to be emptied first and then left dry. At least from the top of St. Stephen's Cathedral one had a good view of the events.

Already on 08.09.1529 the janissaries demanded their "assault money" with emphasis, probably in the belief to have already won. A similar unruly behaviour was already known from the Lansquenets in the west. Carrying numerous horses made the Ottoman army practically a summer army in winter due to lack of food. Lord Kinross[1] uses the example of this campaign to point out the problem of not being able to carry and care for large numbers of prisoners during the retreat. An exception was probably young, attractive boys and girls who promised to make profit on the slave market in Istanbul.

The loss of about 10,000 men[2] on the Ottoman side had actually not yet been decisive for the Ottoman defeat. Ottoman and Turkish historians,[3] thus not only the so-called "court reporters", let the reader believe that the siege was still quite successful because of the destruction and allegedly higher losses of the defender despite early withdrawal, even if wikipedia.tr at the beginning describes the siege as "*başarısız*" - "unsuccessful". The above mentioned deficiencies are largely concealed here. Figures differ partly clearly, as so often. From today's point of view, therefore, can be determined: The siege was not only based on a wrong political/military decision, but also on considerable planning deficiencies of various kinds. The morale even of the elite troops, the janissaries, was impaired. Lord Kinross[4] points out that unrest by the janissaries mostly took place between the campaigns, so long periods of rest endanger discipline. Ottoman/Turkish historians sometimes distort the events, mostly by omissions. A lack of internal critical faculties of the Ottoman army and its leadership was characteristic, so that it did not allow necessary renewals to become visible. Some deficiencies should therefore be repeated as early as 1683 during the 2nd siege of Vienna.

At sea the Ottomans had a great boom in the 16th century. These included the conquests of the islands of Rhodes in 1523 and Cyprus in 1571. A man named Hızır Reis (1478 1546) came to the aid of Sultan Selim I in his conquest of the provinces on the North African coast. He entered the Sultan's service, conquered Algiers and an area on the Algerian coast in 1529. He then became commander of the Ottoman navy under the name Barbaros Hayrettin Paşa[5]. Among the naval battles won, the victory of Barbaros against a numerically superior fleet of crusaders under the command of the Genoese Andrea Doria on 28.09.1538 near Prevesa or Preveze[6] in the Ionian Sea deserves special mention. This became then the Ottoman day of the fleet. In 1560 the reconquest of the Tunisian island Dscherba/Cerbe took place, which brought the Ottoman Empire for a short time to the zenith of naval rule in the Mediterranean.

A prerequisite for the nautical successes was also the production of nautical charts by the Turkish admiral and cartographer Piri Reis. The most important chart was that of the Medi-

---

1 Lord Kinross „The Ottoman Centuries" p. 192.

2 https://tr.wikipedia.org/wiki - *I. Viayana Kuşatması.* - First Turkish siege of Vienna.

3 Among them is even the Sultan Süleyman I himself, who left a "war diary", evaluated by Behrnauer, published in Vienna in 1858.

4 Lord Kinross "The Ottoman Centuries" p.181.

5 Kaptan-ı Derya - captor/ruler of the sea. After his red beard (barbaros) the North African provinces were then called "barbarian states", which endangered the merchant shipping with piracy.

6 https://tr.wikipedia.org - *Preveze Deniz Muharebesi.*

terranean and Black Sea from the year 1521. This book was entitled "*Kitab-ı Bahriye*", "The Book of the Sea". His later publication of a part of a world map around 1501 with the representation of America can be traced back to Christoph Columbus.[1]

Piri Reis primarily fought as commander of two fleets in the Indian Ocean and south of Egypt against the Portuguese. The command for these two fleets was established in 1525, in addition to the existing command for the Black Sea and the Mediterranean. While the Ottomans gained control of the Red Sea against the Portuguese, this could not be achieved for the Indian Ocean. After a defeat Piri Reis was beheaded in 1554.[2]

A momentous defeat at sea was the Battle of Lepanto/İnebahtı[3] in the Ionian Sea in 1571, i.e. during the reign of Selim II, where about 200 galleys and other ships faced each other on both sides, including 12,000 Christian rowing slaves on the Ottoman side. The Holy League, however, owned 6 modern galleys, which could also use large-calibre guns on the side for boarding. Both parties also had cannons on board, which worked lengthwise. The fighters of the League were obviously equipped with considerably more arquebuses; the Ottomans still fought mainly with bow and arrow.

After a lack of enlightenment the Ottomans were surprised and defeated. After a one-day fight and high losses, the deputy Ottoman commander Ali Paşa managed to escape with 30 ships, about 1/6 of the fleet. He was nevertheless honoured in Istanbul with the subtitle "*Kiliç*" = the "sword". Many surviving Christian slaves on the Ottoman ships were freed.

The Ottoman fleet could be replenished within a year, but the naval supremacy in the western Mediterranean was lost. Instead, the Sultan had the North African provinces, the Barbarian states, from which pirates operated. The cause of the Ottoman defeat at Lepanto must be seen, apart from the element of surprise, above all in the more modern equipment of the ships of the Holy League. The event thus marked the end of Ottoman naval domination, at least in the western Mediterranean. The myth of Ottoman invincibility had suffered again.

In the transition to the 17th century, the Ottoman Empire faced growing problems in its interior. In the provinces farmers left the country because of increased tax burden, the Timar system of the Sipahi broke down consequently, uprisings shook the country. The people, the farmers and also soldiers rebelled against an arbitrary administration, non-Muslims also against the military tax/haraç.[4] The so-called "Celali uprisings"/"*Celali ayaklanmalar*"[5] spread over the whole of Anatolia and other provinces in the core period 1596-1609, and were finally suppressed with difficulty.

Even in the capital, the court troops rebelled in 1589-1592, in order to obtain a salary.[6] an "accession to the throne" (*Bahşiş*), and finally also to have a say in the decision about the throne. Lord Kinross also points to the weakness of leadership of sultans after Suleyman I

1 The first map was discovered in 1789 by the Prussian envoy Heinrich Friedrich von Diez, the second one with the handwritten note about Columbus was not discovered until 1929 in Istanbul. Klever, Ulrich „Sultane, Janitscharen und Wesire". p. 267.

2 https://de.wikipedia.org - Piri Reis.

3 https://de.wikipedia.org - Naval battle of Lepanto - *İnebahtı Deniz Muharebesi.*

4 The tax was levied - also with reference to Qur'an 9:103 - as compensation for exemption from military service, for protection under a Muslim regime and as a gesture of loyalty of non-Muslims to the state. The amount of the annual tax was fixed in a *hadis*, i.e. 2.5% - 7% of the assets. Muslims had to pay the "*zekât*", one of the five sacred duties, as an annual donation. The "*haraç*" for non-Muslims later changed to the "*cizye*". After 1856 the "*bedel-i askeri*" was levied as a substitute tax for military service.

5 https://de.wikipedia.org - Celali uprisings. Named after a sheik Celal in Tokat in 1519.

6 Payments of wages were sometimes withheld for a quarter, as in 1513, because of the time differences between the solar year (levying of taxes) and the Islamic lunar year (wage payments). A so-called "disappeared year" - " *sıvış yılı*". Neumann-Adrian, Michael "Turkey" p. 227.

(1520-1566) and to a justified demand of Muslims for access to all public offices, including those of the janissaries: "*The result, through pressure on a line of irresolute sultans, was the opening of official posts in the Sultan's service to all free Muslims, with the right to bequeath their posts to their own sons*".[1] Kinross also reports several times about the unreliability of the palace cavalry, which e.g. in 1593 had to be disciplined[2] by the janissaries again or about desertion of the provincial cavalry of about 30,000 men in 1596.

The Sultan Osman II was murdered in 1622 with the participation of the janissaries, the Grand Vizier Ahmet Paşa in 1632[3] and the Sultan İbrahim ("the mad") in 1648. Afterwards they forced the 15-year-old Sultan Mehmet IV (1648-1687) to execute public servants. In 1687 the janissaries in return deprived him of his power.[4]

With these uprisings the authority of the state was shaken lastingly, the most loyal and disciplined troops had become unreliable. The tradition of coups d'état by the army has continued - with interruptions - up to the present, also revived by Kemalism in the 20th century.

Murad IV had been the last Sultan in the field in the 17th century, later the Sultans left the "military craft" to the grand viziers. It is also known from modern wars that the political leader as military commander-in-chief could very well consolidate the spirit of the troops on the spot.

In the 17th century, the Ottoman Empire led further campaigns in the east against the Shiite Safavids, who in turn exploited the internal weaknesses of the Ottomans caused by the Celali uprisings and their commitment in the west. Nevertheless, the Sultan was able to maintain Baghdad, but not Tabriz and Revan/Erivan.

Confrontations with Poland initially brought territorial gains. Moldova was recognized by Poland as Ottoman territory, and in the Peace of Buças on October 18, 1672 Podolia was also recognized. This agreement marked a historical caesura. In the Turkish history book mentioned above it says: "*Osmanlı Devleti, Buças Antlaşması'yla batıda son kez toprak kazandı ve en geniş sınırlara ulaştı.*". ("With the Buças Agreement, the Ottoman Empire conquered territory in the west for the last time and reached the widest extension". Translation by the author).[5] In Western literature, the year of the greatest expansion is usually set at 1683, the year of the second unsuccessful Siege of Vienna and the incipient reconquest of Gran/ Esztergom/Nové Zámky/Uyvar[6] in then Hungary by troops of the Holy Roman Empire.

The second siege of Vienna lasted with nearly 2 months (14.07.-12.09.1683) clearly longer than the first siege in 1529. The complete Ottoman encirclement of the city therefore quickly led to a lack of food in the city. While the Turkish descriptions of the siege are very brief and hardly suggest any reasons for the defeat, the Western descriptions are very detailed.[7] Once again the impression is gained that Turkish historians are reluctant to report about defeats, and as mentioned above, that some Ottoman errors of the siege of 1529 were repeated. After previous battles in Hungary, the Ottomans were exhausted again, had left the heavy artillery

1 Lord Kinross "The Ottoman Centuries" p. 617.

2 This is also attributed to the far too low leader density in the cavalry, while the discipline of the janissaries was even better to maintain due to a high leader density (about 1:40). Klever, Ulrich "Sultan, Janitscharen und Wesire" p. 222.

3 As early as 1481, the janissaries murdered the Grand Vizier Karamanî Mehmed Paşa during the disputes over succession to the throne. Neumann-Adrian, Michael "Die Türkeu" p.221.

4 The number of the janissaries had risen to about 80,000 until about 1661, but was then temporarily reduced again to about 30,000 by Mehmet IV. Neumann-Adrian, Michael "Die Türkei" p.255.

5 Almost identical in https://tr.wikipedia.org - *Bucaş Antlaşması.*

6 https://de.wikipedia.org – Schlacht bei Gran or https://tr.wikipedia.org - Nóve Zámky.

7 https://de.wikipedia.org. – Zweite Wiener Türkenbelagerung (23 pages). https://tr.wikipedia.org. - II *Viyana Kuşatma* (4 pages).

behind. Important insights are thus left by the wayside. The descriptions of the second part of the operation, i.e. the decisive battle at Kahlenberg,[1] are of equal short length.

The army had made too few logistical preparations, probably hoping for a short battle. Since according to Turkish data of approx. 120,000 men only 60,000 fighters (*muharip)* existed. These were numerically at least 2:1 superior to the defender with 16,000 - 30,000 men, who were protected by walls strengthened since 1529, artillery less strong. Thus the success of special troop formations was of great importance, such as the alleged 5,000 Ottoman miners. The mine war was fought with bitterness and heavy losses on both sides, now using explosive mines, but ultimately did not lead to an Ottoman breakthrough.[2]

The Grand Vizier Kara Mustafa Paşa, commander on site, had undertaken the siege without the consent of the absent Sultan Mehmet IV, which was to cost the Grand Vizier his life after the battle. Other Ottoman failures were the initial lack of a complete blockade of the Danube Canal into the city, and later before the Battle of Kahlenberg, the securing of the Danube bridges, especially near Klosterneuburg. In this battle, the Ottomans were attacked from the east through the Vienna Woods, so they had to fight on two fronts, leaving too many troops in the siege according to Turkish information. The horses suffered from lack of food and were already exhausted.

Due to the arrival of the Polish King Johann III Sobieski, new commander-in-chief for the troops of the Holy Roman Empire, with his reserve army, the fighting strength ratio turned to the disadvantage of the Ottomans, so that they had to give way to the superiority of the Polish

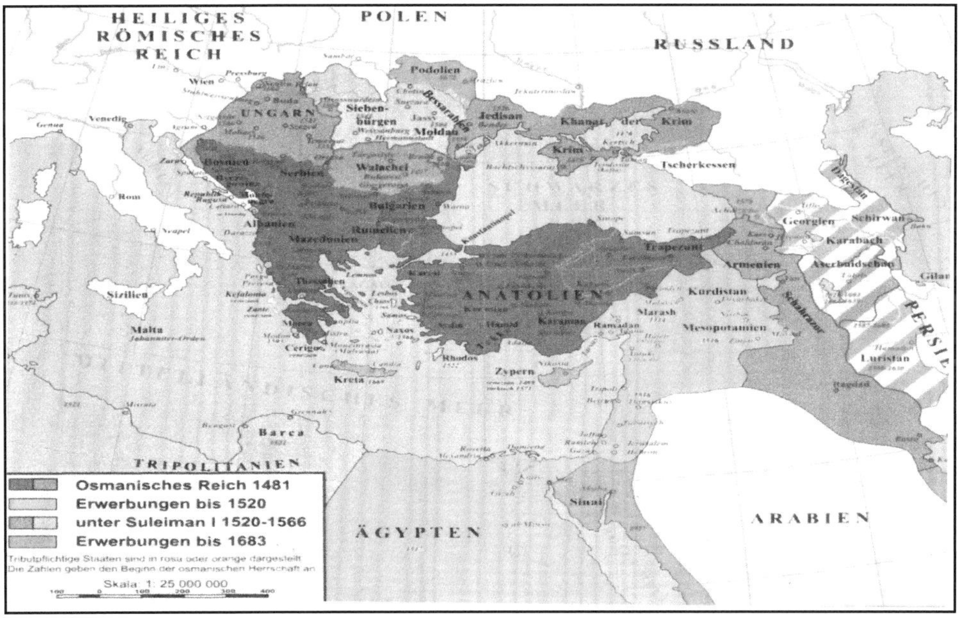

Map 6 Largest expansion around 1683 (Excerpt)

1 https://de.wikipedia.org. – Schlacht am Kahlenberg (4 pages). https://tr.wikipedia.org. - Kahlenberg *Muharebesi* (4 pages).

2 In addition to the janissaries and the sipahi, artillery and pioneer troops had meanwhile been deployed as palace troops, in addition to the troops in the provinces.

cavalry, which stormed down from the mountain in a brave fight on 12.09.1683. This hill had not been secured by the Ottomans before. Morale collapsed and the Ottomans only came to a halt again at the river Schwechat 10 km further east, leaving behind a lot of material and probably many wounded. However, they are said to have taken about 80,000 slaves[1] on the retreat to compensate for some of the financial losses.

The Turkish chronicler summarizes the defeat as follows: "*Psikolojik savaş olarak da Osmanlı üzerinde büyük bir kayıp, Avrupalı ise büyük bir kazanç olarak değerlendirildi"*. ("From the psychological point of view of the Ottomans, the battle was considered a great defeat, but from the European point of view it was a great victory". Translation by the author).

Also faith had its significant place again. The Ottoman Master of Ceremonies names another reason for the defeat: Lack of praise of Allah and the committing of multiple atrocities and sins, i.e. the incensing of the good pleasure of Allah. Also the later strangulation of the defeated and supposedly unrepining grand vizier by order and in the absence of the sultan took place according to a traditional ritual "in due form", i.e. a last concentrated prayer, defiling the body with dust, which was then buried as a corpse without scalp and unwashed.[2] The 5 prayers a day were not waived, nor was the music of several military bands, with emphasis after the last and before the first prayer.[3]

Again a turning point in history was reached. The Sultan and Caliph had to admit that with Austria, and even later with Austria - Hungary,[4] he had an opponent on a par with him, with whom - from a high point of view as the shadow of Allah - negotiations had only been conducted at the level of the Grand Vizier so far.

The agreement of Karlova/Karlovaç/Karlowitz in 1699 brought the Ottoman Empire land losses for the first time in the west, in the Peloponnese, large parts of Hungary, in Podolia. What was now the Ottoman intention? "*Daha önceki batıda ilerleme amacının yerini, bundan sonra, kaybettiği toprakları gerı alma amacı almıştır...hatta gerilemeye başladığını göstermıştır. Bu gerileme, 1921 yılındaki Sakarya Savaşı'na kadar sürmüştür.*"[5] ("Whereas the goal had previously been to advance in the west, the goal now is to regain lost territory...but instead the beginning of a retreat was looming. This retreat was to continue until 1921, the Battle of the Sakarya". Translation by the author).

The long siege of Crete in 1699 brought the island completely under Ottoman control until 1898, when it became Greek property in 1913.

Until the peace of Küçük Kaynarca in 1774, the struggles continued in the west with a break in 1718-1730, the more peaceful so-called Tulip Period/*Lale Devresi*. Until 1774, temporary minor Ottoman successes were also recorded, accompanied by the sending of Ottoman ambassadors to Western countries. A bitter setback was the loss of the Crimea, which was annexed by Russia in 1783.[6] The Ottoman domination of the Black Sea came to an end. But the event also had a religious dimension. For the first time in Ottoman history, a conquered territory, which was also populated by Muslim Crimean Tatars, had to be cleared. Thus now also the belief in the unshakeability of Islam with the promise of victory had suffered, although the Arab brothers in faith had already made this bitter experience long before in the battle of Tour and Poitiers in 732.

---

1 Klever „Sultane, Janitscharen und Wesire" p. 306. According to Klever the total strength of the Ottomans was even 200,000 with the harem included. p. 305.

2 Kretel & Teply „Kara Mustafa vor Wien 1683". p. 199-201.

3 loco. p. 128.

4 Austria- Hungary 1867-1918.

5 Tarih Lise 2 p. 45.

6 Winner was the famous general of Catherine II, Grigory Potemkin (1739-1791).

The trade agreement with Prussia in 1761 was to establish a special bilateral relationship, later between Germany and Turkey, which took its closest form during the First World War. These two countries have - at least practically - never been at war with each other since 1761.

In the won 2nd war with the Russians 1710-1711 on the river Pruth, however, the janissaries again behaved without discipline (*disiplinsiz*) under the Ottoman commander on the spot, Grand Vizier Baltacı Mehmet Paşa, who had to make early peace before a complete victory: "*Ancak Baltacı Mehmed Paşa, Deli Petro'nun ordusunun etrafını sarmışken, isyan belirtileri gösteren Yeniçerilere güvenmemesi nedeniyle barışı kabul etmıştır.*"[1] "Because Baltacı Mehmed Paşa saw that the crazy troops of Peter (the Great) in the surrounding area were going to fraternise and the janissaries showed signs of rebellion, he accepted the peace treaty". Translation by the author).

From the Turkish side, Küçük Kaynarca has been identified:

"Osmanlı Devleti bu antlaşma ile Avrupa devletlerinin üstünlüğü kabul etmiştir."[2] ("With this agreement the Ottoman Empire has recognised the superiority of the European states". Translation by the author).

The Ottoman Empire led campaigns against Iran in the east until 1779, when the river Aras was agreed as the border.

With the invasion of the Napoleonic fleet in Egypt in 1798, a new trouble spot arose there, which was finally eliminated only in 1918. Although the fleet was devastatingly beaten off Abukir by the British Admiral Horatio Nelson, it took further battles to drive the French out again in 1801 with the support of the British and Albanian troops under the command of Albanian-born Mehmet Ali.[3] An immediate consequence was the weakening of the Mamelukes and then in 1805 the appointment of Mehmet Ali Paşa (1769-1848) as an Ottoman provincial governor and thereafter as Khedivian/Vice-King. He was later to help the Sultan again, but also to force him into civil wars in the struggle for power.

In answer to our above-mentioned questions about the mission of the Ottoman army, its relationship to politics, religion and its internal constitution, the 350 years since 1453 can perhaps be summarized as follows, even if the history has only been examined in extracts:

The mission of the Ottoman army was initially still the conquest, with its heyday in the 16th century under Süleyman I. This strategy pursued the constant expansion of the "*dar al-harb*", the "house of war" into the territory of the infidels. However, with the greatest geographical expansion achieved by 1683 and military failures, the focus was now on reconquests. When this was not feasible, however, the new mission had to be limited de facto to the goal of "consolidation", which was not successful either, because until 1921, apart from exceptions, a long series of rearward-looking battles had to be fought, i.e. a slow political and military decline took place. The intervention of changing coalition partners in the respective warring parties created new balances of power; The Ottoman Empire and the Ottoman Army increasingly had to seek allies to achieve their goals.

The loyalty of the army was broken at the latest by the 17th century. Particularly striking examples are the disloyal and partly criminal behaviour of the janissaries and the palace cavalry. Here it was not only about money, but also about co-determination of the state leadership. The army also followed this trend, plus that of the population, who also committed

---

1 *Tarih Lise 2 p. 46. and https://tr.wikipedia.org. - Prut Savaşı.*

2 https://tr.wikipedia.org. – *Küçük Kaynarca Antlaşması.* https://de.wikipedia.org. – Friede von Küçük Kaynarca.

3 https://de.wikipedia.org.- Ägyptische Expedition. https://de.wikipedia.org. - Abukir. https://tr.wikipedia.org. - *Fransa'nın Mısır Seferi.*

insurrections due to the deteriorating economic situation. The author shares the view of Uyar & Erickson:

"The second result was actually not a new issue but rather the worsening of an old problem: Military rebellions and politicization."[1] This problem has continued to the present."

Religion was obviously still a stabilizing factor, even if, according to some authors, the influences of the Sufi orders, especially the Bektaşi order with its proximity to Shia, possibly also had a destabilizing effect. However, the Sultan, since 1517 also Caliph, had the possibility to use his secular and religious authority in cooperation with the *Şeyh ül-İslam.* Surprisingly, this happened much later, namely with the person Abdülhamit II (1876-1909).

The analysis of various battles shows that the equipment of the army, probably also for economic reasons, was not always able to keep pace, while the Ottoman fleet was able to temporarily achieve a supremacy in the Mediterranean and Black Sea.

However, the analysis also shows that defeats were mainly due to poor planning, before and during the battle. Napoleon, on the other hand, had realised that he was in desperate need of expert military advisors/officers in his immediate environment, in peace and war, thus giving birth to the idea of a general staff.

However, the entire secular/religious power and splendour of the Ottoman Empire continued to live on in its symbols, e.g. as with the Ottoman coat of arms (Fig. 8) This has been modified several times in the course of history. It is a combination of figurative representation, especially of weapons and flowers, calligraphy and decoration. The flag on the right symbolizes with the colour red the secular power of the Sultan, here the representation 1793-1844 with crescent moon and still hexagonal star,[2] the flag on the left shows the representation 1517-1844 with the colour green and 3 sickles, the Muslim power of the caliph. The balance in the left part is supposed to represent justice, the two books lying on it the Qur'an and the Kanun, the Sultan's secular law book. At the bottom of the coat of arms are orders. In the upper part a calligraphy and in the circle a *Tuğra.*

Tuğra (Fig. 9) is comparable to a seal of western rulers with a signature. It was already used in the 11th century by the Turkic tribe of the Uigurs and is probably linguistically connected with the Turkish word "*tuğ*". This means a bush of feathers of a bird or tail or tail of a yak or horse. During the campaigns, the Ottoman dignitaries had poles with a different number of tails in front of their tents to mark their rank. (Fig. 10). Thus even today the lowest general rank of the Turks is sometimes called "*Tuğgeneral*", i.e. in the western Armed Forces comparable to the brigadier general.[3]

The Tuğra, which also changed in form and content with each Sultan, contains in the lower part and in the inner left loop the title and name of the ruler, the son of the father with name, if necessary additionally a characterization of the ruler like "permanent victor". In the upper part rising 3 symbolized horse tails, following the first Arabic letter of the alphabet "*alif*". In the right part the extended parallel lines are supposed to represent a dagger (*hançer*) or arm (*kol*). Showing the Tuğra on public buildings was forbidden in 1927 after the previous abolition of the Sultanate (1922) and the Caliphate (1924) by Atatürk, exceptions like at museums

---

1 *„A Military History of the Ottomans" p. 104.*

2 The Turkish flag of today has a pentagonal star and was established in 1936. https://tr.wikipedia.org. - *Turk bayrağı.*

3 The Tugra depicted here is probably that of Abdülmecit I, which would historically fit into the period before 1844. After: Keten "The Ottoman Monograms - Tughra *(Tuğra)*". https://tr.wikipedia.org. - *Osmanlı Imperatorluğu arması.* https://de.wikipedia.org. - Emblem of the Ottoman Empire. https://de.wikipedia.org. - Tughra. The elements of the Tuğra of Mahmut II are explained by colour differentiation e.g. in https://de.wikipedia.org. - Mahmud II.

were allowed. The Ottoman Coat of Arms was only permitted until 1922, the year of the end of the Sultanate.

The army in the 19th century

The 19th century must probably be considered the most difficult century of the Ottoman Empire, culminating in a derogatory term of a "sick man" ("*hasta adam*")[1] (on the Bosporus) and in an International Debt Management.[2] The decline of the economy with the de facto national bankruptcy in 1875 naturally had negative consequences for the maintenance of a powerful army. The 20th century brought further lows with the lost 1st World War and the failed peace treaty of Sèvres in 1920, but then brought the rise again, still in the Ottoman Empire until 1923 under Mustafa Kemal Atatürk, an outstanding personality of the 20th century.

Besides the economic situation, however, the decline of discipline in the army was an important cause of its weakness in the transition to the 19th century, the liquidation of the Janissaries in 1826 (as described before) and the decline of the *Sipahi* system. Already in the 18th century there were strong reform efforts towards a modern army, especially by Selim III (1789-1807), who took advisors from France and tried to implement the ideas. This happened against the will of the Janissaries and the Şeyh ül-İslam, who even pronounced a fatwa/fetwa. In it the Sultan is accused: "*introduced among Muslims the manners of infidels and shown an intention to suppress the Janissaries, the true defenders of the law and the prophets".* This example shows the power the high clergy/Ulema could exercise by denouncing Western secularization tendencies and assigning troops an important function in the defense of Islam. Selim III was assassinated by another opponent, his successor Mustafa IV, in 1807, who in turn had been assassinated by his successor Mahmut II (1808-1839).

Murat IV had already tried before 1640 to recruit a more reliable troop from Bosnia alongside the Janissaries, but the project failed with his death[3]. From 1791 Selim III had also had a new army established in Istanbul parallel to the old one, the "New Order" (*Nizam-ı Cedid*)[4]. It reached a total strength of about 24,000 men[5] and lasted only until 1806. The soldiers had to provide guarantees or bail (*kefalet sistemi*) to prevent desertion. As bodyguard Selim III set up, among others, the "*bostancı"*, who were also gardeners and executioners.

In the 18th century, French, British and German officers stayed in the country as advisors who influenced his reform ideas.[6] During this time, Europeans were especially in demand in theoretical and technical domains such as navigation, engineering or artillery/mortar. Mahmut II (1808-1839) wanted to continue the reform work of Selim III under the name "*Sekban- ı Cedid",* this time with Muslims as instructors. He achieved the approval of the clergy, but not

1 Tsar Nicholas I to British Ambassador in 1852. https://de.wikipedia.org. - Sick man on the Bosporus.

2 After the declaration of the Ottoman state bankruptcy in 1875, Western states introduced an international debt management system in 1881, the "*Dette Publique Ottomane*". https://de.wikipedia.org - Administration de la dette Publique Ottomane. Lord Kinross "The Ottoman Centuries" p. 433.

3 Jorga "History of the Ottoman Empire" Volume III p. 466 ff

4 https://tr.wikipedia.org, - *Nizam-ı Cedid Ordusu.*

5 Mantran "*Osmanlı İmparatorluğuTarihi II". p. 14.*

6 Among them were the French officers Claude Alexandre de Bonneval (after conversion Ahmet Paşa), (1729 - 1738), who founded a school of geometry as part of the training of artillerymen, and François Baron de Tott, who founded a school of mathematics for the navy under Mustafa III in 1773, also for basic training. https://tr.wikipedia.org. - *Mühendishane-i Bahr-i Hümâyun.* An early precursor of today's Technical University. The comprehensive work was continued after him by the Scot Campbell. Changes in personnel also depended on the current state of war. Another advisor was the Prussian colonel and later Major General Karl Ludwig Bogislav von Goetze, who served in Constantinople from 1789-1792.

that of the Janissaries. They had even refused to put on new uniforms[1] in 1807. So he had to give up the new approach already in 1808.[2]

The next more lasting reform step of Mahmut II only took place after the destruction of the Janissaries in 1826 with the establishment of the "Victorious Troop of Muhammad", the "*Asakir-i Mansure- i Muhammediye*". "*Dindarlarin tepkisini azaltmak için Muhammediyye ismi eklendi*"[3] ("To reduce the contradiction of the clergy/the pious, the epithet Muhammediyye/the Prophet was added. Translation of the author).

Starting in 1834, the army was divided into an active part (*Nizam*) with a service period of 5 years and a reserve (*Redif*) with a service period of another 7 years, i.e. in summary 12 years. The army comprised about 90,000 men[4] around 1839. In the navy also served about 10,000 non-Muslims.

The army followed after the organization of the tripartite structure, which is still common today, with the familiar designations for units and ranks: At the top a marshal (*müşir)*, below them a high general rank (*ferik*), below them the lowest general rank (*mirliva*), until then all with the additional designation *Paşa*, below them the *miralay* as commander of a regiment (*alay)*, below them *yüzbaşı* as commander of a battalion (*tabur)*, below them the company commander *başçavuş* with his company *(bölük*).

The *Timar* system was abolished. In the capital, a new police force replaced the Janissaries who had previously been entrusted with this task.

After the dissolution of the Janissary Music Band/*Mehterhane-i Hümâyun* in 1826 a civil/-military modern music corps was established in 1828 and trained by the Italian Giuseppe Donizetti Paşa[5] (1788-1856). The new music corps called itself "First Imperial Turkish Music Band" ("*Ilk Türk bandosu Mûsikâ-i Hümayûn'un*"), today "Symphony Orchestra of the Republic".

However, the reforms of Mahmut II were much more comprehensive, both military and civil. Only a few aspects are mentioned which show that he became the most important sultan after Süleyman I. In 1826, he founded a modern medical academy, which also provided primary education. In 1838 it was moved to the Galata district, to the former property of the School of the Pageboys, called Galatasaray (the castle of Galata), today a well-known grammar school. Besides Turkish, French became the language of instruction. From 1836 onwards, Mahmut II introduced ministries according to the western model. The Janitscharen Ağa was replaced by the *Serasker,* an earlier used term for the commander at the front, with today's designation "Commander in Chief". However, there was no uniformity of military leadership and training below the level of the Sultan as parts of the army were not under the command of the Serasker[6] in peacetime.

The Grand Vizier practically became Prime Minister, outsourcing functions to new ministries while retaining the name Grand Vizier, who later also temporarily held the position of Foreign Minister.

1 Kreiser „Der Osmanische Staat" p.36.

2 https://tr.wikipedia.org. - *Sekban-ı Cedid.*

3 *https://tr.wikipedia.org. - Asakir-i Mansure-i Muhammediyye.*

4 Kreiser "Der Osmanische Staat" p. 37, which probably refers to the active peace strength, because other authors name clearly greater strengths, this time probably including the reserve.

5 A brother of Gaetano Donizetti. https://tr.wikipedia.org. - Giuseppe Donizetti. https://tr.wikipedia.org. - *Mızıka-yı Hümâyun. Mekteb-i Tibbiye.*

6 Jorga "Geschichte des Osmanischen Reiches" Vol. III p. 244, 417, literally translated as "Lord of the Soldiers".

Against initial resistance from the clergy, the Fez replaced the Turban in 1828, also in the military. This had always been regarded as Muslim headgear.

Also noteworthy is the further division of the troops into right and left wings following the above mentioned Qur'an explanations of the companions to the right and left hand respectively. The connection to Islam was thus still very close and was to be increased again l under Abdülhamit II (1876-1909), as he particularly strengthened the caliphate. In anticipation of his reign, another military aspect should already be mentioned.

In 1890, this Sultan, mainly by resorting to Kurds, established the Hamidiye cavalry regiments named after him with the centre in Erzincan for the following reason: *"Bu sebeple, 1890 yılı sonrasında Doğu Anadolu'da bir Ermenistan devletinin kuruluşunu engellemek amacıyla Hamidiye Alayları'nın kurulmasını sağladı."*[1] ("The Hamidiye regiments were established in the 1890s to prevent the foundation of an Armenian state in East Anatolia". Translation by the author). The regiments also partly got out of control of the leadership: "*Hamidiye Alayları daha çok eşkiyalık yapar*". ("The Hamidiye regiments also committed a lot of banditry". Translation by the author).

Nevertheless, as is well known, Armenians temporarily gained their independence in May 1918 and finally in September 1991.

The regiments were in essence irregular troops with a high degree of autonomy, even if they were partly led by paid Turkish officers or were subordinated to higher Ottoman headquarters. As already indicated, looting and collecting unjustified taxes was part of the regiments' livelihood. According to different authors, they are said to have grown up to 24,000 men according to Ternon or 40,000 men according to Kieser or, according to the above-mentioned Turkish file, even to 65,000 men[2] in 1908. With the abdication of Abdülhamit II, the regiments were formally renamed "Light Aşiret Cavallerie"/*Aşiret hafif süvari* [3]and reduced in number to 24 regiments.

In 1913 they were again reorganized and renamed Reserve Cavalry Regiments and placed under the 9th Corps in Erzurum. Among other things they performed the following task: "*Ermenilerin tehcir edilmesinde etkin oldular".* ("They were effective in the resettlement/deportation of the Armenians. Translation by the author).

According to additional information[4] Abdülhamit II was also concerned with getting the partly disloyal Kurds under control. Under Sheikh Ubeydalla/Ubeydullah Nehri, for example, these too had aspirations for autonomy. The everlasting Kurdish problem will have to be dealt with later.

First of all, the view should be directed once again to Egypt and that for the Sultan dangerous striving for power of the Ottoman Albanian-born governor Mehmet Ali Paşa: 1805-1848 provincial governor and Viceroy /Khedive/ Hidiv.[5] He fought for the Sultan in 1807 against the British,[6] 1811-1836 against the Wahhabites[7] on the Arabian Peninsula, 1821 against the

1 *https://tr.wikipedia.org. – Hamidiye Alayları.*

2 Ternon "Tabu Armenien". Kieser "The Armenian Question and Switzerland 1896-1923".

3 Nomadic tribe.

4 https://de.wikipedia.org. - Hamidiye cavalry.

5 *https://de.wikipedia.org. - Muhammad Ali Pasha. https://tr.wikipedia.org. - Kavalalı Mehmet Ali Paşa.*

6 https://de.wikipedia.org. – Britisch-Türkischer Krieg (1807) Alexandria Expedition.

7 The Wahhabis, (Turkish Vahhabi), named after their founder Abd al-Wahhab, have held an extremely puritanical view of Sunni Islam since the 18th century. After an agreement with the Arab royal house Saud in 1744, a Saudi-Southern claim to power has been added to the religious claim to power with the aim of unifying Arab tribes. In 1833, Mehmet Ali was able to reconquer the Holy Places, but they were finally lost to the Ottoman Empire during the 1st World War against the British (Edward Lawrence of Arabia). The

Greek freedom fighters, against Russia in the Crimean War 1853-1855. Ali had largely got rid of the Mameluken in a bloody action in 1811. The Janissaries, in turn, had mutinied for lack of pay and murdered their local commander Hüsrev Paşa. Mehmet Ali had a clear path after that. He led 3 campaigns against the Sultan 1831-1841 .

He, more effective than the Sultan, had early on brought military advisors to modernise his army from Italy (navy), Spain (artillery), Poland (cavalry), but above all from France, whose men brought the experience of the Napoleonic wars. The French Colonel Joseph Anthelme Sève came to the country in 1815 and later became chief advisor in all military matters under the name Süleyman Paşa. In addition, Mehmet Ali introduced compulsory military service for the "Fellachen" (peasants), some of whom then tried to avoid military service by mutilating themselves.

Mehmet Ali demanded from the Sultan the rule over Syria and Crete and occupied Kütahya in Anatolia in the 1st civil war 1831-1833. In this emergency, the Sultan concluded the assistance contract of Hünkâr İskelesi (on the Bosporus) in 1833, true to the Turkish proverb: "*Denize düşen yılana sarılır*" ("On the sea one (even) embraces the snake").(Translation by the author).

After the Russians entered the Bosporus, the local Egyptian commander, his son İbrahim, had to acknowledge the peace of Kütahya,[1] but Syria remained in the possession of Ali. A second civil war flared up in 1839 in Nizip[2] on the Euphrates, in which the Prussian Hauptmann Helmuth Moltke (later: von Moltke) also took part (Fig. 11). This battle was lost by the Ottoman field army commander Hafız[3] Paşa against İbrahim Paşa, Moltke lost his records during the retreat.[4] The fighting power of the Sultan's army had only been partially used, his troops had been positioned unfavorably. Before that, Hafız had fought a civil war against the Kurds, who of course tended to desert as forced recruits in battle afterwards.

After an intervention of Great Britain, Russia, Austria and Prussia in Syria, the 3rd Civil War, Mehmet Ali had to give up Crete and Syria in 1841, now no longer supported by France, which was laid down in the London Treaty[5] of 1840. The conceded dynasty of the Egyptian viceroys was then to remain in existence until the beginning of the 1st World War.

Internal national conflicts of the Ottoman Empire were now increasingly internationalized, partly because of the weakness of the Central Army, which led to further dependencies and interference by foreign states.

However, the main cause for further uprisings, civil wars and revolutions in the Balkans were undoubtedly the thoughts of the French Revolution of 1789, reinforced by other factors including the influence of the other states.

In the case of Serbia, conquered by the Ottomans in 1459, the trigger of the first comprehensive uprising in 1804 was the execution of 72 *Knezen*/Village Rulers under the responsibility of commanders and the *Ağa* of the Janissaries. In the Turkish history book it says

---

radicalism of the Wahhabis may have been a godfather to the emergence of radical currents such as the Taliban, Al Qaeda and the "Islamic State" (IS). https://de.wikipedia.org . - Wahhabi. https://de.wikipedia.org. - Ottoman-Saudi War.

1 https://de.wikipedia.org. - Treaty of Kütahya. https://tr.wikipedia.org. - *Kütahya Antlaşması.*

2 https://tr.wikipedia.org. - *Nizip Muharebesi.*

3 A Muslim who can recite the Koran by heart. The Pasha was quite resistant to advice from Moltke's recommendations; instead Commander Hafız preferred to follow the incompetent military advice of the Muslim clergy/the Ulema at the staff.

4 That is why he made some time mistakes in his book „Briefe über Zustände und Begebenheiten in der Türkei aus den Jahren 1835-1839"

5 https://de.wikipedia.org. – Londoner Vertrag 1840.

frankly: *"Bölgedeki yeniçeri ağalarının halka karşı sorumsuz davranmaları."*[1] ("The local irresponsible actions of janissary commanders against the people". Translation by the author)

Although the commanders were subsequently punished by Sultan Selim III, the fire was lit. Belgrade fell for the first time in 1807, followed by further Serbian uprisings (1815-1817), resulting in autonomy in 1829, temporary independence in 1878 and final independence in 2006.[2] Further causes of the revolution were also to be found in Ottoman tax policy, the obligation to use forced labour and probably also in the support of the Serbs by Russia. This political relationship, also of religious nature, was to continue through all further turmoil in history up to the present.[3] It should not be underestimated that religion, in this case the Serbian Orthodoxy towards Islam, can also strengthen national feeling.

This probably also applies to the next example of a planned successful revolution, Greece and Greek Orthodoxy.[4] The Greeks and many Ottoman citizens of Greek/Byzantine origin, the "*Rum*"[5] so called by the Turks, including the Greek Orthodox Patriarch Grigorios V and the Phanariots/"Greeks" in Istanbul, pursued the revolutionary idea of the *Megali Idea*, that of a great empire of the Greeks, including the revival of at least parts of the Byzantine Empire; an idea that was finally buried in 1923 under the Lausanne Treaties. The rebellion[6] began in 1821 in the Peloponnese, supported by Russia, and by 1827 at the latest also by Great Britain and France. In 1825 Mahmut II called on Ali Paşa from Egypt for help, but despite initial successes he was ultimately unable to prevent defeat on land and at sea in the Battle of Navarino in 1827[7]. It was the last great sea battle exclusively with sailing ships, with about 22 ships on the side of the British, French and Russians against about 78 of the Ottomans including the Egyptians. However, the ships of the allies were superior to those of the Ottomans in terms of artillery, their men also in terms of experience: "*Ayrıca müttefik gemilerinin kaptanları ve mürettebatları Napolyon Savaşların'da muharebe alanında önemli tecrübeler edinmişlerdi*"[8]. ("In addition, the captains and crews of the ships of the allies on the Napoleonic battlefields had gained great experience". Translation by the author).

As mentioned above, the Janissaries had been destroyed by the Sultan in a major action in 1826. Thus, after 1826 there was neither a powerful army nor an operational navy in the Ottoman Empire.

In 1828-1830 Russia also waged a successful war against the Ottoman Empire. During this war, many Greek and Bulgarian soldiers cooperated with the Russians in the course of the emerging nationalism, which led to the fact that subsequent Ottoman armies - with few exceptions - were only recruited from Turks. [9]

In the Edirne Agreement of 1829, a southern part of present-day Greece thus became independent, Wallachia and Moldavia became autonomous.

The map below shows the territorial permanent and temporary expansions of Greece since independence until 1947 with the largest expansion after the Balkan wars in 1912/1913,

1 *Tarih Lise 2 p. . https://de.wikipedia.org. – Erster Serbischer Aufstand.*
2 https://de.wikipedia.org. – Zweiter Serbischer Aufstand.
3 https://de.wikipedia.org – Geschichte Serbiens.
4 https://de.wikipedia.org. – Griechische Revolution. https://tr.wikipedia.org. – *Yunan İsyanı.*
5 Greeks are referred to by Turks as "*Yunanlı*"
6 The so-called "Protected" in the Ottoman Empire, i.e. the Christians and Jews, were actually not allowed to carry weapons. They were also exempt from military service. Nevertheless, obtaining weapons should not have been a major problem for the rebels.
7 https://de. wikipedia.org. – Schlacht von Navarino.
8 *https://tr.wikipedia.org. - Navarin Deniz Muharebesi.*
9 Uyar & Erickson „A Military History of the Ottomans“ p. 41.

mostly at the expense of the Ottoman Empire. Further disputes between the Ottoman Empire or Turkey and Greece should therefore join. Bilateral tensions continue to radiate to the present day e.g. in the Cyprus conflict or even within NATO.

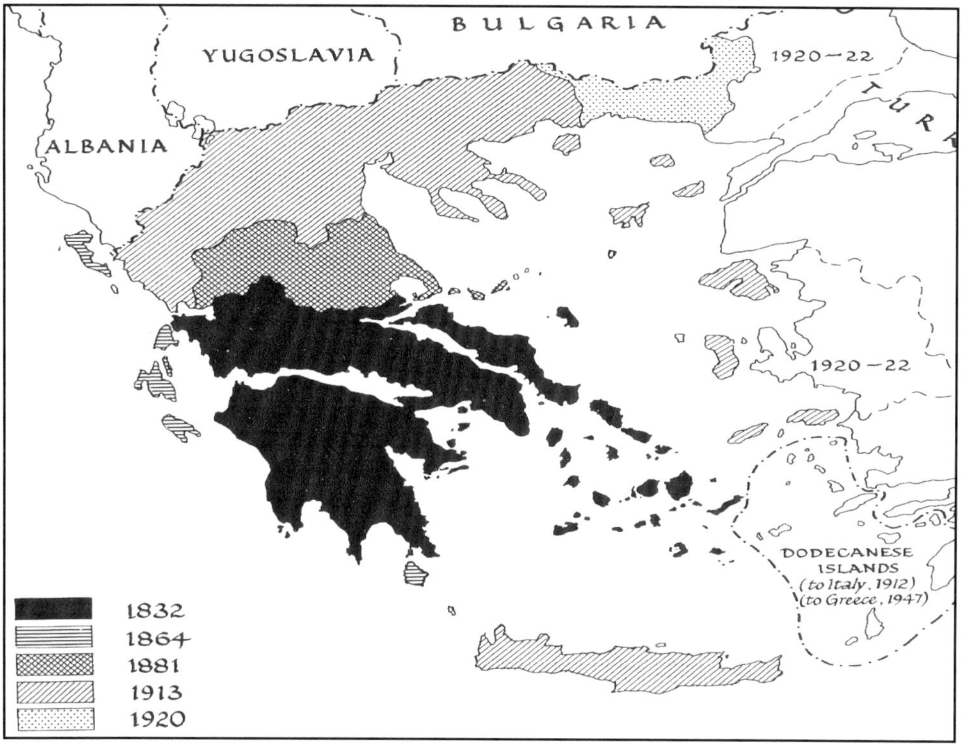

Map 7 The territorial extensions of Greece

Before dealing with another major war in the long series of Ottoman-Russian wars,[1] the Crimean War 1853-1856, however, it is necessary to first take a look at the Sultans' domestic political measures, which had also been demanded by European states. This refers to the period of the *Tanzimat*[2], which lasted from about 1839-1876, ending with the year of the 1st Constitution and the beginning of the 1st Constitutional Monarchy (*Meşrutiyet*). The first stage was a sultan's edict from 1839 with the name " *Hatt-ı Şerif of Gülhane* ", also called "*Tanzimat Fermanı*" or "Charitable Ordinances". The decree declared the equality of all citizens, but within the framework of Sharia/*Şeriat* law. In addition, the half-hearted general Recruitment Act of 1846 meant that exceptions were still made for non-Muslims, clergy and their students, artists, residents of the Holy Places of Mecca/Medina and rich people who could be freed or

1 https://de.wikipedia.org. – Russisch – Türkische Kriege.
2 *https://de.wikipedia.org. - Tanzimat. https://tr. wikipedia.org. - Tanzimat Fermanı.*

represented[1]. After all, the law produced a recruitment quota of about 25,000 men per year.[2] The duration of military service was limited to 4 years, in 1846 it was changed to 5 years. In the decree of 1839, the term "*vatan*" -"fatherland" appeared next to the previous term "*yurt*"- “home", a sign of an increasing national feeling after territorial losses, parallel to the emerging nationalism around 1848 in Western Europe.

The Crimean War, however, changed the focus in the meantime. Russia had invaded Transylvania/*Eflak* and Wallachia/*Boğdan* in1853, had burned down the Ottoman fleet in Sinop on the Black Sea in November and had devastated the town, thus conjuring up a coalition with Great Britain, France, Sardinia/Piedmont and the Ottoman Empire. The Crimea was conquered, but with the Paris Agreement of 1856, the status before the war was largely restored[3].

From a military point of view this so-called 8th Russian-Ottoman War had shown important progress and provided insights. First of all, there was the strategic insight that wars were becoming more global with considerable consequences for troop transports and supply lines. As is well known, the Crimean War had also taken place in locations further away than just the Black Sea. The second finding was that wars are increasingly determined by the exploitation of all civil/military resources, and thus, of course, by the formation of the warring parties. In case of paralysis in positional wars like before Sevastopol/Sivastopol, material battles were fought with high personnel losses. This meant that modern armament was first of all important, as the Ottoman fleet in Sinop had to painfully experience. They were not only surprised in the harbour, but also defeated by modern ship artillery. Conversely, the Russians were at a disadvantage with outdated rifles, e.g. against the British, who already used the rifled barrel.

The strategic/tactical exchange of information was accelerated by the transition from optical/mechanical to electromagnetic telegraphy. In this war, the first telegraphic message was sent to Istanbul via Edirne in 1855. Around 1876, large parts of the Ottoman Empire were networked. A special Turkish Morse[4] code was developed for this purpose. However, Abdülhamit II also used the network to receive spy messages from his surveillance agents.

Propaganda became more effective by using modern photography. According to experts, the renewed army - in contrast to the overpowered Ottoman fleet - had fought brilliantly with British/Indian support at Silistria/Dristra in present-day Bulgaria; only one Ottoman division was deployed in Crimea.

Significant findings were made above all in the fields of medicine and care of the wounded. According to British sources, there were more victims as a result of hunger, thirst and disease than of combat. The high personnel losses on both sides of more than 200,000 each inevitably put the medical service with all its components in a central position as an important factor.

British nurse Florence Nightingale[5] became famous with her team of 38 nurses, who set up a modern military hospital on the Anatolian side in Istanbul, in the Selimiye Barracks. A small museum in the northeast tower of the present barracks still reminds us of this. Nightingale established a nurse school in London after the war. Her egagement together with the subsequent one by Henry Dunant was instrumental in paving the way for the Red Cross and Red Cres-

1 Uyar & Erickson "A Military History of the Ottomans" p. 156. Actually, inhabitants of Jerusalem as the third most holy place should also been excluded.

2 Jorga „Geschichte des Osmanischen Reiches“ Volume V p. 424, .

3 https://de.wikipedia.org . – Krimkrieg. https://tr.wikipedia.org. – *Kırım Savaşı.*

4 Lewis "The Emergence of Modern Turkey" p. 181.

5 ttps://de.wikipedia.org. - Florence Nightingale.

cent/Kızılay[1] movement. The subsequent First Geneva Convention of 1864 was the beginning of the development of a far more comprehensive international law of war, which was then incorporated into what is now known as International Humanitarian Law.

At this point it should be mentioned that numerous soldiers from other countries went into Ottoman service on the basis of individual decisions, some of them succeeded and even took over command functions. These adventurers or de facto mercenaries were no longer bound by any instructions of their countries of origin, converted to Islam if necessary and adapted to the Muslim lifestyle. A striking example is the Prussian Ludwig Karl Friedrich Detroit alias Mehmed Ali Paşa and who as a young man completed an Ottoman cadet school under futile Prussian protest, joined the Ottoman army in 1853, immediately participated in the Crimean War, and later in numerous other wars. In 1865 he became Paşa, in 1877 he became marshal, *(müşir)* after having commanded the Ottoman troops on the Danube front in Bulgaria as commander-in-chief. During the Berlin Congress, he was even a member of the Ottoman delegation, to the displeasure of German Reichskanzler Otto von Bismarck, who called this a "lack of tact". Ali Paşa married a Muslim woman, had four daughters and died in battle in 1878[2].

In addition to the horrors of war, humour was sometimes not neglected, here in the form of a caricature from 1855, but its serious core indicates that religion and the use of clergymen also played a major role on the side of Christians during the war[3] (Fig. 12).

In the Paris Agreement of 1856, 18 days after the armistice, a passage was added which reflects the second stage of the Tanzimat Reforms aimed at, the *Islahat Fermanı*/Reform decree of the Sultan from the same year, also called *Hatt-ı Hümayun*/Handwriting of the Sultan[4]. According to the decree, non-Muslims should now be able to become civil servants, attend military schools and do compulsory military service. Instead of this, however, a substitute military service tax could be paid, which in principle still applies today. Finally there should have been created the complete equality for all Ottomans[5], also in terms of taxes, which met with resistance not only on the side of the Muslims, but surprisingly even among non-Muslims.

"Çünkü Osmanlı tebaası olan gayrimüslümer, Müslümanlarla eşitlik değil bağımsızlık istiyorladı." [6] ("Because the unbelievers as Ottoman subjects did not want equality with the Muslims, but independence". Translation by the author). Ultimately, therefore, the non-Muslims, despite many disadvantages, wanted to retain their privileges, which were associated with the "*Millet*" system and exemption from military service against payment of a special tax. The reform efforts thus petered out.

The *Millet* system was also changed and favoured a nationalistic way of thinking up to the conceptual level. The Turkish word "*millet*" was no longer understood only as "religious community", but in Turkish and translated literature it was misleadingly understood and referred to even as "nation". With the permission to give to the millets own constitutions the Sultan ac-

---

1 Henry Dunant founded the International Committee of the Red Cross in Switzerland in 1863 after the Battle of Solferino (1859). The Ottoman Empire used the Red Crescent as a comparable symbol in the Russian-Ottoman War 1876-1878. The literal translation of "Kızılay" is "Red Moon".

2 https://de. wikipedia.org. - Mehmed Ali Pasha. https://tr.wikipedia.org. - Mehmed Ali Paşa (müşir).

3 Thus the author learned that the plans of the NATO staff in Istanbul also provided for the participation of 6 clergymen, both imams and representatives of the Christian denominations.

4 An addition was still made in 1860. https://tr.wikipedia.org. - *Islahat Fermanı.*

5 Thus, although the head tax "*cizye*" was abolished for non-Muslims in 1857, the substitute military service tax "*bedel*" was introduced. A still limited general conscription should be enforced only at the beginning of the 20th century, but the exemption against payment should remain until today.

6 Lise 2 p. 63.

tually wanted to meet the non-Muslim religious communities and integrate them, but unintentionally promoted separatist efforts. The bloody clashes with the Ottoman Armenians in the 19th and 20th century were an indirect consequence and had - like the solidarity of wide circles of Ottoman Greeks with Greece - very negative effects on the cohesion of the Ottoman army.

A further reform approach was possibly to be expected from the first Ottoman elections, the first ever in the Islamic world,[1] leading to the 1st Ottoman Constitution/*Meşrutiyet* of 1876.[2] Their enactment and the appointment of Sultan Abdülhamit II had been preceded by activities of the Young Ottomans[3] and a bloodless revolt of the Young Turks/*Jön Türkler*, in which Sultan Abdülaziz had been encircled by army and navy in his Dolmabahce Palace and again overthrown in a "*Fetva*" with the approval of the clergy. The constitution established a kind of constitutional monarchy. It should have indeed restored equality for all Ottomans, but in practice it had no effect. Indeed, Abdülhamit II had already sent the first Ottoman Parliament on compulsory leave for 29 years, without formally dissolving it, less than a year later in 1877. With the establishment of the official language "Turkish" in the constitution a further step was taken in anticipation of a unified "Turkish" nation, while the Sultan continued to pursue conservative Muslim-Ottoman policies.

However, before we take a closer look at the Young Turks and the revolutionary events, let us first examine the work of some German[4] military advisors and reformers, starting with the officers around Hauptmann Helmuth Moltke from 1835 up to the beginning of World War I and General Liman von Sanders.

Moltke (later von Moltke)[5] served from 1835 to 1839 as a retired Prussian captain in the Ottoman Empire during the time of Mahmut II, at the invitation of the Serasker and with the approval of the Prussian King. The later fame of Moltke, also supported by Turkish historians, distorts the influence that Moltke and his sent comrades had on the thinking or even the structure of the Ottoman army. Already during the battle against the Kurds or against the troops of the Egyptian governor Ali Paşa with local leadership of İbrahim Paşa near Nizib 1839, the Ottoman troop leader Hafız Pasha (Fig. 11), a quickly promoted protégé of the sultan, was reluctantly advised, although Moltke's advice and intervention was successful at least twice. A Paşa, who can recite the Koran, does not listen to an unbeliever in the rank of captain. Instead, the influence of the Mollas/Clergy is still very important:

"...Pasha Effendimis convoys a divan of the Mollas, dozens of whom we have here now and who take the pas in front of the general lieutenants (probably until the fetwa is issued)". p. 319.

And still on this page: "The Mollas can tell you whether the war is just - but whether it is wise, you alone can judge. The whole situation of the circumstances, the intentions of the Grand Lords, the European courts, - the strength and position of all our corps and of the enemy corps, the country's resources, the accumulated stocks, etc., all these things would have to

---

1 Lewis "The Emergence of Modern Turkey". p.164.

2 https:// tr.wikipedia.org. - *Kânûn-ı Esâsi*. https://tr.wikipedia.org. - *Meşrutiyet*.

3 *Yeni Osmanlılar* - "New Ottomans". Civil/military revolutionary secret organization existing 1865-1878 with strong relations abroad. Most famous representative of their poets was Namık Kemal. https://tr.wikipedia.org. - *Yeni Osmanlılar*.

4 The term should exactly refer to Prussian, Saxon (instead of German) and other reformers before the foundation of the German Reich in 1871.

5 At that time the Prussian general staff officer Moltke did not yet have a title of nobility and was not promoted, not even to a higher Ottoman rank. „Briefe über Zustände und Begebenheiten in der Türkei in den Jahren 1835-1839".

be available to give advice on this highly important matter, and neither the Mollas nor I nor anyone else but you know all these things. All the honor and responsibility falls on you, and you can't expect advice from anyone else.

But that is not what he wants to hear. Religion and superstition did the rest. The Hafiz Paşa read in old writings, was convinced that the conqueror of Syria would wear dark trousers according to a prophecy and that his dreams would give him valuable hints". "Mollahs and Hodjas were now his preferred company"[1].

Hptm von Mühlbach had to learn that the removal of his beard, even if it had to be done for temporary health reasons, had caused horror among the Turks because it was a sin and meant misfortune.

In addition, the discipline of the troops was poor. "*In some relationships, subordination was quite poor, especially among the higher officers*".[2]

Some Kurds had been recruited by force, against whom war had been waged before. Moltke had frustratedly offered his resignation, which was rejected by Hafiz Paşa. The subsequent defeat of Hafız was no surprise for these and many other reasons. The consequence for the Sultan was, however, that he had temporarily no more operational army after the battle, but also no fleet, because it had been sold by his unfaithful admiral Ahmet Fevzi with advice of the French to the Ottoman viceroy in Egypt ![3]

Moltke's letters also describe the state of the empire and especially of the army with critical words (p. 92): "*The Ottoman monarchy needs above all a regulated administration, with the present one it will hardly be able to feed even the weak army of 70,000 men in the long run*".

Moltke's influence could be seen more positively, e.g. with the production of maps of the Bosporus at the scale of 1:100,000 and the associated studies on artillery. Actually, the Ottomans were suspicious of these activities on the grounds that these maps could fall into enemy hands, so that their own advantage of terrain knowledge would be lost. A map had already been produced before, e.g. in 1764 by the Hungarian captain and engineer Baptist von Reben[4]. Even during the war of 1878/1879 against Russia, the lack of useful maps was still a complaint.[5] Later, the Ottomans were happy to have at least partially more precise maps than their opponents.

Moltke and his comrades had handed over 11 memoranda and 20 plans to the Serasker after explorations in the terrain, especially at the straits, but these were not implemented to a large extent, except for some measures concerning artillery and fortifications. "*All remained a lost labour of love*".[6] Of course, the reason was probably the lack of money.

Even more successful were proposals for armament, which was especially noticeable in the period from 1883-1895 when the Prussian officer LTC (later marshal) Colmar von der Goltz was in charge. Especially the procurement of more modern guns paid off, e.g. in 1915 when defending the Dardanelles.[7] The superstition of earlier years and the anti-progressive influence of the mullahs, e.g. the closure of the Istanbul observatory in 1580 after only 3 years of ope-

---

1 *Moltke p.249.*

2 *Wagner „Moltke und Mühlbach zusammen unter dem Halbmond 1837-1839". p. 105.*

3 Jorga „Geschichte des Osmanischen Reiches" Vol. V p. 387.

4 Copies of both maps in possession of the author. As is well known, special emphasis was placed on the training of Prussian general staff officers, especially in this subject, to produce artillery shooting documents.

5 Uyar & Erickson "A Military History of the Ottomans" p. 201.

6 Wagner "Moltke und Mühlbach zusammen unter dem Halbmond 1837-1839". p 59.

7 It is said that due to his influence about 500 guns were procured from 1885 onwards and over 500,000 modern rifles. https://de.wikipedia.org. - Deutsche Militärmissionen im Osmanischen Reich.

ration[1] or the obstruction of the Ottoman-Turkish art of book printing still in the 18th century[2], after Ottoman Armenians and Jews had operated it for a long time[3], slowly gave way to the realization that one cannot close oneself to Western technology.

After the victories against Austria in 1866 and France in 1871, German military advisors became attractive to the Sultan, so that they increasingly displaced the French, who were still feeding on the fame of Napoleon. The first official German military mission was sent out in 1880/1882, including a number of officials. With the exception of von der Goltz[4], however, the officers were not very successful, because Sultan Abdülhamit II in reality did not want a powerful army and, for good reasons, feared for his life, prohibited exercises in open terrain, especially with live ammunition, and used German officers more as figureheads in relation to the other states. Even the frustrated von der Goltz wanted to resign several times, but was repeatedly persuaded by the Sultan to stay. Von der Goltz managed to push through some reforms to a limited extent, due to his sensitive mentality, his quickly acquired Ottoman language skills and his profound military-political knowledge. Even after the upheavals of 1908/-1909, he managed to remain recognized as an expert and advisor under the new regime of the Young Turks, supported by the officers he had previously trained.

After his first stay in 1883-1895 von der Goltz returned to the Ottoman Empire several times and continued his reform efforts (1908, 1909, 1910) until his final stay in 1914-1916, which resulted in a total stay of about 15 years. His work was comprehensive and concerned all areas of the army with its main components man, materiel, training, planning. Thus he influenced a new army constitution, initiated the Recruitment Act of 1885[5] with the aim of "universal conscription", even though equality was still not achieved. He worked out plans for a new structure and operation plans for deployment and operations; he led through accompanying terrain discussions and maneuvers with a focus on Eastern Thrace, probably anticipating the Bulgarian threat there. In 1909, he accompanied a manoeuvre in the Selanik/Thessaloniki area and Manastır/Monastir/Bitola (in the Balkans), also with this crisis area in mind. He underpinned his efforts by producing maps and translated training documents. He dedicated himself to the so-called internal service, hygiene and medical care. He succeeded in abolishing corporal[6] punishment, at least for officers, but not yet for non-commissioned officers and simple soldiers. Moltke already had still reported on the administration of beatings with a stick to the group of subordinate officers.

Von der Goltz' main field of activity and original mission, however, was education and training, especially of army officers. He modernized the military curricula and reorganized military education and training according to Prussian pattern. Von der Goltz devoted himself to both the Basic Training (Kriegsschule)/*Mekteb-i Harbiye* [7] of army officers in the 1st level,

1 https://de.wikipedia.org. - *Taqi ad Din.*

2 https://tr.wikipedia.org. - İbrahim Müteferrika. https://de.wikipedia.org. - İbrahim Müteferrika.

3 The German Johannes Gutenberg had already succeeded in inventing it in the 15th century.

4 https://de.wikipedia.org – Colmar von der Goltz. https://tr.wikipedia.org. – Colmar von der Goltz.

5 In 1868 a general compulsory military service for Muslims was again introduced. Von der Goltz „Der Thessalische Krieg" p. 253.

6 Lieutenant to Captain. The staff officers were obviously not beaten, but could "lose their heads" after a lost battle.

7 A term that was also still used in the German army. https://de.wikipedia.org - Kriegsschule. Comparable also with the French officer's school St. Cyr, which was founded by Napoleon in 1802 and may have been the godfather. The Ottoman school was founded in 1834. In 1877, however, only less than 10% had passed through the *Mekteb-i Harbiye*.. Uyar & Erickson "A Military History of the Ottomans" p. 177. https://tr.wikipedia.org. - *Kara Harp Okulu*. https://tr.wikipedia.org - *Mekteb-i Ulum-u Harbiye*. The school in Istanbul was located in Maçka Barracks behind Taksim Square, which also had a mosque.

the war school as well as the promotion of suitable graduates in the 2nd level, in the General Staff School/*Erkan-ı Harbiye* comparable to the Prussian War Academy (Kriegsakademie)[1].

"Üst kademede, dikkati en fazla çeken yenilik, bir Kurmay Okulu'nun (Erkân-ı Harbiye Mektebi) kurulmasıdır: Bir tür askeri akademidir bu; içindeki eğitim de, öteki büyük askeri kurumlarda olduğu gibi -Fransiz ve Prusyalı- Avrupalı uzmanlarca sağlanır". ("The highest level was reformed with the greatest care and a general staff school[2] was established: On the one hand, it was a kind of military academy within which education/training was provided by European specialists as in the other large military academies in France and Prussia". Translation by the author).

Further 1st level military schools were then founded until 1875 in Bursa, Edirne, Manastır, Damascus, Erzurum and Baghdad. In the period 1876-1896 then again some more in the whole country[3]. The Ottoman school names and structures underwent various changes before and after. Thus, the schools were also merged and the "*Harp Akademisi*" was established in Istanbul as the highest military school next to the Technical University. After the coup of 2016, a new form of top-level education for officers was conceived.

Mustafa Kemal (Atatürk) e.g. underwent this training in the period 1899-1905 as number 1283, first the army school, then the war academy[4]. This period lasted 3 years and concerned only 25 officers of about 1.000 per year[5]. The shortage of General Staff officers continued for years and then mainly affected the Division command level, where there was little expertise on the "battle of combined arms". Enver Paşa completed this training in 1896-1902, 3 years before Mustafa Kemal.[6] This put Enver in the forefront of his career, and in 1913, after taking power by leaping to the highest level of the Minister of War, he used it. Rivalries between these two strong personalities later arose, even after the end of the war in 1918.

One completed the training at the war academy as a captain, after 1899 with now 40 participants per year This corresponded to a share of 5-10 % of a year group[7]. The German rank addition to the officer rank " i.G." - "in the General Staff" corresponded to the Turkish "*Erkan-i Harp sabiti*" or the addition "*kurmay* - "General Staff" as part of the rank.[8]

It was clear that there would be tensions in the transition from the old to the new system, even before von der Goltz became active[9]. In the earlier system, in the army it was mainly the regimental commanders (*alay* - regiment) who decided on the careers of their subordinates (*alaylı* - a regimental member), based on practical service and personal assessment, while school graduates (*mektebli*) were assessed and promoted by teachers according to more neutral performance criteria. In addition, the higher conservative strata of the population were

1 https://de.wikipedia.org. - Prussian War Academy. In the Bundeswehr, the General Staff School would be comparable to the Command and Control Academy (Führungsakademie) in Hamburg. Prior to this, the German officer goes through officer training schools in the branches and services. In France comparable to the Ecole Superieure de Guerre from 1876-1992.

2 A general staff obviously existed already since 1880 under the name "*Erkân-ı Harbiye-i Umûmiye Riyaseti*". It was under the authority of the Serasker until 1908, then the Minister of War, from 1920 the head of the cabinet and in 1924 it left the cabinet as an independent organization. Today's name is "*Genelkurmay Başkanlığı". http://www.tsk.tr/TSK Hakkinda/Tarihce Türk Silahlı Kuvvetleri Genelkurmay Başkanlığı.*

3 Uyar & Erickson "A Military History of the Ottomans" p. 203.

4 A vivid presentation of his school class in the Military Museum (*Harbiye*) in Istanbul.

5 Uyar & Erickson "A Military History of the Ottomans" p. 207.

6 https://tr.wikipedia.org - Enver Paşa.

7 Tröndle „Mustafa Kemal Atatürk" p. 31.

8 In the Bundeswehr, the additional title is linked to the service post, so it does not necessarily require training in the General Staff. E.g., the additional designation is not used in command functions.

9 E.g., Admiral Staff Officers of the Bundeswehr also omit the additional designation. One feels one belongs to the elite, but does not show it. This is the result of the subsequent military career anyway.

sceptical of western-oriented non-Muslim education systems[1]. Very soon the *mektebli* had career advantages. When von der Goltz initially taught in French, the later General Pertev (Demirhan)[2] translated into Turkish.

The Turkish officer corps still today pays von der Goltz the greatest respect and recognition for its long and successful work in the Ottoman Empire, especially its work in the military schools: "*Von der Goltz, askeri okullarda köklü reformlar gerçekleştirip genç subaylar yetiştirilmesi için önkoşulları oluşturdu*". ("Von der Goltz made radical reforms a precondition for the training of young officers in military schools". Translation by the author).

The armed forces have each maintained or are maintaining their own military schools: The Navy since 1773 the "*Deniz Harp Okulu*"[3], the Army since 1834 the *Kara Harp Okulu*,[4] the Medical Service since 1898 the *Gülhane Eğitim ve Araştırma Hastanesi*[5] and the Air Force since 1951 the *Hava Harp Okulu*.[6]

It should not go unmentioned that by sending more Ottoman officers to foreign troop units and training institutions, the level of training could be increased, also linguistically, and that personal relationships were established which were to be very helpful for German and Turkish soldiers in World War I.

1877-1878 there was another conflict with Russia[7], in Turkish historiography called "*93 Harbi*" ("War of 93"), because it began in 1293 according to the so-called Rumi calendar[8], which is based on the Muslim calendar[9]. The Russians, as part of their Pan-Slavic strategy and their drive towards the (ice-free) Mediterranean, attacked both in the Caucasus and in the West, supported by Romania/Romanya, Serbia/Sirbistan, Bulgaria/Bulgaristan and Karadağ. Despite considerable Ottoman initial successes, also favoured by modern American rifles, the Ottomans had to give way to superiority. After the fall of Edirne in 1877[10] and the Russian advance on the Çatalca line 60 km west of Istanbul in the peace of San Stefano/Ayastefanos/Yeşilköy[11] and the Berlin Congress[12] the Ottomans had to make considerable concessions. The intervention of the fleets of France and Great Britain had at least prevented the further advance of the Russians.

The above-mentioned Balkan countries, except Bulgaria, gained independence. Bulgaria became a principality tributary to the Ottoman Empire and declared its independence only in 1908. Bosnia-Herzegovina, where uprisings had already been suppressed by Ottoman troops in 1875, came under Austrian administration. With Eastern Rumelia, the Ottoman Empire also regained its old capital Edirne, temporarily lost the area to Bulgaria again in 1908, only to finally regain it in 1923. In the east, territory was lost including the cities of Kars, Ardahan

1 Thus the coexistence of the two development stages existed as early as 1858; von der Goltz only developed them significantly in terms of content. https://tr.wikipedia.org. - *Mekteb-i Erkân ı Harbiye.*

2 Demirhan „Generalfeldmarschall Colmar Freiherr von der Goltz".

3 https://tr.wikipedia.org. - *Deniz Harp Okulu or http://www.dho.edu.tr/Deniz Harp Okulu.*

4 https://tr.wikipedia.org. - *Kara Harp Okulu or http://www.kho.edu.tr/Kara Harp Okulu.*

5 Training and research hospital in Gülhane/Istanbul. Since 2016 assigned to the Ministry of Health. https://tr.wikipedia.org. - *Gülhane Eğitim ve Araştırma Hastanesi*. Previous designation "*Gülhane Askeri Tip Akademisi*".

6 https://tr.wikipedia.org. - *Hava Harp Okulu. http://www.hho.edu.tr/Hava Harp Okulu.*

7 https://de.wikipedia.org. – Russisch Osmanischer Krieg (187-1878).

8 https://de.wikipedia.org . – Rumi Kalender.

9 https://tr.wikipedia.org. – *93 Harbi.*

10 An armistice was concluded in Edirne on 31.01.1878. https://de. wikipedia.org. – Waffenstillstand von Edirne.

11 https://de.wikipedia.org. – Frieden von San Stefano. https://tr.wikipedia.org. – *Ayastefanos Antlaşması.*

12 https://de.wikipedia.org. - Berlin Congress. Text at https://de.wikisource.org. - Treaty between Germany, Austria-Hungary, Great Britain, Italy, Russia and Turkey (Berlin Treaty). https://tr.wikipedia.org. - *Berlin Antlaşması.*

and Batumi/Batum. However, final contractual arrangements for this territory were not made until the end of the Ottoman War of Independence in 1923. [1]

On the Russian side, the use of field telegraph lines and the use of torpedoes in naval warfare was remarkable from a technical point of view.

At this point we should also remember the numerous deaths on all sides and the fate of the refugees and displaced persons who flocked to Anatolia, e.g. from the lost Ottoman territories, such as in 1783 when the Crimea was lost in the order of 300,000. When meeting the local people, there were often riots, which made it necessary to use Ottoman Jandarma or even military force. In the Turkish file on the "*93 harbi*", a rough estimate of the number of refugees of Turkish origin from the western theatre of war is given: *"Mülteci sayıları 130,000 - 1.5 milyon arasında farklı tahminlerle ifade edilmektedir"*. ("The number of refugees is estimated to vary between 130,000 and 1.5 million". Translation by the author).

The many riots in the Ottoman Empire made it necessary to maintain a police force not only in the cities, but also in the countryside. This should relieve the army in peacetime, and as paramilitary troops with the appropriate training and equipment be available for peace and wartime operations.

The date of foundation of the *Jandarma*[2] under the name "*Zabtiye*", which is difficult to determine, was set at 1839, as shown in the coat of arms. (Fig. 13) The name "*Jandarma"* was not introduced until 1879.[3] The Italian Carabinieri, which had already been established in 1814, may have served as a model for the foundation. The connection of the Jandarma and its predecessors to the army was always very close. While until 1826 the Janissaries were also responsible for security and order under the leadership of the Janissary Ağa/*Yeniçeri Ağası*, especially in the capital, Mahmut II then assigned the task to the so-called *Serasker* as commander of the army, and from 1908 onwards he called him Minister of War/*Harbiye Nezâreti*. Since the institution of the General Staff was also created in 1908, there was now a particularly close connection to it. The Minister of Defense/*Milli Savunma Bakanı*, established from 1920 onwards, took on personnel/material support tasks for the armed forces, but not for training and operations.

From the outset, however, it was difficult to assign or subordinate the two-faced paramilitary Jandarma, since the governors were primarily responsible for security and order in their provinces/*Eyalet (later Vilayet)*[4]. The governors, however, were subordinated to the Minister of the Interior/*Dahiliye Nezâreti*, who was established in 1835 (from 1922 *İçişleri Bakanı*). After a long military assignment, the Jandarma was even temporarily only subordinated to the Minister of the Interior in 1912, and assigned to the governors in the provinces. However, the strong ties with the military remained intact. Thus the Jandarma has been associated with departments in different deployments in Turkey and abroad[5] and from 1956 on also took over border patrol tasks. Their equipment and strength were constantly adapted. With the establishment of the command of the coast guard/*Sahil Güvenlik Komutanlığını* in 1982 as the 5th branch/Service of the Armed Forces the tasks of the border guard were also adapted.

In 1983 after the military coup, there was a double subordination, i.e. in police operations to maintain security and order, to the Ministry of the Interior and in wartime operations, including preparatory training in peacetime, to the General Staff with a duty of notification to

---

1 Lisec „Der Unabhängigkeitskrieg und die Gründung der Türkei" p. 54-56.

2 *Scheben „Verwaltungsreformen der frühen Tanzimatzeit"*.

3 Uyar & Erickson "A Military History of the Ottomans" p. 212.

4 Homepage *Jandarma Genel Komutanligiö File Tarihçe* (History).

5 As in World War I and the subsequent war of liberation E.g. 1974 also in Cyprus.or 2018 ın North Syria.

Fig. 1 The Army Coat of Arms

Fig. 2 The Navy Coat of Arms

Plate II

Fig. 3

Fig. 4

Figs 3,4
The Caps of the Scythians
and Jannissaries

Fig. 5 The Akinci Riders

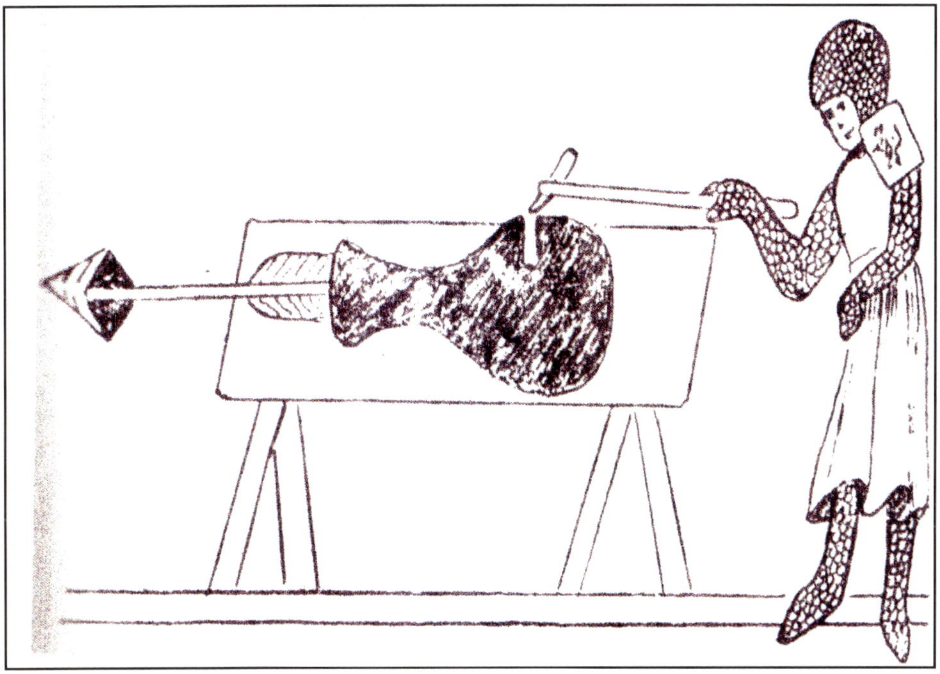

Fig. 6 First Cannon around 1326 in Florence

(Commons.wikimedia.org – Early Cannon de Nobilitatibus or wikipedia.org – Walter de Milemete)

Fig. 7 The Fireworks Book from 1470

Plate IV

Fig. 8 The Ottoman Ccout of Arms

Fig 9 The Tuğra

(İsmet Keten „ The Ottoman Monograms Tughra – Tuğra)

Plate V

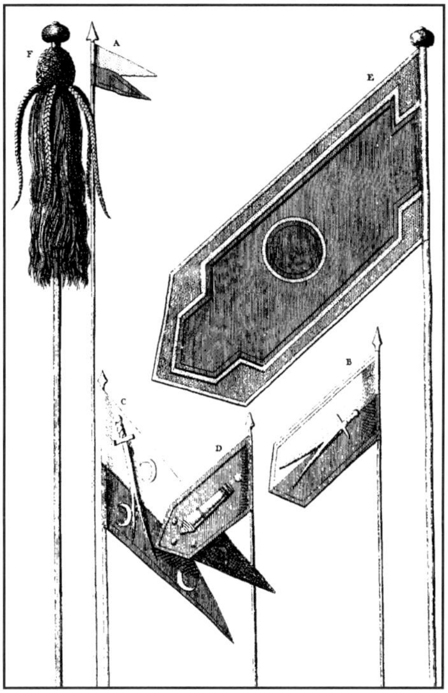

Fig. 10 (Standards and field signs)

(Luigi Ferdinando Marsili, Bologna, 1930 in Kretel & Teply "Kara Mustafa vor Wien 1683" S.79)

Fig. 11 Moltke (left) reports to his commander General Hafiz Paşa (middle) (1839) :https://commons.wikimedia.org. – Hafiz and von Moltke at Nezib)

Plate VI

Fig. 12 The Clergy in War
(https://commons.wikimedia.org. – Die Gartenlaube (1855)

Fig. 13 Coat of Arms of the Jandarms
(https://wikipedia.org – Jandarma Logosu)

Fig 14 The Turk turns his back on Abdülhamid II in 1909
(hhttps://commons.wikimedia.org. – Abdulhamid Cartoon 1909)

Fig 15 The Cruiser Hamidiye
(https://commons.wikimedia.org. – Savuranoğlu Hamidiye).

Plate VIII

Fig. 16 The triumvirate of power 1913 - 1918
Ismail Enver Pasha Mehmed Talât Paşa Ahmed Cemal Paşa

Fig. 17 The future lies in the skies (Atatürk 1925)

the Prime Minister. The Jandarma was therefore always included in the organization charts of the General Staff as the 4th element alongside the classic 3 branches of the armed forces and the coast guard as the 5th element with the same status of double subordination. With the current constitution of 2017 and the Law on the Armed Forces as amended on 02.01.2017, footnote 2 therein states[1] that the Jandarma and the Coast Guard are no longer part of the armed forces. As of 02.01.2017, this affected a Jandarma force of 194,700 men. According to article 118 of the current constitution the Jandarma Commander is also no longer a member of the National Security Council/ *Milli Güvenlik Kurulu (MGK).* The coast guard was not represented in it anyway. Thus, the total strength of the army in peace has changed, but not necessarily the strength in a state of emergency or war[2]:

"*Savaş ve seferberlik hallerinde Komutanlığın, Genelkurmay Bakanlığı'nın, görüşü alınarak Bakanlar Kurulu kararıile belirlenecek bölümleri Kara Kuvvetleri Komutanlığı emrine girer, kalan bölümleri ise normal görevlerine devam eder".* ("In war or during an operation, fixed units of the (Jandarma) Command, according to the coordinated view of the General Staff and the Cabinet, come under the command of the Land Forces by decision, while the remaining units continue their normal service. Translation by the author).

The mission/*görev* for the Jandarma is now in summary [3]:

"*Adli, mülki ve askeri görevler: * Emniyet asayiş ve kamu düzeni *Ceza ve tutukevlerin dış korunması *Adli kolluk hizmetleri*". ("Justice tasks, civil and military tasks: *Public safety and order *Public protection from criminals and prisoners *Penalty tasks". Translation by the author).

In this brief description, pure police tasks are listed, which corresponds to the now clear subordination to the Ministry of the Interior. It further states: "*15 Temmuz askeri darbe girişminin ardından ilan edilen olağanüstü hal kapsamında çikan 25. Temmuz 2016 tarihli ve 668 sayılı Kanun Hükmünde Kararname ile Jandarma yapısında sivilleştirmelere gidilerek tamamen İçişleri Bakanlığına bağlanmıştır".* ("In view of the coup d'état on July 15th 1916 and the state of emergency declared thereafter, Law No. 668 of July 25th 1916 gives Jandarma a civil structure and makes it fully subordinate to the Ministry of the Interior. Translation by the author).

In the above mentioned file and the file of the Jandarma homepage[4] it is additionally stated identically: "*Askeri görevler: Kanunlara ve Cumhurbaşkanlığı kararnameleriyle verilen askeri hizmetleri yerine getirmek*". ("Military tasks: Execution of tasks within the limits of the law and based on the decisions of the President of the Republic". Translation by the author).

A bond with the military therefore still remains, especially in war. A later look at the mission of the armed forces will make it clear that these changes are essentially about the allocation of competencies between the Defense Ministry and General Staff on the one hand and the Ministry of the Interior on the other. When it comes to the deployment of forces within the interior, the Minister of the Interior now has the say. A shift to the civilian side can also be seen in the assignment of secret services, which is not discussed in this book, however. Here, too, the intention was obviously to strengthen the Ministry of the Interior.

Towards the end of the 19th century, the Ottoman army had another two successes in the Greek-Ottoman war of 1897[5], but the political fruits could not be reaped. The war took place

1 Law No. 681: "*Turk Silahlı Kuvvetleri İç Hizmet Kanunu*".
2 https://tr.wikipedia.org. - *Türkiye Cumhuriyeti İşişleri Bakanlığı.*
3 https://tr.wikipedia.org. - *Türkiye Jandarma.*
4 www.jandarma.gov.tr.
5 https://de.wikipedia.org. – Türkisch – Griechischer Krieg. https://tr.wikipedia.org. – *Osmanlı - Yunan Savaşı* (1897). https://en.wikipedia.org. – Greco Turkish War (1897).

on two separate battlefields, on Crete and the Greek mainland in Thessaly with a secondary battlefield in the Ottoman Epirus. Thessaly was only awarded to Greece in 1881 after the Berlin Congress.

After an uprising of Greek Orthodox population in Crete/Candia/Girit, which since 1669 belonged completely to the Ottoman Empire, Greek troops intervened within the framework of the above mentioned "*Megali Idea*" and the Unification/Enosis. In the war that followed, the Ottoman troops were victorious. This time the Ottomans were politically "supported" in the peace negotiations by Italy, Great Britain, France and Russia, but had to appoint a Greek governor/Vali under Ottoman administration IAW the Istanbul Agreement of 1897[1]. In 1898, the island received the status of an international protectorate with a Greek high commissioner. The new so-called "Cretan State"[2], however, became more and more under Greek influence, also due to the political turmoil in the Ottoman Empire. The island became Greek at the end of the Balkan wars after the Athens Agreement of 1913[3], as did Thessaloniki/Selanik.

The Ottoman army was also successful in the so-called 30-day war in Thessaly April - May 1897 and in Epirus. "*Ancak savaşın yavaş tempoda cereyan etmesi üzerine, büyük devletlerden gelebilecek bir müdahaleyi önlemek için Sultan II Abdülhamid, Edhem Paşa'ya yıldırım harbi emrini verdi."* ("But the war took place at such a pace that the great powers could no longer intervene before Sultan Abdülhamid II Edhem Paşa had given the order for a Blitzkrieg"[4]. Translation by the author).

The Ottoman intervention was a reaction to the Greek intervention in Crete, but also to unrest in what later became Northern Greece. Probably the reasons for the rapid defeat of the Greek army were on the one hand a political/military overestimation of its own capabilities, as it will again come to light later in the Turkish struggle for independence in 1919-1922, still a lack of operational/tactical preparation, and on the other hand the previous effective reforms under von der Goltz. The latter has analysed the war on the mainland and comments in detail on the Turkish army[5]. Basically, he sees the army still in transition to the acceptance of the initiated reforms, also in the selection of personnel for the leaders. He sees particularly good progress in the leadership by the "Grand General Staff", on the ground in the infantry and artillery, but less good progress in the cavalry, transport, supplies and medical services. He also criticises the leadership performance at and below divisional level and sees the causes in a suppression of initiatives in peace, from which lack of independence arises in war. He also criticises the slow pace of action, and generally sees the army as not yet sufficiently mature for mobile operations. "*If one judges the achievements of the army as a whole, it must not be overlooked that the army was by its very nature much more suitable for passive national defence than for offensive war.* (p. 252) Marshal Liman von Sanders 1918 still held the same opinion.

What is not mentioned by von der Goltz is the incomprehensible behaviour of the Sultan: Of the approx. 700,000 (!) modern "Mauser" rifles, the Sultan had only 1 of 10 divisions equipped[6]. Probably again because of the panic fear of his army.

German advisors participated on both sides. At the capture of Larissa/Yenişehir on 21. 04. 1897, for example, the German Lieutenant Colonel and later General/Paşa Viktor Karl Ludwig

---

1 https://tr.wikipedia.org. – *İstanbul Antlaşması* (1897).

2 https://de.wikipedia.org. – Kretischer Staat. https://tr.wikipedia.org. – *Girit Devleti*. In the Turkish file, the state is called "*otonom*" - "autonomous".

3 https://tr.wikipedia.org. – *Atina Antlaşması* (1913).

4 https://tr.wikipedia.org. - *Osmanlı-Yunan Savaşı* (1897). https://commons.wikimedia.org. - Battle of Domokos map.

5 Von der Goltz „Der Thessalische Krieg und die Türkische Armee".

6 Uyar & Erickson "A Military History of the Ottomans" p. 211.

von Grumbkow[1] participated there as artillery instructor, who had joined the military mission in 1882, but had to leave the battlefield again on the orders of the German Emperor. Here his close relationship to the Greek royal family played a role. The decisive battle took place in Dömeke/Domokos south of Pharsalos - where the Romans were already fighting in 48 B.C. - with subsequent pursuit of the Greeks towards Golos/Bolos on the Aegean coast and with the threat of an advance on Athens. *"Fakat Avrupa Devletleri'nin aralarında anlaşması üzerine Rus çarı II Nikolay II Abdülhamid bizzat telgraf çekerek savaşın durdurulmasını durdurulmasını telep etti"*. ("But in order to give the European states (temporal) space for an agreement, the Tsar Nicholas II has called on Abdülhamid II in a personal telegram to end the war". Translation by the author).

It is therefore gratifying that a strategic "hotline" could already be operated back then using modern telecommunications. As a result, the Ottomans did not have to vacate the occupied territory afterwards. It should not have been the last conflict between Greece and Turkey, while tensions still persist today, both bilaterally and within NATO.

Looking back on the 19th century the Ottoman Army during this period is marked by turbulence and a further political/military decline.

The mission of the army at the beginning of the 19th century was initially an internal one, namely to implement the first two reform attempts of Selim III and Mahmut II, which failed due to the resistance of the conservative military and the *Ulema*. The army could only react to partially successful separatist efforts in the West, South and Northeast as well as to attacks from outside and was dependent on the help of others. After the radical cut in 1826 and the success of the third comprehensive attempt at political/military reforms under the probably greatest reformer, Mahmut II, the new army was able to recover gradually, but was not yet able to effectively counter internal and external threats. The implicit mandate to the army was, of necessity, although naturally not propagated, to remain defensive at first, to become stronger and to maintain the status quo as far as possible, because it was now too weak to attack and possible territorial expansion.

In relation to the sovereign and to politics, the army acted like the population in general. The reforms during the *Tanzimat* period and in the course of the establishment of the 1st Constitutional Monarchy in 1876 had partly been brought about under European pressure, although not without effect in the long term. The equality of Muslims and non-Muslims was not really supported by the broad majority, the parliament was condemned to inactivity by the Sultan for 29 years. Resistance arose among parts of the army, the civilian population and among opinion leaders abroad under the name Young Ottomans and Young Turks, who demanded reforms and increasingly propagated the national idea, also influenced by the ideas of freedom of the French Revolution 1789.

The army benefited not only from the reforms of Mahmut II, but also from the work of initially French/British reformers, later mainly German. Especially under von der Goltz Paşa a fresh breeze came into the training and equipment of the army, while the navy was lagging behind in terms of armament technology up to World War I. Until 1914, e.g. Admiral Sir Artur Henry Limpus[2] from the seafaring nation of Great Britain took care of the navy, and the French General Baumann, based on a long experience of the French with their gendarmerie[3],

1 https://de.wikipedia.org. - Viktor Karl Ludwig von Grumkow. He died in 1901 on the return journey to Germany.

2 http://mentalfloss.com/article/30568/world was in centenial mission implausible.

3 http://egm15-3.blogspot.de/2007/04/la gendarmerie . The origins of the French gendarmerie go back to 1720, the formal designation to 1791. The gendarmerie also knows the civil/military double subordination.

took care of the Jandarma, until the Germans took over the helm here too. The sending of officers to Western countries parallel to the exchange of ambassadors also brought important insights.

The relationship of the army as well as that of the population to religion remains close, which in part even combined with archaic superstition influences military decisions. Not only Moltke reports about this. The *Ulema* is fundamentally opposed to military reforms, but is also increasingly convinced by the superior Western armament technology when it comes to the fate of the empire. Abdülhamid II uses his caliphate specifically to maintain power. Later. Mustafa Kemal (Atatürk) himself had to tread carefully with the *Ulema* until 1924 in order not to jeopardize his reform work with the goal of a "Republic".

The Military Coup of 1909 and the Young Turks

In 1889 another conspiratorial group was formed, this time by four military medical students. The group, which became known as "Young Turks/*Jön Türkler*", was soon joined by other soldiers and civilians. They also established relations abroad and after a change of name they founded a party called "*İttihat ve Terakki*",[1] "Unity and Progress"[2]. The Young Turks were possibly influenced by the national unification thoughts of the Italian group of the Carbonari,[3] which had formed at the beginning of the 19th century. Lewis briefly describes the ideas of the Young Turks: "*Their political ideas were simple and rudimentary - freedom and fatherland, the constution and the nation.*"[4]

Leader of a first failed coup attempt in 1896 was General Kâzım Paşa, Commander of the 1st Division in Istanbul, who, like the 78 co-conspirators, surprisingly escaped with his life. From 1906 onwards, further revolutionary cells were formed in Damascus, where Mustafa Kemal had been transferred to after his time at the military academy and after revolutionary activities, but after that to the III Corps in Thessaloniki. There conspirators were, among others, the later Minister of War Enver Paşa and Minister of the Interior Tâlat Paşa. An attempt by the Sultan to get the situation in Macedonia under control ended with the assassination of the seconded Şemsi Paşa. In the meantime, the II Corps in Edirne also showed solidarity with the conspirators. On 21.07.1908 the Sultan was given an ultimatum by telegraph, on 24.07.1908 he had to call new elections, recall the parliament and put the constitution into force, with which the 2nd Ottoman constitutional period/*İkinci Meşrutiyet* [5] began.

The constitution, which was amended several times until 1918, basically continued the contents of the two above mentioned *Tanzimat* decrees from the 19th century. Among other things, it stipulated that the Sultan remained commander-in-chief of the armed forces and could make promotions (Art. 7). With Art. 62 it was stipulated that the members of the Senate, the 2nd chamber, must have held at least the general rank of a divisional commander of the land or naval forces (*Ferik*). The constitution did not contain any statements about the mission of the armed forces or a general conscription.

With the 1st Turkish Constitution of 1921 as Law No. 85,[6] the work of Mustafa Kemal, the Ottoman Constitution of 1876 got a deadly competition, was buried in 1923, replaced by the Republican Constitution in 1924 and thus ended the double constitutional period.

1 https://de.wikipedia.org. – Jungtürken. https://tr.wikipedia.org. – *Jön Türkler*.
2 https://tr.wikipedia.org. - *İttihat ve Terakki*. https://de.wikipedia.org. _ Committee for Unity and Progress.
3 https://de.wikipedia.org. – Carbonari.
4 Lewis "The Emergence of Modern Turkey".
5 https://tr.wikipedia.org . – *İkinci Meşrutiyet*.
6 https://de.wikipedia.org. – Türkische Verfassung von 1921.

However, the revolutionary spirit of parts of the army did not sleep. Albanian conservative Islamist officers of the I. Corps in Istanbul, who saw the *Şeriat* endangered, made a counter revolution in Istanbul on 12.04.1909, whose demands were first fulfilled by Abdülhamid II, e.g. the deposition of the Grand Vizier,[1] Among them were many older "*Alaylı* officers", i.e. the "regimental officers", who, contrary to the "*Mektebli* officers", had not gone through the war school system and had worse career chances. Some of them also fell victim to the purges, but later had to be reactivated for the Balkan wars.[2]

This in turn infuriated the nationalist wing of the Young Turks and the military in Thessaloniki. They marched under the commander of the 3rd Army, General Şevket Paşa[3] with some troops[4] to Istanbul and prepared on 24.04.1909 an end to the spook. "*Hareket Ordusu ittihatçılerin, 1909 yılında, 31 Mart Ayaklanması'nı bastirmak için Selanık'ten Mahmut Şevket Paşa komutasında İstanbul'a gönderdikleri ordudur. Kurmay başkanı ise Kolağası Mustafa Kemal Bey'dir"*. ("The Ittihat Actionist Intervention Force was sent from Selanik to Istanbul on March 31, 1909 under the army commander of Şevket Paşa to suppress the uprising. The chief of staff was, after all, Mustafa Kemal". Translation by the author).

He had been a member of the party[5] as number 322 since 1907, but then he left the party in September 1909[6] because he did not find support with a basic idea. This was, among other things, the strict separation of party membership and officer status. If two "chains of command" were mixed together, military discipline would otherwise suffer. This important principle was also strictly adhered to by him when the Republic was created; it was to be groundbreaking to the present day. Mustafa Kemal then served only as a soldier until his abdication or dismissal in 1919 during the beginning of the War of Independence. He banned the party in 1923.[7]

The Sultan was deposed (Fig. 14) and the office was finally removed from power as soon as Mehmet V took office. The key positions were newly filled and new laws were enacted, which pointed the way to a repressive Turkish nationalism. Once again the ideals of equality and tolerance fell by the wayside after initial euphoria.

The loss of territories such as Crete to Greece, Bosnia-Herzegovina to Austria-Hungary in 1908, the Serbs' declaration of independence in the same year, threatening losses on the North African coast due to the Italian attack in 1911 aggravated the situation. It was also leaked that the Tsar and the British King announced in Reval 1908 their intention to divide the Ottoman Empire.

The new regime resisted the internal and external threats with all its might, and even introduced compulsory military service for the first time in Ottoman history,[8] even before the Balkan wars, on 7 August 1909. For the first time non-Muslims were also conscripted to about 2/3. However, at the beginning of 1914 the use of non-Muslims at the front was already ended again by the Young Turks.

Italy attacked Tripoli/Trablusgarp[9] in Libya in October 1911. The Ottomans, who had owned the area since 1551, could send neither a fleet nor an army because the British refused

1 The following day was 13 April 1909, according to the Rumi calendar 31.03.1325. Therefore the event was called "*31 Mart Vakası*", the "event of 31 March". https://tr.wikipedia.org. - *31 Mart Vakası.*

2 Uyar & Erickson "A Military History of the Ottomans" p. 221.

3 https://tr.wikipedia.org. - Mahmud Şevket Paşa

4 Called "*Hareket ordusu*" - task force. https://tr.wikipedia.org. - *Hareket Ordusu.*

5 *Ittıhat ve Terakki.*

6 Tröndle ‚Mustafa Kemal Atatürk" p. 39.

7 https//tr. wikipedia.org - *Ittıhat ve Terakki.*

8 Uyar & Erickson "A Military History of the Ottomans" p. 221.

9 To distinguish Tripoli in Lebanon, the city is called Trablusgarp, which means "Trablus in the West".

access via Egypt. So only a few officers, among them the captains Enver and Mustafa Kemal, partly under disguise and on adventurous paths, were able to reach the area to defend it with weak forces and with the support of the local Senusi/*Sanusiya.*[1] The Italians, on the other hand, were able to mobilise naval forces to stop Ottoman naval operations and to relocate their troops. The balance of forces was about 1:3 to the disadvantage of the Ottomans. After Ottoman initial successes in Derna (under Mustafa Kemal) in March 1912, Tobruk and Benghazi (under Enver), the Ottomans were then forced to sign the peace treaty of Ouchy/Uşi (near Lausanne)[2] on 18.10.1912. Additionally the Italians had occupied the Dodecanese Islands, bombed Dardanelles forts in April 1912, attacked in the Red Sea and fought a battle near Beirut. With the following agreement, Tripolitania and Benghazia became autonomous or came de facto under Italian control. The Dodecanese came only temporarily under Italian control and went to Greece in 1948.

The Sanusiya continued to fight for years against the Italians through guerrilla warfare, with several major losses on the Sanusiya's side, also under a poison gas attack in 1928. The Italians declared Libya a colony in 1934; the country finally gained independence in 1951.

THE OTTOMAN - ITALIAN WAR 1911-1912

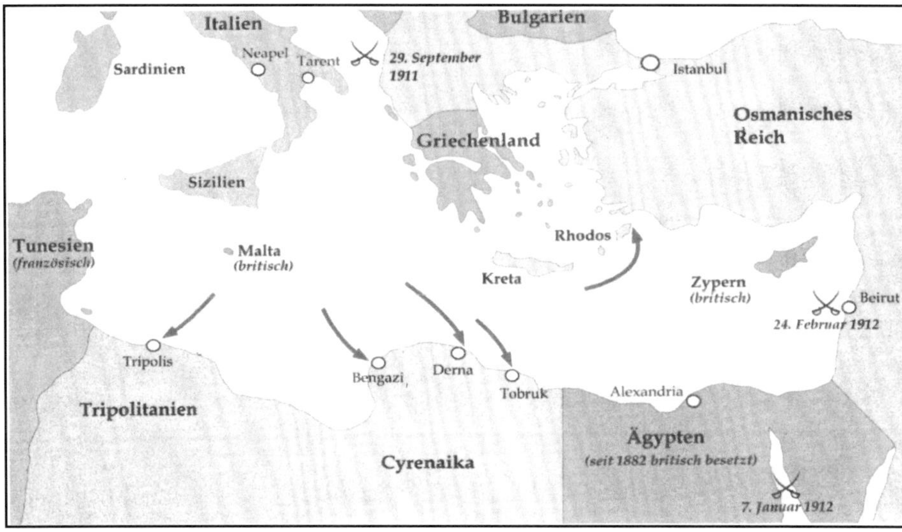

Map 8 https://commons.wikimedia.org. – File Bellum 191.png

Militarily remarkable was the use of Italian airships with bombs and airplanes.[3] The Italians already had 2 airships and 22 airplanes available, while on the Ottoman side there were no anti-aircraft guns on the ground nor any aircraft. On 22. 10. 1911 the first Italian reconnaissance flight over the remote battlefield took place with a Blériot XI, on 01.11.1911

1 An Islamic Sufi brotherhood in Libya 1843-1969. https://de.wikipedia.org. - *Sanusiya.*

2 https://tr.wikipedia.org. - *Uşi Antlaşması.*

3 In the presence of the author one Italian speaker gave a conciliatory speech in Istanbul 2011 about the aircraft deployment, the centenary of the Turkish Air Force.

also an attack flight with dropping of 4 bombs: "*Giulio Gavotti ise 1 Kasım günü Etrich Taube model bir uçakla Libya'daki Osmanlı kuvvetlerine karşı bir hava saldırısı düzenlemiş ve bu saldiri, ilk hava saldırısı olarak tarihe geçmiştir. Herhangi bir hava taşıtı savunma silahı olmayan askerleri ise tüfek atışıyla bir uçak düşürmeyi başarmıştır".*[1] ("Giulio Gavotti even flew an air attack against Ottoman forces in Libya on November 1 with an Etrich Taube aircraft, historically the first air attack. In the absence of an anti-aircraft weapon, the soldiers then crashed the plane with rifle fire". Translation by the author).

"*10 Mart günü İtalyanlar güdümlü balonları P-2 ve P-3'ü*[2] *getirerek, Türk mevzilerini bunlarla bombardıman ettiler".* ("On March 10, the Italians deployed the two airships P-2 and P-3 by bombing the Turkish positions". Translation by the author). The Italians also used cameras for reconnaissance.

In the above mentioned ongoing peace negotiations the 1st Balkan War began on 08.10.1912 against Greece, Serbia, Bulgaria and Montenegro. These states had formed the Balkan Union[3] with Russia, which provided for the division of the Ottoman territories in the Balkans. Fighting took place on 4 fronts, the most dangerous of which was the one in Eastern Rumelia with the Bulgarian operation on Edirne. After growing up with the enemy, the approximately 340,000 Ottomans in the Balkans were confronted by about 1.3 million soldiers. The Ottoman Empire still had forces tied up in Yemen and in the north-east of Anatolia, where it feared a Russian invasion. The Greek navy forced the Ottoman to retreat to the Dardanelles, with the notable exception of the cruiser Hamidiye.[4] (Fig. 15) The ship attacked the Bulgarian coast around Varna at the end of 1912, bombed Greek installations at the beginning of 1913, "neutralized" (sunk) the Greek cruiser "Makedonya" and later 6 Greek merchant ships. Commander was Rauf Orbay,[5] the later Turkish Navy Minister.

The Turkish history book describes the state of the Ottoman Army accurately, albeit with astonishing justification:

"Osmanlı yöneticileri savaş öncesi Rusya'nın Balkanlara saldırmayacağı düşüncesiyle ordunun büyük bir kısmını terhis etmişlerdi. Balkan Savaşı başladığında Osmanlı Ordusu düzensiz bir durumdaydı. Orduda siyası bölünmeler vardi. Bu nedenlerle Osmanlı ordusu her cephede yenildi."[6]

("Before the war, the Ottoman leadership had not believed in a Russian-induced uprising in the Balkans and had dismissed a large part of the army. At the beginning of the Balkan war, the Ottoman army was in a disorderly state. Only parts of the army were fit for war. Therefore the Ottoman Army was inferior on every front." Translation by the author).

In a Turkish file, the number of dismissed soldiers in the Balkans is given as 75,000 with the same reasoning. An important factor was also the release of Albanian soldiers with the shedding of Albania: *"Balkanlarda Arnavutlar Osmanlılara ihanet itti."* ("Among the inhabitants of the Balkans, the Albanians have committed treason against the Ottomans". Translation by the author).

There was inner disruption in a now politicized army. The rivalry between two competing parties had some temporary impact on the army: After a coup against the ruling party "Hürriyet ve İtilaf Fırkası" (Freedom and Unity Party) in January 1913 by the the Young Turks,

1 https://tr.wikipedia.org. - *Trablusgarp Savaşı*. The relatively small bombs were still dropped by hand.
2 P - Parseval.
3 https://de.wikipedia.org. - Balkan League.
4 https://de.wikipedia.org. - Hamidiye (cruiser). https://tr.wikipedia.org. - *Hamidiye (kruvazör)*.
5 https://tr.wikipedia.org. - Up Orbay.
6 Tarih Lise 2. p. 70.

the "İttihat ve Terakki Fırkası" (Unity and Progress Party) prevailed. This party thus held power from 1908 - 1918 with a brief interruption in the period February 1912 - January 1913.

The Ottoman Empire, and with it the army, also had a quality problem in the area of infrastructure, as the lack of efficient railway lines and roads made the deployment as well as the logistics difficult. Some of the military equipment was outdated and discipline was fragile. There is no other way to explain why in Selanik about 26,000 capitulated to the Greeks, in Yanya/Joannina the Greeks were able to take about 33,000 prisoners of war and the Bulgarians about 65,000. According to Turkish information about 115,000 were taken prisoner, i.e. about 30%.[1]

Mahmud Muhtar (Katırcıoğlu) Paşa,[2] who as commander of the 2nd Eastern Army in 1912, relentlessly described the state of the army in the Balkan War in the last chapter of his book "Betrachtungen".[3] He says that they were not defeated by the Bulgarians, but by their own serious shortcomings even in the run-up to the war. One of the causes of the many desertions of Turkish soldiers was the desertion of the "Rum", i.e. the “Greek-born” soldiers, and the shirking of the "sarıklı", the turban-wearers and Islamic clergy. Muhtar Paşa demands that religious trust and devotion to Allah be coupled with military feeling, national consciousness, good training and equipment. *"The fear of God does not eliminate the fear of bullets"*. (p. 164). In addition, Muhtar also mentions the serious lack of clothing and equipment, but also e.g. the forced passivity of 12 aircraft without pilot. The honor of the navy had saved the above mentioned Hamidiye. Summing up, he quotes a Turkish proverb, which in translation reads: "The highest knowledge lies in the recognition of one's own shortcomings".

With the London Agreement of 30.05.1913 the 1st Balkan War was ended, Albania became independent; Balkan territories divided into Greece including Selanik and Crete, Serbia and Bulgaria up to the Midye-Enez line, which corresponds to the above mentioned Catalça line. Large flight movements of Muslim parts of the Ottoman population from the Balkans set in towards Eastern Thrace and Anatolia of well over 1 million civilians, because according to Turkish information 6.1 million Ottomans lived in the Balkans in 1912 out of a total of 28 million in the Ottoman Empire. Heinz Richter e.g. has thoroughly examined the problems of population exchange agreements and expulsions between the Ottoman Empire and neighbouring states in the north-west and north-east during the last century and reported on the suffering associated with them.[4]

It should not be left unmentioned that after the devastating course of the 1st Balkan War for the Ottomans, discussions were held about the reasons why even the German military advisors/reformers were partly to blame for the defeat. It must be noted here that although von der Goltz had sent advisors again and again after his 12 years' stay, another military mission was not sent until 1909, but these could exert little influence. In the Balkan war itself the Ottoman Minister of War Nâzım Paşa wanted to do without German assistance. Nevertheless, German pilots flew missions and Oberstleutnant Otto von Lossow (later general) even - for the first time with official German approval - successfully led a division.[5]

1 https://de.wikipedia.org. – Balkankriege. https://tr.wikipedia.org. - *Balkans Savaşları*. First Balkan War. https://tr.wikipedia.org. - *Birinci Balkans Savaşı*. 2nd Balkan War: https://tr.wikipedia.org. - *İkinci Balkan Savaşı*

2 https://tr.wikipedia.org . - Mahmud Muhtar Katırcıoğlu. https://de.wikipedia.org. - Mahmud Muhtar Pasha.

3 Mahmud Mukhtar Pascha „Meine Führung im Balkankriege 1912“.

4 Richter, Heinz „Die Griechen im Osmanischen Reich 1913 – 1923“.

5 https://tr.wikipedia.org. – Nâzım Paşa. Kriegsminister 08.01.1912 - 23.01.1913.

In the Turkish personal description of the Minister of War Nâzım Paşa[1] rather large planning deficiencies are seen with the 1908-1913 acting Chief of General Staff İzzet Paşa. [2] He was responsible for the reduction in personnel and did not follow the strategic defense plans of von der Goltz, who had attached great importance to mobilisation, deployment and operation planning. In addition, İzzet Paşa was not available on the ground, as he was busy suppressing unrest in Yemen.

Already during the war, tensions between the victorious powers became apparent, leading to a new constellation at the beginning of the 2nd Balkan War.

With the view that Bulgaria would have been too big a cake, Serbs, Greece, Montenegro, the Ottoman Empire on 11 July 1913 and later Romania joined forces against Bulgaria in June 1913. The latter had to accept defeats and finally ceded territories again. Ottoman troops under Enver advanced on Edirne and marched there again on 21.07.1913. In the bilateral Istanbul agreement with the Ottoman Empire of 23.09.1913, Eastern Thrace was returned to the Ottoman Empire; the border became the present border river Maritza/Meriç Irmağı. Western Thrace went to Bulgaria, later to Greece. In another bilateral agreement with Greece in Athens on 14.11.1913, the Ottoman Empire renounced the region around Selanik, Crete and islands in the Aegean Sea.

In Istanbul the lost war against Italy in 1911 and the course of the 1st Balkan War had political consequences. On 23.01.1913 the Young Turks and the military under the leadership of Enver revolted against the government, which in their opinion was too liberal and weak *"23 Ocak 1913 tarihinde Enver Bey öncülüğünde silahlı bir grubun Bâb-ı Ali'de toplantı halindeki hükûmeti basması, Harbiye Nazırı Nâzım Paşa'yı öldürmesi ve sadrazam Paşa'nın kafasına silah dayarak istifa zorlaması ile İttihat ve Terakki, askeri darbe ile iktidar ele geçirdi".* (" On January 23, 1913, an armed group led by Enver Bey staged a coup d'état at a meeting in the government building, killed[3] the Minister of War Nâzım Paşa, held a gun to the head of Grand Vizier Kâmil Paşa, forced him to resign and thus took power through a military action together with the Ittihat and Terakki party." Translation by the author).

IAW Turkish sources Enver had been promoted to Colonel on 18.01.1913, but shortly after the coup he became (i.e. made himself) General/Paşa. When the new Grand Vizier Şevket Paşa was assassinated on 11.06.1913 the new government developed towards a military dictatorship with a powerless Sultan, with a party in the background and a largely powerless or time dissolved parliament.

Enver later formed a triumvirate in the new cabinet with another officer named Cemal and a civilian named , (Fig. 16) a leading member of the party. Now Enver Paşa became Minister of War, Talât Paşa Minister of the Interior and Cemal Paşa Minister of the Navy. But since Cemal Paşa took over the 4th Army in Damascus at the end of 1914 and also became Vali over a large area, Enver Paşa de facto led the office of the Navy Minister in personal union until the end of 1917;[4] the centre of power shrank to a duumvirate. Enver Paşa continued the reforms in the army already begun by the Minister of War İzzet Paşa, which were continued with verve with the arrival of the German military mission under Liman von Sanders at the end of 1913. The reforms included a reduction of the reserve troops to about 40% in favour of the active ones, the dismissal of about 1,300 officers, the streamlining of training, also of the newly drafted ones, the execution of exercises, especially for the cooperation of the troop

1 Lisec „Der Völkermord an den Armeniern im 1. Weltkrieg – Deutsche Offiziere beteiligt?“. p. 41.

2 https://tr.wikipedia.org. - Ahmet İzzet Furgaç. 23.07.1908-11.06.1913. Title *"Erkân-ı Harbiye-i Umûmiye Riyaseti"*

3 The murderer probably had been Yakup Cemil.

4 Lisec „Der Völkermord an den Armeniern im 1. Weltkrieg – Deutsche Offiziere beteiligt?“ p. 64.

categories in the so-called "battle of combined arms". Even the keeping of a war diary (harp ceredesi) is taught. The orders are to be written in a certain format with 7 sections.[1] NATO has laid down a similar procedure e.g. also in a Standardisation Agreement (STANAG).

As already mentioned, on the Ottoman side, after the later established date of foundation of the Turkish Air Force in 1911, (Fig. 18) Ottoman aircraft also took part in the Balkan Wars of 1912/1913. As the Turkish Air Force did not yet have its own aircraft industry, they were acquired abroad and each pilot/tayyaretci and observer were initially trained there.

The history of the Ottoman Air Force 1911-1918 is described comprehensively and in great detail in a five-volume Turkish-language work entitled "Türk Hava Kuvvetlei Tarihi" by Ajun Kurter from 2006,[2] apparently a commissioned work for the Turkish Air Force Command with a focus on the Ottoman/Turkish Air Force, which operated under Ottom[3]an/Turkish sovereign insignia.[4] This means that e.g. German aircraft which operated under German insignia in the Ottoman Empire during World War I are only marginally mentioned, also because comprehensive knowledge about them was not any more available.

The cooperation with the German Air Force 1911-2011 is described in the bilingual German book "Askeri Havacılıkta 100 yıllık Türk Alman İşbirlıği" or "100 Years of German/Turkish Cooperation in Military Aviation", a commissioned work for the Ankara office of EADS company with the participation of the author,[5] further Turkish and German authors. With recourse to both works and further literature as well as available official and private files on the INTERNET, a quite complete picture of the development of the Turkish Air Force up to the present day is thus obtained. Here first the development until 1914 and the missions in the Balkan wars.

First flight attempts with human muscle power were allegedly made as early as 1630 from the Galata Tower in Istanbul by Ahmet Çelebi, in Germany demonstrably by Otto Lilienthal, who crashed fatally in 1896, and in the USA by the Wright brothers around 1901. In 1903 Orville Wright also managed the first powered flight over a very short distance. On 25.07.1909 the Frenchman Louis Blériot flew with a machine of the same name over the Channel to Great Britain. The French then became leaders in aircraft construction, which is why the Ottoman Empire also sought cooperation with them above all. In 1911 France held all the "world records".

This cooperation was preceded in 1912 by experiments with two German tethered balloons of the type Dragon, acquired by the Ottoman Empire, and in 1913 with an airship of the type Parseval, the technology of which Germany, in turn, had focused on for too long until the First World War due to sceptical thinking on the part of the military. Count Ferdinand von Zeppelin's controlled airships (Güdümli balon) with an aluminium skin became particularly famous. The Istanbul district Yeşilköy became a testing ground, thc site of later flight schools (in 1912 the 1st school for pilots and observers, in 1914 as the 2nd school a naval flying school and in 1917 stationing of an operational fighter squadron to protect the capital) and the modern Atatürk Airport. Captive balloons and airships were still used in the Ottoman Empire with German and Ottoman crews in World War I: Balloons for reconnaissance and as barrage against enemy aircraft, e.g. at the straits and off Izmir, and airships e.g. over the Black Sea for

1 Erickson „Ottoman Army Effectiveness in World War I" p. 9-11.

2 In the possession of the author. To his knowledge only in Turkish. Without ISBN number. With a preface by Orgeneral Faruk Cömert.

3 https://tr.wikipdia.org. - *OsmanlıTayyare Bölükleri.*

4 In aircraft acquired by Germany, almost exclusively in World War I, the national emblem was only a square with the Iron Cross painted over in black, later the crescent moon with star.

5 Since only a small edition was published, the book is at least borrowable in the German library system. ISBN 978-975-8559-13-8.

reconnaissance and weaponry. They operated from Jamboli/Yanbolu in Bulgaria from 1915 to 1917, also to guard Ottoman coal transports on the Black Sea coast. The advent of spark telegraphy with a range of about 100 km, further developed into "directional telegraphy" with the ability to determine location, and the establishment of a suitable reporting network in the Ottoman Empire also increased the temporal effect of the reconnaissance results. Towards the middle of the First World War, however, balloons and airships were replaced by "heavier-than-air" planes, all of which were fixed-wing aircraft.

Mustafa Kemal (Atatürk) was one of the first officers to inspect the new means of war in September 1910 in Picardy/France during a manoeuvre together with the military attaché Fethi Bey. 14 airplanes and 4 airships were used. When Atatürk had taken over the responsibility in Turkey he promoted this new third classic division of the services with the famous two words "İstikbal Göklerdedir". ("The future is in the skies". Translation by the author). Also stated in the coat of arms of of the Turkish Air Force school (Fig. 19) The date of foundation of the school is given as 1951.

The Minister of War Mahmut Şevket Paşa,[1] also a sponsor, bought French, British and German aircraft between 1911 and 1914, had Ottoman pilots trained abroad, who then transferred aircraft to Istanbul in 1912. On 26.04.1912 the first flight of an Ottoman pilot, Captain Fesâ Bey, on an Ottoman aircraft of type R.E.P. took place in Yeşilköy.[2] At the beginning of the Balkan War, the Ottoman Empire owned 10 mission aircraft of 5 different types as well as 4 aircraft for training.[3] After the 1st armistice on 03.12.1912 the operational stock had shrunk to 6. The opposing states also operated some machines. For observation purposes 2 sets of binoculars were then procured from the German Zeiss company. The Greeks now also used naval aircraft of the type Maurice Farman Hydravion.

Due to the scarcity of financial means, the Osmani population also collected money for the purchase of airplanes, which will be repeated in the War of Independence 1919 - 1922, but also for the purchase of modern ships before World War I. These were signs of great common solidarity, but also a strongly emerging national feeling. German pilots also transferred 4 aircraft and entered Ottoman services as pilots or airborne observers, supported by maintenance personnel.

This is how the German pilot Mauricio Scherff describes, among other things, an adventurous joint mission with a biplane type Mars over Eastern Thrace with a Captain Kemal.[4] With hits from Bulgarian gunners on the plane and a twisted propeller, both landed safely again in strong winds and at nightfall in Yeşilköy. In general it must be stated that according to statistics, about 50% of the losses in World War I were not caused by enemy fire, but by weather, lack of training, tactical errors and technical failure. As the aircraft were still unarmed at the beginning of World War I, apart from a pistol or small hand bombs in the cockpit, and the MG was only slowly being scaffolded from 1915 onwards, the first mission of the crews was that of reconnaissance anyway, not the destruction of troops or installations on the ground or on the water nor enemy aircraft. Other tasks were then added, such as passenger transport, courier services and logistics. It was also astonishing how pilot and observer could communicate with each other; the case of soldiers of two nations occurred even more frequently: E.g. the pilot Fethi Bey and his German observer Birkner, again in a Mars biplane. Since the observer was the more important person on a reconnaissance mission, later also the weapon operator and radio operator, he usually wore a higher rank than the pilot.

1 Minister of War and Grand Vizier in the period 1910 -1913. https://tr.wikipedia.org. - Mahmud Şevket Paşa.
2 Kurter Cilt I, sayfa 83.
3 Kurter. Cilt I, sayfa 115.
4 Not to be mixed up with Atatürk. He never entered an aeroplane.

Again, as in many wars with Russia before, the Ottoman Empire is now threatened by a pincer movement.

Since in the Balkan wars, similar to the above mentioned war against Greece, Germans fought on both sides, it is proven that it almost came to an air fight between two German pilots.

In the end, by 1914 the Ottoman Empire had acquired at least 24 aircraft,[1] with the insurmountable disadvantages of a large variety of types and a technical reliability still in its infancy. Due to the lack of hangars in the area for protection against weather and camouflage, highly specialized training of the pilots, which made interchangeability difficult, and lack of qualified maintenance personnel, fuel shortage and also Bulgarian successes, it was not surprising that the operational readiness of the few aircraft was low and had shrunk to about 2 aircraft at the beginning of World War I. (Fig. 20) This made a new start necessary at the end of 1914, which also began in March 1915 with the arrival of German aircraft. From the Air Force's point of view, the period of the Balkan wars was therefore a time of training, experimentation, education of personnel and gaining knowledge.

WARS WITH RUSSIA

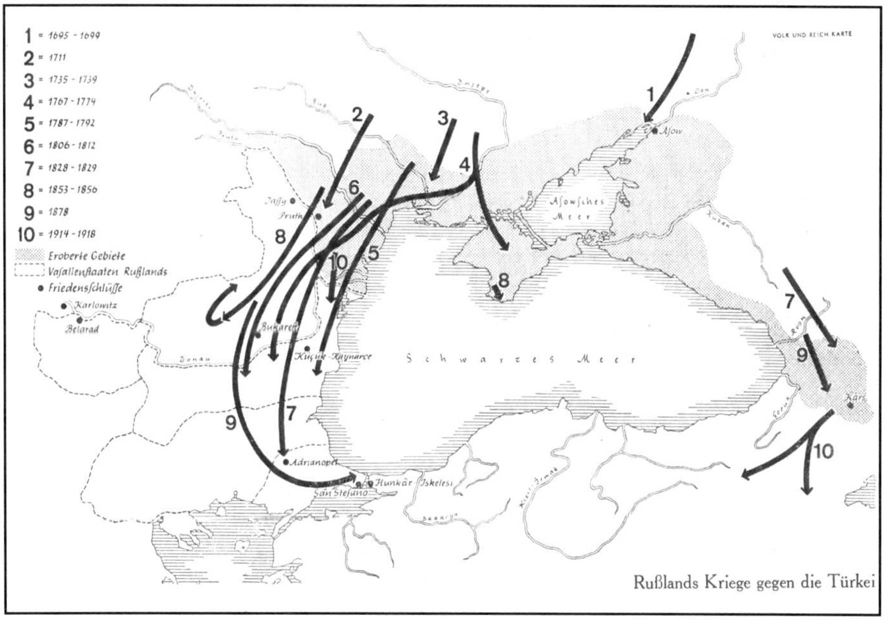

Map 9

Enver Paşa as Minister of War since 1913 also had the ambition to let long-distance competitions take place as in Western Europe, such as over 2,500 km from Istanbul to Egypt over the Taurus with 13 stopovers, as air-to-air refuelling was not yet possible. So Captain Fethi as pilot with his observer First Lieutenant Sadık started on 08.02.1914 with a Blériot XI

1 Kurter Cilt V, sayfa 30.

B named "Muavenet-i Miliye" ("National Assistance"); but they crashed fatally in bad weather on 27.02.1914 near Lake Tiberias. Shortly afterwards, the same fate was suffered by First Lieutenant and pilot Nuri with a Deperdussin named "Prens Celalettin", while the observer Captain Hakkı survived. In May 1914, Captain Salim and his observer Major Kemal made the first long-distance flight from Beirut to Alexandria on a Blériot named "Edremit". The flying monument near the Fatih Mosque in Istanbul is one of the reminders of the heroes of the early years.

The conclusion for the Ottoman Empire and its army for the 20th century until the beginning of the 1st World War is devastating from a political/military point of view. Neither politics nor the army were able to prevent the enormous territorial losses in the Balkans and the last territories on the North African coast.

- The mission of the army was in principle unchanged, i.e. at least to maintain the status quo. It has not succeeded in doing so.

- A rift ran through the army as well as through society as a whole, as evidenced by the chain of revolutionary events from 1908 to 1913. With regards to the relationship to politics or loyalty, the question had to be asked: "To whom"? The parliament or the respective government, led by the Grand Vizier or the Sultan? The Sultan had lost his authority, the governments changed and the idea of a "parliamentary army" introduced by Mustafa Kemal from 1920 onwards, which is still valid, was not yet in sight. The rift, or even the rifts, ran between the religious conservatives and the progressives, between the more liberal and the hardliners, between two competing parties, one of which was to gain the upper hand in 1913 and with the triumvirate, later duumvirate, caused a phase of practical dictatorship until 1918.

- The army's traditional relationship to religion still existed, but was now overshadowed by the rise of nationalism. Among the conflicting ideologies, those of Islamism (İslamcılık) and Ottomanism (Osmancılık) fell behind Panturanism (Turancılık), represented by Enver Paşa, and Türkism (Türkçülük) as well as Western orientation (Batıcılık), represented by Mustafa Kemal (Atatürk).[1].

- The internal condition of the army was deplorable, due to lack of money and internal strife. Even the reformers and foreign advisers could do little to change this. The navy was weak and outdated, the army geographically dispersed among the unstable periphery of the empire and the threat/war fronts. The technological backwardness vis-à-vis the West was particularly evident in the establishment of the third classical branch of the armed forces, the air force. Only much later has Turkey been able to close this important technological gap through research, development and its own production, made possible also by the economic situation.[2]

The Ottoman Army in World War I

The abundance of events in the First World War and in the run-up to it allows only a small selection that seems relevant in the sense of our central questions. The Ottoman Army is to remain the central focus of the study, very soon in a "brotherhood of arms" with the German army. The environment will only be addressed within the necessary framework. The general course of the First World War is assumed to be largely known, the campaigns in the Ottoman Empire are only briefly outlined. The deployment of Ottoman troops outside the Ottoman Empire in Galicia, Romania and Macedonia is also not considered, apart from an inevitable weakening of the Turks at home.

1 Due to limitations of the subject matter of this book, the ideological approaches will not be explained further. However, they can already be derived from the terms.

2 "Turkey seeks to use mainly local defense tech by 2020" Article in Hürriyet Daily News dated 19.06.2017.

At the request of Sultan Mehmed V a German military mission arrives again in Istanbul on 14.12.1913 under the leadership of General Liman von Sanders, the later Marshal/*Müşir,* with him initially 10 further officers. Again, the aim is to restore the Ottoman army to a more efficient state after the recent defeats. (Fig. 21) Von Sanders did not suspect then that he and his advisors in the further growing military mission until the delayed outbreak of World War I in the Ottoman Empire on 29.10.1914 in cooperation with the Minister of War Enver Paşa would only have just less than 11 months time. After the outbreak of war in the West and the defensive alliance with Germany on August 2, 1914, this time was overlaid by conscription, mobilization and deployment.

In November, von Sanders took over the command of the 1st Army in Istanbul until March 1915, in April 1915 - April 1918 the command of the 5th Army in Gallipoli/Çanakkale and in April 1918 the command of the army group "F"/*Yıldırım* north of Jerusalem. In these functions, whenever there was time, he of course continued training of the troops, from night marches to shooting and from fortifications building to conduct in combat. In his staffs, von Sanders preferred to work with Turkish officers, because he wanted to ensure the connection with the subordinate predominantly Ottoman troops.[1]

Almost on a par with Enver Paşa had von Sanders, equipped with the necessary command authority, freedom of action in the training of the soldiers, could also soon make an impression in the form of a parade in front of the Sultan in Istanbul and international observers early in 1914. However, it could not hide the fact that the good impression could only be achieved by concentrating resources; the situation of the remaining troops in the Ottoman Empire remained deplorable. The predominant view of the experts then remained that the Ottoman army was only capable of "defense", less of mobile combat in attack or delay. This was to prove true in war, was also recognized by Mustafa Kemal and was partially corrected in the fight for independence from 1921 onwards. The other major deficit was the persistence of "command tactics" as opposed to "mission tactics", which required more independent action on the part of the leaders and subleaders. Here also religion sometimes led to some passivity, even to fatalism. Mustafa Kemal, who had the opposite temperament, had also recognized this weakness and had already set impressive examples in the Gallipoli War of 1915 through his independent action in specific situations.

However, there was also the danger of underestimation on the part of the British, French and Russians, especially the Turkish soldier, who developed astonishing abilities in infantry fighting, based on faith and love for his country. In contrast to Western Europeans, the Turkish soldier in particular proved to be tough and undemanding. In the absence of rifles or ammunition he also switched to close combat. Arab troops did not have this quality and also became more unreliable after the Arab rebellion in Mecca mid 1916. Armenians and Ottomans of Greek origin, the so-called "Rum", were already placed in worker - battalions or transferred to less sensitive posts in the army at the beginning of 1915. In this respect, the fighting Ottoman army was essentially reduced to a Turkish army. It was not surprising that the Turks were tired of war after such long years of war, and desertions could also be explained by the care of the family at home.

The outcome of wars is usually already determined by the Allies on both sides, in the case of the two world wars mainly by the participation of the USA. Even operational or tactical victories cannot change this, not even the greatest willingness to fight or exceptional bravery. The German Field Marshal General Erich von Manstein later boldly described this with the

1 Liman von Sanders „Fünf Jahre Türkei".

title of his book: "Verlorene Siege" (Lost Victories). A new strategy or new means of war can also bring about a decision or shorten a war, like the US atomic bomb in World War II. Furthermore, the strategic resource situation plays a very important role, as do other geostrategic factors such as the depth of space or the distances to the various theatres of war. In individual cases, other factors can also play a role, such as the duration of the war or e.g. the domestic political situation of the USA in the Vietnam War 1955-1975.

E.g. in World War I, the Entente, formed by Russia, Great Britain and France among others, joined by Greece, Italy and Romania in addition to the USA, would have severe consequences for the Ottoman Empire until the peace negotiations in Lausanne in 1923. Bulgaria later joined the triple alliance of Germany, Austria -Hungary and Italy. whereas Italy later left it.

For the Ottoman Empire the 1st World War began on 29.10.1914 with the invasion of the Ottoman fleet under the leadership of the German Admiral Wilhelm Souchon into Russian Black Sea ports at the insistence of Germany and with the approval or prepared instructions of Enver Paşa. The Sultan as commander-in-chief was only informed afterwards, the Grand Vizier was passed over, Talât Paşa was involved and the Naval Minister Cemal Paşa was allegedly not, according to his statements, which is hard to believe. The following text corresponds to the current state of research[1], even if the role of Germany is not mentioned.

"*Gerçekten, 22 Ekim'den başlayarak, Enver, Karadeniz'deki Rus limanlarına saldırma emrini verecektir Amiral Souchon'a. Kimi üyeleri savaşa girmeye karşı olan Osmanlı kabinesinin son duraksamaları görülür. Ne var ki, 29 Ekim'de zarlarlar atılmıştır: Aldığı emirlere uygun olarak, Türk donanması, Odessa, Sivastopol ve Nevorossisk'i topa tutacaktır".* ("In fact, Enver gave Admiral Souchon the order to attack the Russian Black Sea ports on October 22. After all, some Ottoman cabinet members wanted to prevent the start of the war at the last moment. However, on 29 October the decision was made "In accordance with the given orders, the Turkish fleet will bomb Odessa, Sevastopol and Novorossiysk". Translation of the author)[2].

After evaluation of the Turkish file on World War I (https://tr.wikipedia.org.- *I Dünya Savaşı*) and many other documents the strength ratios on the ground of the Ottoman Empire can be estimated. The Triple Alliance (*İttifak Devletleri*) brought in about 3 million soldiers, of which about 2 million were on the front lines, over 90% of them provided by the Ottoman Empire. Although Germany in summary had about 30,000 soldiers of all 3 services of the armed forces on the ground until the end of the war, Austria-Hungary about 7,000-10,000 men[3] from the army and Bulgaria an unknown number of ships with subordination of its navy in 1915, one can quantitatively speak of an Ottoman army, although formally it was a coalition army of 4 states. The contribution of Germany and Austria-Hungary was mainly qualitative, in the case of Germany also material. The growth of the German Military Mission has so far been presented in the literature in a consistently incomplete and misleading manner.[4] Of the

1 In many Turkish accounts, Enver's role is still played down as if the attack had been launched by Admiral Souchon (meaning Germany) alone, as if Enver had only given permission for reconnaissance. So for example in https://tr.wikipedia.org. - *I Dünya Savaşı: "26 Ekim'de Osmanlı donanması bir keşif tatbikatı için hazırlanma emri aldı ..." (*"On October 26th, the Ottoman Fleet was ordered to conduct a reconnaissance operation..." Translation by the author). See also Wolf "Gallipoli" p. 50 ff. or Wallach "Anatomie einer Militärhilfe". p. 165 or Mühlmann "Deutschland und die Türkei 1913-1914". Annex 9.

2 Mantran "Osmanlı İmparatorluğu Tarihi II" p. 275. Zürcher „Turkey – A modern History.

3 Meier-Welcker "Seeckt".

4 Jung & Mötz „Die K.U.K. Streitkräfte im Ersten Weltkrieg 1914-1918" p. 33 In addition to extensive artillery, the Monarchy provided above all logistics troops, medical units, instructors and specialists for various tasks, from telegraphy to mining and cable car construction. They were deployed throughout the Ottoman Empire.

30,000 soldiers mentioned above[1], about 2/3 were deployed internationally with double German/Turkish subordination, about 1/3 nationally with purely German subordination. With an officer quota of about 8%, it can be assumed that about 2,400 German officers served in the 3 branches of the armed forces. With regards to German personnel management, however, all German soldiers were assigned to the military mission, which had to account to the German Reich.

The numbers of the Entente (*İtilaf Devletleri*) on the battlefields of the Ottoman soil, including troops from many other countries, are difficult to determine in total; ultimately, the balance of power on each front is decisive for the individual battles. The Ottoman Empire, strengthened by Germans and Austrians, fought on 5 main fronts and 3 secondary fronts, which will be briefly discussed below.[2]

The battles in the north-east on the Caucasus front lasted from 24.10.1914 - 30.10.1918.[3] The impatient Enver Paşa went to the front with his German chief of staff General Bronsart von Schellendorf, took over command of the 3rd army on 21.12.1914, attacked the Russians and suffered a bitter defeat in a winter campaign without sufficient preparation at Sarıkamış. "*130.000 kişilik asker mevcudunun 90.000'i çarpışmalarda veya soğuktan donarak hayatını kaybetti*". ("Of 130,000 soldiers, 90,000 died in battle or from cold. Translation by the author).

Because several thousand defected Armenians had also fought on the side of the Russians and these had been deliberately deployed at the front, an Ottoman dagger thrust legend was created in connection after another defeat at Van (19.04.-06.05.1915).

"Bu mevcuda dört tane olan Ermeni Gönüllü Tugayları iki tugay katılmıştı. Diğer iki tugay İran Cephesinde bulunmaktaydı". In this number 2 of 4 Armenian volunteer brigades were deployed here, the other two on the Iranian front". Translation by the author).

The Ottoman Armenians were disarmed in early 1915, similar to the "Greek-born" "*Rum*", and transferred to worker- battalions or to less critical posts. Enver Paşa returned to Istanbul already at the beginning of January 1915.

In the final phase of the fighting, Nuri Paşa conquered Baku on behalf of Enver after the Russian October Revolution and the Russian vacuum left behind with the "Islamic Army" on 15 September 1918 in pursuit of the above-mentioned "Turanian Idea", also in order to have a bargaining chip for the subsequent peace negotiations. The total losses in the north-east including prisoners of war and sick persons are estimated at 300,000. The Germans had deployed only a small number of leading personnel in this area, including two division commanders. From mid-1918 German troops landed in Georgia and were very soon sent to Istanbul, after a temporary political/military tension with Enver Paşa regarding Baku. Of course, Germany was also very interested in the oilfields of Baku.The few air planes were practically not effective in northeast due to the terrain, weather and the necessary logistics with difficult access to the front.

Before dealing with the Çanakkale/Gallipoli front, one should first take a look at the command powers resulting from the top-level military/political structure. (Fig. 22) Supreme local warlord and commander was the Sultan, his deputy was the Minister of War Enver Paşa. He also held the office of the Minister of the Navy for Cemal Paşa until the end of 1917, because he was not available in Istanbul as commander of the 4th Army and Vali in Damascus. The Grand Vizier was not directly in the military hierarchy, but like the other ministers he

1 Lisec „Der Völkermord an den Armeniern – Deutsche Offiziere beteiligt?" p. 46 ff. Thus the estimate of the number of German generals / admirals is correct at about 33, but not the number of officers in https://tr.wikipedia.org. - *Alman Askeri Misyonu*. See also Nutku „Alte Kameraden". p. 174.

2 https://tr.wikipedia.org. – *I Dünya Savaşı'nda Osmanlı cepheleri.*

3 https://tr.wikipedia.org. – *Kafkasya Cephesi.*

THE FRONTS

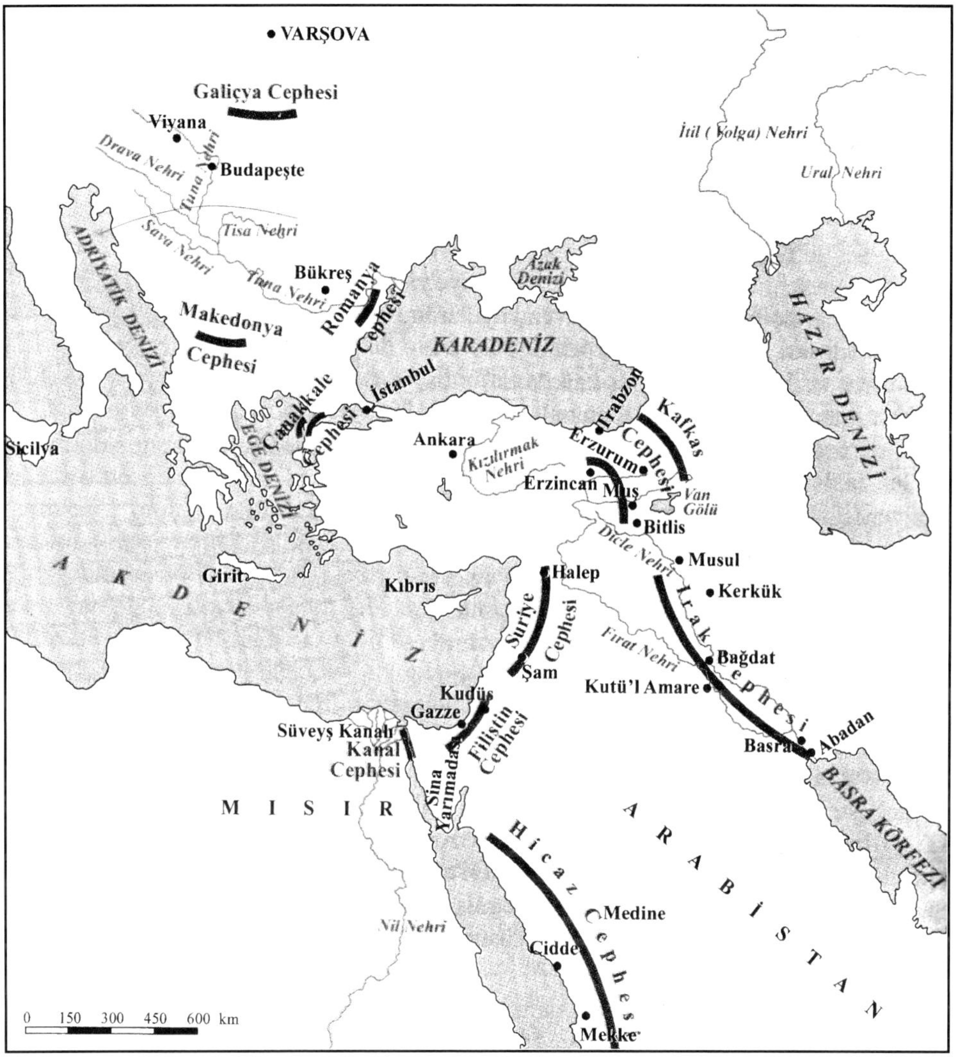

Map 9

participated in the decision-making processes, among these with growing influence the Minister of the Interior Talât Paşa, who also became Grand Vizier in 1917.

Liman von Sanders represented the German military interests for the German Emperor at the head of the German military mission, the political ones the German Embassy. The General Staff, which was subordinate to the Minister of War and nominally led by him, was de facto led by the Chief of Staff, General Bronsart von Schellendorf[1], and from the end of 1917 by General Hans von Seeckt. The staff had 13 departments, most of which were headed by Germans. The "floating" navy or fleet with the German commander Admiral Souchon[2], who was in charge of the Ottoman Navy and the Bulgarian Navy when Bulgaria joined in 1915, was under the command of Enver Paşa. He also had under his command the German Admiral Guido von Usedom, responsible for the coastal fortifications and the mines along the straits, who in turn was sub-commandant for the Bosporus and the Dardanelles. It was precisely this organisation, which mainly operated the forts at the Dardanelles, used artillery and mines and had some ships at its disposal, which was to gain great importance in the Battle of Gallipoli.

Already here it should be mentioned that in the general staff also officers of the navy and the air force served, it was therefore not only a pure land - oriented army staff. In the end Enver led all 3 services[3], provided by 4 nations, so that the uniformity of command was given and quick decisions could be made without lengthy consultations.[4] Due to the expertise in his staffs in Istanbul he was also able to lead triphibious operations like the first big battle of this kind in Çanakkale/Gallipoli. Previously, historically, no major air forces or ships – including submarines - had participated in a similar operation. In this respect, the main battle of Gallipoli from the end of 1914 to the beginning of 1916 is a military-historical lesson, which will be repeated e.g. to some degree in World War II with the landing in Normandy in 1944.

THE THREAT TO THE DARDANELLES AND ISTANBUL

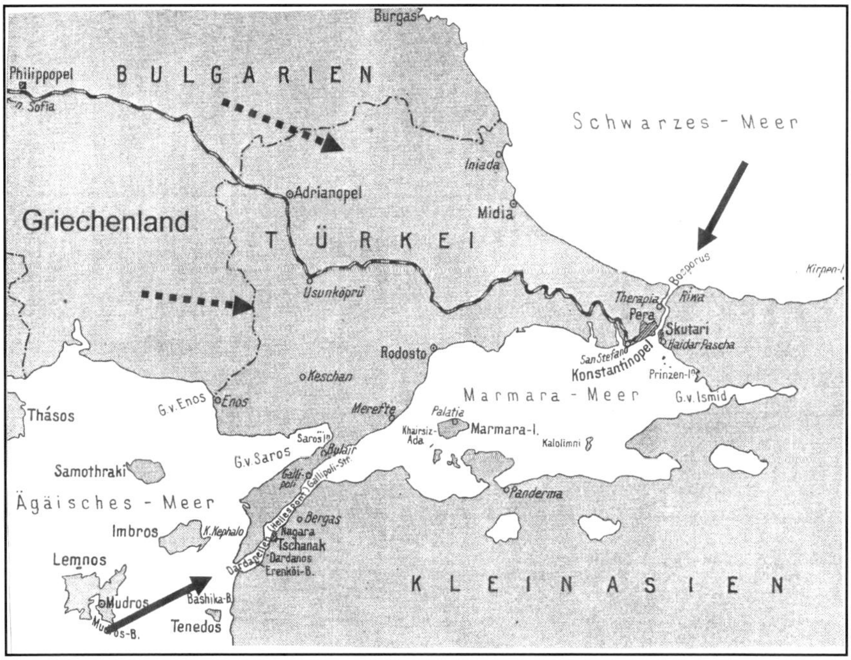

Map 11 The Dardanelles

1 Uyar & Erickson "A Military History of the Ottomans" p. 238.
2 Admiral Souchon was also in charge of incoming German ships, such as submarines, when they operated in his coastal waters.
3 Even though the Air Force was not yet a separate service of the German and Ottoman Empire at that time.
4 In NATO terminology called "Joint" (all branches of the armed forces) and "Combined" (several nations).

The battles at the Dardanelles[1] lasted from 03.11.1914 to November 1918, because already at the beginning of the war British and French ships bombarded the outer forts at the Dardanelles in reaction to the events in the Black Sea. Afterwards the intensity of the operations decreased but reached a first climax in the naval battle on 18.03.1915. After another break the land war began on 25.04.1915, which ended with the withdrawal of the Entente States at the beginning of 1916. Until the end of the war mainly air war operations of lower intensity followed. Istanbul, however, was never in serious danger until the armistice, since no threat emanated from Greece or Bulgaria in Eastern Thrace and this region could be thinned out by troops in favour of the capital and other theatres of war; nor were the Russians able to realize their intention to advance to Istanbul via the Bosphorus or by land and unite with the other Entente troops there. These geostrategic conditions favoured the victory of the Ottoman/German/Austrian troops, along with other geostrategic factors such as long distances for the Entente states including India, Australia, New Zealand and the (enforced) treatment of Gallipoli by the Entente as a secondary theatre of war with less effort than operations in the West. A decisive contribution to these strategic, but above all also subsequent operational mistakes or the underestimation of the enemy was made not only by the entire British/French leadership, but especially by the British Navy Minister Winston Churchill, in this case with regard to the naval war. The outcome of this battle was astonishing for the world public.

Istanbul and the Dardanelles were threatened from various directions: The main threat was from southwest by Great Britain and France - aiming at the Gallipoli peninsula, perhaps via the Gulf of Saros. In the north-east Istanbul was threatened from Russia via the Black Sea. At the beginning, it remained unclear how Greece and Bulgaria would act.

The shelling of the outer forts from 03.11.1914 by 4 ships from Great Britain and France was rather an emotional reaction and from an operational point of view almost counter-productive. For the defender it was a wake-up call, which now bundled all forces on site and thus he was prepared on 18.03.1915. British, French and Russian citizens in the Ottoman Empire were now under threat and not evacuated yet.

On the eve of the 17.03.1915 the German military pilot Erich Serno arrived in Çanakkale. "*Almanlar, Turk askeri havacılığını yenids teşkilatlandırma işini üstlerine aldılar. Bunun için Üsteğmen Erich Serno görevlendirilmi"*. ("The Germans had assumed the responsibility of rebuilding Turkish air forces. Oberleutnant Erich Serno had been entrusted with this task." Translation by the author).

On 17. March 1915 a Rumpler B I had arrived on the ship at Nagara/Nara Naval Air Base north of Çannakkale on the Asian shore[2]. Serno reported to Admiral Usedom. It was the 1st German machine of about 500, which reached the frontlines during the war in the Ottoman Empire and about half of them were used under Ottoman or German flag each. Together with the Ottoman Blériot XI-2 already operating on the ground, both aircraft formed the core of the mixed 1st Squadron to be established.

After a test flight in the evening of 17th March 1915, Serno and the observer Naval Captain Carl Schneider would start a risky reconnaissance flight over sea against the island of Tenedos/Bozcaada in the morning of March 18th. They spot about 40 ships approaching Gallipoli and report this immediately to Admiral Usedom on their return. For successful verification of the report, First Lieutenant Mehmet Cemal Durusoy with his Blériot and

1 https://tr.wikipedia.org. - *Çanakkale Savaşı*. https://de.wikipedia.org. - Schlacht von Gallipoli. www.gallipoli1915.de. Wolf „Gallipoli 1915". http://fr.wikipedia.org. – Bataille des Dardanelles. Richter, *Gallipoli 1915*

2 From March 1915 an additional airfield for army aviation was built near Çanakkale, and from June 1915 another one north of Gallipoli on the peninsula. This airfield with the flying squadron was then placed under the command of General Liman von Sanders.

Lieutenant Frank Seidler with Navy Captain / Denizyüzbaşı Hüseyin Sedat as marine observer, again with the Rumpler, repeated the reconnaissance. A prime example of cooperation between two nations in the air as in the previous Balkan wars.

THE RECONNAISSANCE FLIGHTS ON 18.03.1915 WITH ARMY PLANES OVER SEA FROM CANAKKALE TO THE ISLAND LIMNOS

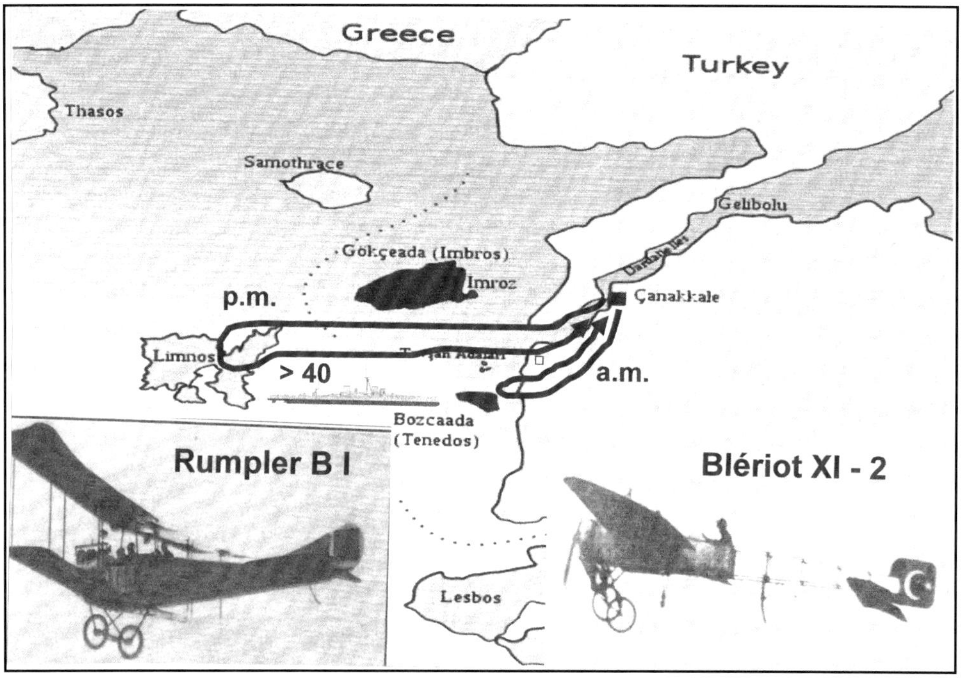

Map 12

In the ensuing naval battle, the defender is assisted not only by the skill and bravery but also by luck, favoured by the omissions and mistakes of the attacker. The fire of the attacker's naval artillery had little effect against the forts with their ramparts on either side of the waterway, because the cannons of the attacker cannot shoot steep fire. Since the ships themselves are endangered, they have to keep moving[1], which worsens their own effect. The lack of steep fire cannot be remedied later in the landbattle in April 1915, even when the attacker directs the fire from balloon ships or airplanes. Nevertheless, the procedure of airborne observers has proven to be very effective up to the present, with the role now being taken over by drones.

Another deficiency is evident in the clearing of mines, in that the small unarmoured mine clearance vehicles are exposed to the action of the Ottoman coastal artillery, including that of the 14 mobile batteries with changeable positions connected by telephone, since "thick ships"

1 Thus determined after a British/French dispute, in which the French admiral Emile Gueprattte argued against shooting out of calm: "*Je jugeais que cette tactique offrait de graves inconvénients pour les unités engagées*". In "L'Expédition des Dardanelles 1914-1915" p. 57.

cannot clear the way. While this artillery could not yet be eliminated by aircraft, it would have required infantry on land, on both sides of the waterway.

The battleships, in turn, proceed in 3 rows, alternating with each other and then again turning into opposite directions. But here they already make the mistake when testing the procedure before 18.03.1915 to always turn at the same place parallel to the coast off Erenköy. (Fig. 24) As countermeasure here in a night operation already on 08.03.1915 the above mentioned mine bar marked No. 11 was laid at a depth of 4.5 m, which was not discovered despite aerial reconnaissance. The attacker recorded the total loss of 3 warships with many dead and the damage of another 4, a loss rate of 7/20. Damage was also caused by mobile Ottoman artillery, especially operating on the Asian shore. The attacker withdrew as a result. There had been 1 Russian, 15 British and 4 French warships.

The 40 m long Ottoman minelayer Nusret, (Fig. 23) built in Germany in 1911, handed over to the Ottoman Navy in 1913 thus became famous. The battle-critical observation and idea was a joint German/Turkish effort by the mixed crew [1] under their commander Lieutenant Captain Hafız Nazmi (Akpınar) and the leadership of the minelayer flotilla. A replica of the ship is now in the Naval Museum in Çanakkale, but unfortunately there is no indication mentioning the close cooperation of both nations, apart from the place where the keel was laid.

This statement also applies to the other museums and memorials to the Gallipoli battles: Almost no mention of the Germans or Austrians, but extensive tributes to Mustafa Kemal (Atatürk). However, the Germans also refused to erect any memorial.

In an interim conclusion, it should be noted that the British Admiralty, in particular, negating the results of earlier German and British studies and opinions[2], believed that they could force a breakthrough to Istanbul at sea without land forces, only because this had been achieved much earlier under different circumstances. Churchill held this view even after the defeat of March 18th 1915[3]. Moltke had already claimed, *"If the artillery materiel at the Dardanelles is in order, I believe that any enemy fleet in the world would dare to sail up the road; it would always be necessary to debark troops and attack the batteries in the throat"*.[4]

That was certainly true of the steamships as well. Already the most important bottleneck south of Çanakkale could not be overcome by the attacker, whereupon another mine and artillery bar at the height of Çanakkale was still waiting for him. And how could the ships have survived in Istanbul with only a small number of marines on board. There the Ottoman fleet was also waiting in the Bosporus under their flagship the Yavuz/Goeben with Admiral Wilhelm Anton Souchon.

The British Minister of War Horatio Herbert Kitchener had probably also recognized this. On 16.02.1915 he demanded 50.000 men land forces for the time "after the breakthrough of the navy", but these were only granted on 10.03.1915.

Finally, on 25.04.1915, the troops of the Entente, in addition to about 200 ships of the navy and the air force, started with 5 army divisions under the command of the British General Ian Hamilton: Two British, one French and the ANZAC[5] large unit with one Australian and one

1 The 5 Germans on board were among others the engineer named Arnholt Reeder under the command of Admiral Usedom. Wolf "Gallipoli 1915". p. 90 .

2 A British staff study from 1906, a contrary opinion of Winston Churchill from 1911 (in Robert James "Gallipoli"), the opinions of the British military attaché Col Cunliffe - Owen, the British admiral Sir Arthur Henry Limpus and others.

3 Churchill "Die Weltkrise 1911-1918 Band I" p. 602. The risks of the army (he means the land forces) were greater than those of the fleet.

4 Moltke „Briefe über Zustände und Begebenheiten in der Türkei aus den Jahren 1835-1839. p. 100. Moltke visited the Dardanelles 5 times for inspection and rated the forts at the 1.3 km wide constriction south of Çanakkale as the most important.

5 Australian and New Zealand Army Corps.

New Zealand division, i.e. about 75,000 men from the army. Again, the Entente had no common commander-in-chief, e.g. in London, unlike the defender in Istanbul.

The 5th Ottoman Army[1], newly formed a month earlier, was able to deploy 6 divisions, i.e. approx. 84,000 men under the command of General Liman von Sanders with headquarters (HQ) in Gallipoli/Gelibolu, in addition to the Navy and the Air Force. Both sides will, however, introduce considerable reinforcements in the course of the battle, whereby the initial ratio of forces of approx. 1:1 will worsen to approx. 2:1 to the disadvantage of the Entente. Taking into account the above mentioned geostrategic factors, the Entente was faced with a critical operational situation from the beginning, even though its fleet and air force were clearly superior. Moreover, the difficult sandy terrain clearly favoured the defender. Tactical factors and planning mistakes on the part of the Entente, which could have been avoided, were added to this, such as water shortage, poor maps, lack of ammunition, completely inadequate medical services, and later the poor training of the reinforcements for the Suvla Bay operation.

Very surprising, also for Liman von Sanders, was the local approach of the attack forces: The French division on the Asian side near Kumkale for a simulated attack, the British Royal Naval Division (an infantry division) in the Saros Gulf off Bulayır, an isthmus of about 4 km width, also with a fictitious attack to irritate the defender. In fact, von Sanders took some time to recognize the deception in the Saros Gulf, but then reacted by redeploying forces and deploying operational reserves. He had even had this practised across the waterway in both directions. The advantage of the feint attacks for the defender, however, was that the Entente was initially only able to deploy less fighting force. The next surprise was that the British placed their 29th division at the southern tip of the peninsula, furthest away from Istanbul. A sickle cut out of the Bay of Saros would have been operationally desirable, but had been rejected by the British Navy due to the nature of the shore conditions. To make matters worse, the ANZAC troops landed in the wrong place[2] on the west coast at *Arı Burnu*, where they had to fight against a steep treeless karst terrain, against a defender who could hold them down from the hills, despite heavy counter-fire from the Navy. The *Alcı Tepe* in the south was after all 240 m high, the *Kocaçimen Tepe* opposite ANZAC even 320 m.

While in the south of the peninsula the defender was able to effectively delay the attacker's action, the situation worsened in relation to the Anzac troops. Now the famous situation arose in which LTC Mustafa Kemal (later Atatürk) flashed his military class. Although he had to perform the army reserve with his 19th division, i.e. he should only have been allowed to act with the permission of Liman von Sanders, he instinctively recognized the situation. He shouted at fleeing soldiers: *"Neden çekiliyorsunuz? Düşmandan kaçılmaz, düşmanla savaşılır. Cephaneniz kalmadıysa süngüleriniz vardır. Süngü tak, yere yat!"* ("Why are you backing away? You do not flee from the enemy, you fight. If you have no ammunition left, you still have your bayonets. Fix bayonets![3] Lay down!" Translation by the author).

The opponent was initially irritated by this behaviour and perhaps sensed a feint. Mustafa Kemal immediately gathered all troops within reach, regardless of whom they belonged to and urged them to attack with the words:

"Size ben taaruz emretmiyorum, ölmeyi emrediyorum. Biz ölünceye kadar geçecek zama zarfında (içinde), yerimize başka kuvvetler ve komutanlar kaim (yerine) olabilir (gelebilir)". ("I am not ordering you to attack, but to die. In the meantime, while we die, other troops and commanders will take our place". Translation by the author).

1 http://tr.wikipedia . org – 5. ordu (Osmanlı).
2 The mystery was solved by releasing documents in the British Imperial War Museum in 1975 and publishing Steel "Gallipoli". p. 108 ff. It was about human weakness, as it often happens in war.
3 https://tr.wikipedia.org - *Çanakkale Savaşı*. Language variant in Erickson "Ordered to Die".

The measure was successful. It was a prime example of well understood military "mission oriented tactics" taught in modern armies. Mustafa Kemal received a written recognition despite or rather because of the arbitrary action and was then promoted to colonel. As a further distinction in a follow - on crisis situation, von Sanders gave Mustafa Kemal the command of the Anafarta Group, comprising 2 corps[1] on 09.08.1915, where he was also to distinguish himself again.

On Gallipoli approx. 1,500 Germans of the armed forces (with approx. 10 army commanders) including the Special Command Usedom as well as the air force fought, without taking into account temporarily deployed ship crews of the fleet[2]. The Germans provided only a few units, but mostly staff personnel, specialists and material. The Austrians provided mortar and artillery units with over 1,000 men from November 1915 onwards.

In the land war, the most important innovation was the introduction of the MG, (Fig. 25) which the Ottomans already owned in the Balkan Wars. It meant an enormous increase in infantry firepower, even though initially only 2 MG were available for each Ottoman division. Because of forced inactivity on the Yavuz/Goeben and the Midilli/Breslau a small unit of Marines with 8 MG and 44 men was deployed on 03.05.1915 at the Dardanelles under the command of Oberleutnant zur See Boltz. It grew up again and again after heavy losses and reached in the meantime on 27.07.1915 a strength of 153 men with 12 MG, operated afterwards also as mixed German/Turkish "landing division". The firepower was very important because the defender suffered from a severe shortage of large-calibre artillery ammunition, which could not be supplied from Germany due to an interruption of the railway line before Bulgaria entered the war and could not be manufactured locally in Istanbul.

With the transition from water-cooled MG to the light air-cooled one, it became possible to equip the guns on aircraft. The enemy also came into possession of 15 Japanese mortars, which could be fired from the trenches, but which also quickly ran out of ammunition. He procured periscopes from the navy to avoid to be hit when firing. In addition, he manufactured hand grenades from jam jars in a mass production facility on site, so-called "Jam Tin Bombs". Both hand grenades and mortars still left the defender behind. It must be emphasized that no flamethrowers or poison gas were used in Gallipoli.

For all branches of the armed forces, modern means of command and control became increasingly important[3]. In the Ottoman Empire there already existed, as mentioned above, a stationary strategic Telegraph network, which was supplemented by a few stationary spark telegraph stations after the war began. With the hub in Istanbul at Çamlıca height and the main station in Nauen[4] northwest from Berlin e.g. an operation had been possible over 6,000 km to Damascus and Baghdad. Morse operation took place here. Occasional telephone calls could be made as during the Balkan wars. More and more field telephone networks were installed in the troops, (Fig. 26) but they were initially not able to follow a mobile battle. However, it was already possible to operate semi - mobile radio stations that could be deployed for a few important users at army and corps level, which were still relatively cumbersome.

Although many facets of the land war on Gallipoli would still have to be discussed, the other services should also be mentioned and some new means of war discussed.

1 https://tr.wikipedia.org. – *Birinci Anafartalar Muharebesi*. Ruşen, Eşref, Ünaydın „*Anafartalar Kumandanı Mustafa Kemal ile Mülâkat*".

2 Uyar & Erickson "A Military History of the Ottomans" p. 259, according to which of the 80 commanders and 23 chiefs of staff on Gallipoli only 8 were German.

3 In addition, even older technical means of communication were used, such as the heliograph/heyograph, i.e. a means of transmitting messages by means of light signals according to the Morse code. Thus the navy also used signal lamps or Morse lamps long after the 1st World War.

4 First operation from 1906. https://de.wikipedia.org. - Large radio station Nauen.

The development of the air force has been particularly rapid on both sides. The local Ottoman Flying Squadron of land planes received a total of 8 aircraft, with a personnel of 7 pilots and 11 observers from both nations in July 1915. Nevertheless, the Entente achieved air superiority in a ratio of about 7:1. They operated from the islands, temporarily also from a provisional airfield at the southern tip of the peninsula and from "aircraft mother ships". With this procedure, take-off and landing were still carried out on the water. Aircraft carriers with flight decks were already tested in World War I, but were no longer used because of fatal incidents. The air superiority did not have such a strong effect, however, because the operational readiness of the aircraft was low, also for weather reasons, as was their weapon effect.

From May 1915 onwards, a seaplane squadron was set up at the Dardanelles by the defender with an influx of 8 seaplanes. Due to technical problems they could only insufficiently fulfil their mission of surveillance and submarine combat; a verifiable sinking by a seaplane did not take place, but by different means. In May 1916 a further seaplane detachment was stationed in Istanbul/Yeşilköy, also with the participation of the later German Grand Admiral Karl Dönitz.[1] Only with the arrival of the 3 German Fokker E II[2], superior in aerial combat, and the withdrawal of the Entente troops at the end of 1915 the air superiority was transferred to the Ottoman/German side. "*Fokker av uçaklarının Çanakkale harekat bölgesindeki tartışılmaz üstünlüğü devam ediyordu*" [3] ("The Fokker fighter planes achieved the air superiority in the Çanakkale battle without any doubt". Translation by the author).

Until the armistice on 31.10.1918 Istanbul could remain largely protected against the threat from the air, even though the Entente continued to drive the arms spiral with improved aircraft. E.g. it resulted in a naval aircraft with a torpedo under the shades. This machine of the type Short 184 could achieve several sinkings.

Even though the main burden of the battle at the Dardanelles was borne by the land forces in the second phase, the navy continued to play a major role. The operations of the German Kapitänleutnant Otto Hersing[4] with U-21 were decisive for the victory. The British had already noticed the approach of this submarine, which they knew well, in the Mediterranean Sea. Out of fear of it they soon withdrew the valuable thick ships from the Dardanelles, including their flagship the Queen Elizabeth. The British author Mackenzie wrote: *"The Royal Navy has never executed a more demoralizing maneuver in the whole of ist history"*[5]. Hersing sunk the "Triumph" on 25.05.1915, despite protection with anti-submarine nets, and escaped the subsequent pursuit by a risky submersion of the sinking ship. Two days later he sank the "Majestic". Hersing achieved further successes, becoming the German submarine commander with the second highest number of ships shot down in the First World War.

In general, the defender at the Dardanelles was quite successful in the fight against Australian, British and French submarines and surface vessels, even though Entente submarines were able to overcome the barrage nets and enter the Marmara Sea time and again. Successes of the defender were among others the sinking of the British submarine E-14 by artillery on 28.01.1918 near Kumkale[6], the French submarine *Joule* on 01.05.1915 after mine

1 Dönitz „Mein wechselvolles Leben".
2 This single-seater Fokker was an agile fighter plane which achieved several kills in early January 1916 as a result of an interrupter gear with synchronized MG which could shoot through the propeller. https://de.wikipedia.org. - Fokker.
3 Kurter "Türk Hava Kuvvetleri Tarihi" Cilt II. p. 225.
4 http://de.wikipedia.org. – Otto Hersing.
5 Mackenzie „Gallipoli Memories".
6 https://en.wikipedia.org. – HMS E14.

collision[1], the British *Goliath* by the *Muavenet-i Milliye*[2] on 13.05. in the Morto Bay, the British submarine E-7 in the Marmara Sea[3] on 04.09.1915, the French submarine *Mariotte*[4] on 26.07.1915 off Kephez, the British destroyer HMS *Louis* by artillery on 31.10. 1915 in the Suvla Bay[5]. The French submarine *Turquoise* was captured on 30.10.1915 near Nagara[6]. It should be added that German submarines operated very successfully in the whole Mediterranean Sea and thus provided indirect support for Gallipoli. A later success was the sinking of the British aircraft mother ship *Ben my Chree*[7] near the island Kastelorio in the Mediterranean Sea on 11.01.1917 by Captain Mustafa Ertuğrul rukwith its coastal artillery[8]. This ship had been partly responsible for the initial British air superiority at the Dardanelles.

Also on the side of the defender large losses were to be deplored, among them the loss of the Midilli/Breslau in the minefield in front of the entrances to the Dardanelles on 30.09.1917 under the new German commander of the fleet Admiral Hubert von Rebeur-Paschwitz with 336 dead. At the end more than 50.000 dead are to be deplored in these Gallipoli fights on both sides. In 1934 Atatürk had a conciliatory speech read out by addressing the relatives of all the victims in Gallipoli, which is carved in stone there, and once again expressed his love of peace. It culminates in his famous saying, which he had already formulated in 1931 and which is a call: "*Yurtta sulh, yihanda sulh!*" (In more recent Turkish *"Yurtta barış, dünyada barış!")* ("Peace at home, peace in the world"! Translation by the author). This legacy of Atatürk is especially addressed to the politicians and military. It is to be considered as a core building block of Kemalism and to be added to the famous 6 Principles/*Altı ok.*

After the clearing of the southern section on 09.01.1916 by the Entente troops and from today's point of view, it can be said in retrospect that the victories in the Gallipolis battles at the end of 1914 to the beginning of 1916 had and still have outstanding importance for the Ottoman Empire and Turkey of today. The world public looked unbelievingly at the shown efficiency of the Ottoman army. Turkey celebrates the Victory Day on 18.03. as Çanakkale Day, but since 1985 it also takes part in the ANZAC Day /*ANZAK Günü* of Australia and New Zealand on 25.04., the beginning of the land battle.

The other battles in the 1st World War on Ottoman soil recede behind these successes, but shall also be treated briefly. Practically at the same time as the campaigns described above, the attack on the Suez Canal/*Süveyş kanalı* also began at the insistence of Germany, in order to make it more difficult for Great Britain to connect with India and to bind forces of the Entente.

In the course of the war, after failures on the Suez Canal and subsequent stagnation on the Sinai Peninsula, the front shifted steadily across Palestine to Adana, where, before the armistice in Adana on 31 October 1918, the command of the Ottoman/German/Austrian troops was transferred from Liman von Sanders Paşa to Mustafa Kemal Paşa. In the east, following the British/Indian/Egyptian/Australian/New Zealand/French troops, Bedouin divisions under Arab/British leadership fought with the British officer, originally a man of the secret service, Lawrence of Arabia in the course of the Hijasbah/Hicaz railway line. On the entire front (*Sina ve Filistin Cephesi*) with very different climate zones, larger contingents of Arab and German troops also fought on the Ottoman side, from mid-1917 under the designation "*Yıldırım*"[9] or

1 Pages14-18.mes.discussions.net. –joule marin sujet.
2 *https://de.wikipedia.org. – Muavenet-i Milliye. https.de.wikipedia.org – HMS Goliath (1898).*
3 https://en.wikipedia.org. – HMS E7.
4 *Pages14-18.mesdiscussions.net. – mariotte marin sujet.*
5 https://en.wikipedia.org. – HMS *Louis* (1913).
6 www.opex360.com. – la mission impossible du marin turquoise.
7 https://de.wikipedia.org. – HMS *Ben my Chree.*
8 https://de.wikipedia.org. – Mustafa Ertuğrul Aker.
9 Turkish: the "Lightning". Also named after the surname of Sultan Bayezit I.

Army Group "F" under the German General Erich von Falkenhayn. The Entente was able to include supporting naval fire war, and also more and more air forces, with which they were to achieve air superiority for the rest of the campaign as early as October 1917.

ADVANCE ON 14.01.1915 ON THE SINAI/SINA

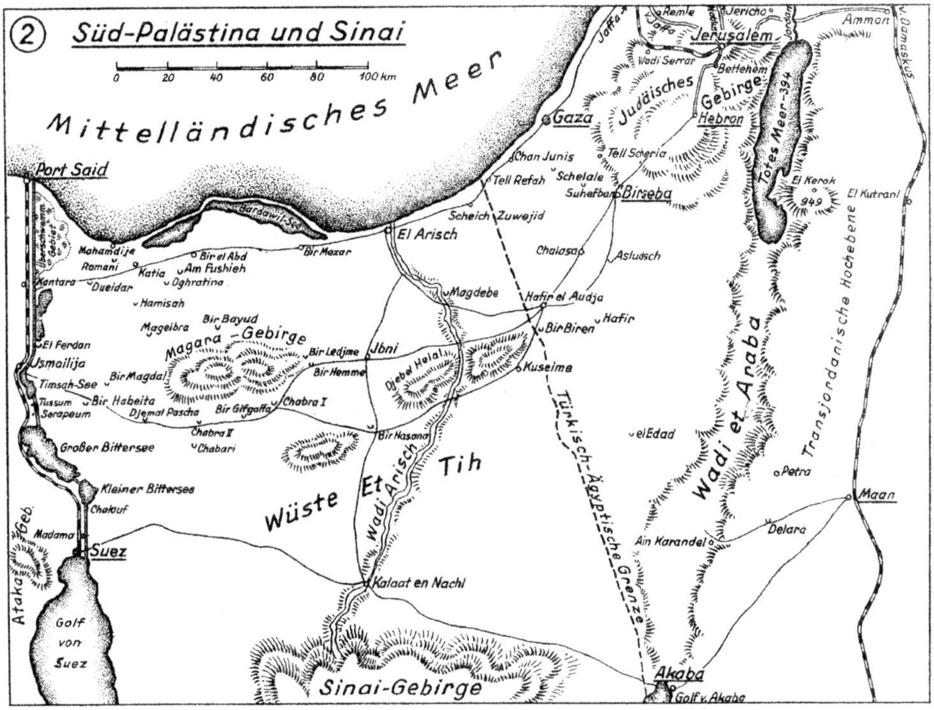

Map 13 *Kress von Kressenstein – Mit den Türken zum Suezkanal)*

By the end of September 1914, Ottoman forces, mainly Arabs, were already seeping across the de facto border into the Sinai Peninsula, with skirmishes over Kantara on the Channel and British bombardment of Aqaba on 14 November 1914. The 1st serious advance began on 14.01.1915 with about 20.000 men and 5.000 camels without airplanes under the leadership of Mehmet Cemal Paşa (From Mersin - Mersinli) as Commanding General, who in turn was under the command of Ahmet Cemal Paşa and the 4th Army in Damascus. In the staff of the "Little Cemal/*Kücük Cemal*" the German Colonel Kress von Kressenstein. Some of the Ottoman troops were without shoes and knapsacks to carry water or provisions. The artillery made very slow progress in the sand. Water was very scarce, despite the beginning of well and water pipeline construction, also with the help of German experts. Turkish officers generally did not speak Arabic, which made it difficult for the command of Arab units. The approach was already cleared up by the British from the air on 17.01.1915. After deployment of pontoons at the canal and the formation of a first bridgehead the attack was repelled, on 03.02. the army command gave the order to retreat.

On 29.12.1915, Kress von Kressenstein, who had previously led the operations on the Sinai as "Commander of the Desert" from Ibni, was assigned an expeditionary corps with the HQ in

Birseba/Beersheba. Until July 1916, only sabotage operations, minor "pinpricks" and operations against the Channel continued under British air threat, aggravated by heat, plagues of locusts, thirst, hunger and lack of wood.

The situation improved with the arrival of the German contingent Paşa I with about 2,000 men from April 2016 with artillery, mortars, radios, experts for well and railway construction as well as with the Army Aviation Squadron 300.

It came very soon to the 1st aerial fight over the Suez Canal on 28.05.1916 against a Farman machine with rear engine and front MG, from which the perforated Rumpler could just about withdraw. The Rumpler could only defend herself with pistol and rifle. Very soon the 300 Squadron had also managed to realize the synchronization between MG and rotor for 2 machines with "on-board means", whereby at least equal opportunities could be established with aircraft of the Entente. In September 1916 6 "synchronized" Rumplers and 2 Fokker E III arrived. Now the air superiority was transferred to the Ottoman side for about 1 year. Cemal Paşa reported Enver Paşa among others on 18.09.1916: *"İngiliz uçakları hava muharebesine girmekten kaçınmaktadırlar"*[1]. ("The British planes avoid air battles". Translation by the author). However, they continued bombing, so on 29.09.1916 on the airfield in El Ariş.

In May and June 1916 air raids against the British aircraft mother ship "Raven"[2] were flown with partial successes, then again on 01.09.1916 during the attack with 5 Rumplers on military important facilities in Port Said. However, due to the heat, flying had to be limited to the evening hours most of the time. It also suffered from sand winds, contaminated aviation gasoline and lack of gasoline. The additional aircraft, which came in 1916/1917, had radio on board, initially only in Morse broadcasting mode, i.e. no receiving mode.

At the same time as the Germans, an Austrian contingent arrived with over 1,000 men, artillery, trucks, a medical facility and a music corps. Altogether the Austrians deployed about 3,500 men in the Ottoman Empire, including specialists for ski training in Erzurum, in mining, for the creation of a radio relay network for airships, in surveying and mechanical engineering[3].

A 2nd big attack started on 09.07.1916 from Birseba/Birüssebi/Beerşeba, reached Romani east of the canal, but was stopped already at the beginning of August. One went over to the delaying operations. In February 1917 the front again reached the de facto border; further delay fights followed. The Ottoman troops suffered additional losses due to cold. In March 1917 the front ran between Gaza and Birseba. The Entente had already reached a scope of 156,000 men with 13,000 men in the Labour Corps. Their railway line from the canal had meanwhile reached El Arisch.

The proclamation of the Grand Scherif of Mecca Hussein ibn Ali[4] on 27.06.1916 did not remain without effect on the fighting morale of the Arabs on all fronts. After promises of Great Britain, he hoped to unite Arab tribes against the young Turkish government and to establish a Hashemite kingdom. His son, the Emir Faisal I al Auwal, together with the British officer Thomas Edward Lawrence and Bedouin warriors on the side of the Entente, will then successfully operate guerilla tactics and thereby accelerate the Ottoman collapse on the Palestinian front. The Ottoman Empire, however, succeeded in defending the holy city of Medinae/Yesrib[5] with heroic resistance until 10.01.1919 under the command of Fahrettin Paşa[6], who as late as September 1918 had rejected a request for the surrender from General

1 *Kurtər " Türk Hava Kuvvetləri Tarihi," Cilt II, p. 355.*
2 https://en.wikipedia.org. - HMS Raven II. Originally a German ship.
3 Jung & Mötz „Die KuK Streitkräfte im Ersten Weltkrieg 1914 – 1918“.
4 https:// de. wikipedia.org. – Hussein ibn Ali (Hedschas)
5 https://tr.wikipedia.org. - Medine Müdafaası.
6 He had handed over the 2nd Army on the Caucasus front to Mustafa Kemal in March 1917.

Edmund Allenby, who in turn wanted to avoid a bloody house-to-house fight. He finally left Medina out. Thus, long after the armistice, the last act of war of the Four-Association in World War I took place here. Fahrettin Paşa also succeeded in saving important relics of the Muslims for the Topkapı palace in Istanbul. Stays in Medina were normally avoided by non-Muslims, and flights over Arab terrain therefore mostly undertaken by Muslim crews.

Pilots of the 300 Squadron undertook three sabotage flights behind enemy lines in the period April-August 1917 and were able to achieve temporary interruptions of the railway lines, telegraph and power lines as well as the water pipeline in the area around Salmana at the border to Sinai peninsula. The German squadron leader reports that in the period April 1916 - September 1917 no aircraft was lost to enemy action, but 16 aircraft were shot down. The technical equipment of the aircraft was improved by send/receive radio communication and the installation of a camera, a so-called "Reihenbildner" (*Seri fotoğraf*), which films the area for the subsequent production of map material on a scale of 1:100,000. Power generators were installed at the airfield, so-called "Lichtwagen". By setting up dummy airports it was also possible to deceive the enemy.

The 1st British attack on Gaza took place surprisingly on 26. March 1917, after General Archibald Murray had demanded reinforcements for the "defense" in vain. The battle ended in a fiasco due to serious tactical/operational mistakes: Insufficient forces, excessive distance to the railroad, no use of reserves, lack of water, lack of communication resources, delayed starting due to morning fog. The use of British gas grenades, of which there were 4,000, was ineffective because either the detonation point was too high or the heat made the gas evaporate. Conversely, the defenders under the leadership of now Paşa Kress von Kressenstein defended toughly with 2 divisions at the line Gaza-Birseba, especially the key area southeast of Gaza, the Mount Ali Muntar, where an Austrian artillery observer was also posted. Despite the numerical superiority of the Entente's planes in a ratio of about 3:1, including modern Bristol Scout (fighters), the defenders were able to avoid own losses and achieve two more kills. Cemal Paşa then wisely prohibited a subsequent pursuit on the ground.

During the 2nd British attack on 19.04.1917 on Gaza with emphasis in front of the freshly introduced 53rd Ottoman division and an advance attack between Gaza and the coast, probably also to deceive about the center of gravity, General Murray this time attacked with stronger forces in a ratio of about 2:1, among them 8 tanks of the type Mark I 4 and armored cars of the brand Rolls Royce. Of the cumbersome tanks, a new means of war in World War I, 4 fell out.

The coming months were marked by considerable troop reinforcements on the Entente side, including the incorporation of French/Italian forces, as well as the assumption of command by General Edmund Allenby on 29 June 1917, who would lead until the end of the campaign. After the entry of the USA into the war and pilot training there, also for the allies, the Entente air force also experienced a strong growth in material and personnel.

On the Ottoman side, the above mentioned army group *Yıldırım* with 3 armies is formed on 27.10.1917 under the command of General Erich von Falkenhayn immediately before the beginning of the 3rd Gaza Battle on 30.10.1917. The general not only replaces Kress Paşa, but as marshal he also does not get along with the demoted Cemal Paşa (Büyük - the great) as commander of the 4th army. Both experienced and influential officers, whereas Cemal also as Vali, leaves this theatre of war, Kress after the 3rd Gaza Battle on 02.12. with the handover of the 8th Army[1] to Cemal Paşa (Mersinli), who then takes over the 4th Army from his namesake. For this the again outstanding Mustafa Kemal Paşa takes over the newly formed 7th Army[2]

1 https://tr.wikipedia.org. - 8._*Ordu (Osmanlı).*
2 https://tr.wikipedia.org. – *7. Ordu (Osmanlı).*

from 05.07.- 09.10.1917, hands it over to Fevzi (Çakmak) Paşa[1] , to take it over again on 07.08.1918 - 07.11.1918. Then Mustafa Kemal Paşa will again encounter the proven arrangement with Liman von Sanders Paşa as commander of the army group since 01.03.1918, although in an extremely critical overall situation.

The 3rd Gaza Battle is lost on 08.11.917 after a break-in at Birseba and a breakthrough at the 8th Army, with a superiority of Allenby of approx. 2:1, strong cavalry, among others provided by the Desert Mounted Corps[2] and again tanks. A use of chlorine gas again remained fortunately ineffective. The defender did not possess any gas masks. From now on, the Entente fighters control the airspace until the end of the war. The navy of the Entente supported with artillery from sea and with airplanes.

On request Enver Paşa Beirut became submarine base in February 1917. In May 1917 28 submarines of Germany and Austria operate in the Mediterranean and sink considerable British tonnage, e.g. on 14.04.1917 off the Syrian coast the British cruiser "Veronika" by UB 42 , on 11.11.1917 the British destroyer "Staunch" and the British monitor M 15 off Gaza by UC 38[3]. This German submarine has sunk 43 ships in the Mediterranean Sea in 1917 alone[4].

Gaza falls on 07.11.1917, Jerusalem/Kudus, the holy place of 3 religions and the most important place for the Muslims after Mecca and Medina, on 09.12.1917. Major Lawrence enters with his Arab troops beside General Allenby; on his side now also Armenian volunteer units as well as Jewish ones.

The German contingent Paşa II, also called Asian Corps, now enters Palestine with about 15,000 men, including 5 further Army Air squadrons. From February 1918 on, another 4,000 men (after the painful relocation of "Reserve Hunter Regiment" 11, a German infantry unit) are added, so that the Paşa contingents, which were deployed in Palestine alone, will ultimately comprise about 21,000 men. In the winter of 1917/1918, the troops suffered from cold, rain and muddy ground as well as from the undermining of railway sections.

Liman von Sanders Paşa reorganized the Army Group Staff on March 1, 1918, when he took over command of the Army Group in his sense, especially by including Turkish officers, with Colonel Kazım Bey as his trusted representative and Chief of Staff. Liman also rejected the Vali (civil governor) function offered by Enver Paşa. There should now be loss-filled retreat battles, interrupted only by isolated tactical victories: For example, in the Jordan battles the recapture of Es Salt east of the Jordan on 30.04.1918. The balance of power at this time is about 1:4 in favour of the attacker[5]. Von Sanders must realize that his troops are no longer suitable for attack operations for various reasons. In addition, Ottoman air reconnaissance is prevented due to British dominance in the air. In July 1918 the number of desertions increases significantly[6], also due to lack of food, clothing, etc. Leaflet actions by General Allenby further undermined morale. His Desert Mounted Corps with about 12,000 riders enables him to be highly mobile, also for the pursuit and capture of about 8,000 men in September, including about 3,000 Germans. On 28.09.1918 von Sanders dissolves the 8th army, still owns the 7th army under Kemal Paşa and the 4th under Cemal (Mersinli) Paşa, whereby just Kemal Paşa again proves his leadership art. Because of riots by non-party Arabs, the II Ottoman

1 https://tr.wikipedia.org. - Fevzi Çakmak.

2 https://de.wikipedia.org. - Desert Mounted Corps. Including ANZAC troops and camel divisions.

3 Staunch: uboat.net/wwi/ships_hit/5763.html. Monitor M 15: https://en.wikipedia.org. HMS-M15. The name "Monitor" is borrowed from the 1st US armoured ship of this name, a ship for shallow waters to bomb the coast. https://de.wikipedia.org. _ USS_Monitor.

4 uboat.net/wwi/boats/successes/uc38.html.

5 https://tr.wikipedia.org. - *Sina ve Filistin Cephesi.*

6 Uyar & Erickson "A Military History of the Ottomans" p. 277, according to which the number of deserters in the entire Ottoman Empire reached about 300,000 in 1917 and about 500,000 in 1918.

Corps under Colonel Ali Bey in southern Amman even was allowed by the British to keep weapons in order to defend himself against the Arabs. A "gentleman's gesture".

THE 2ND GAZA/GAZZE BATTLE OF 19.04.1917

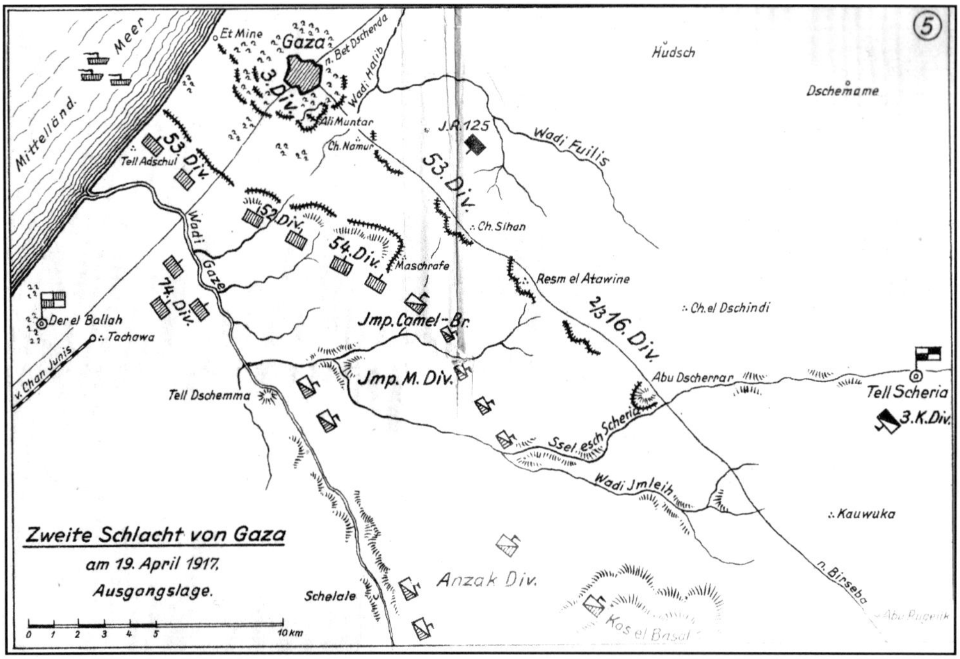

Map 14 *(Kress von Kressenstein – Mit den Türken zum Suezkanal)*

After the armistice of Bulgaria, the interruption of the railway line to the north from 12.10.1918 and the massive impact of about 700 Entente planes, the opponent troops moved into Damascus on 1.10.1918.

On 13.10.1918 the Ottoman Cabinet resigns, İzzet Paşa bundles the functions of Grand Vizier, Minister of War and Chief of General Staff for a few days. On 25.10.1918 Aleppo is evacuated and on 30.10.1918 at the armistice Liman von Sandes Paşa is relieved from office with the formation of an honorary company in Adana. Mustafa Kemal takes over the army group, initially refuses to surrender without a fight, but then has to agree to its dissolution with a final total of about 18,000 men on 7 November 1918.

In the captivity on Malta, Marshal (ret.) Liman von Sanders writes soberly, realistically and accurately: "*It seems that the thoughts of the fairy tales of the Arabian Nights or the mirages of the Arabian desert had clouded the sharply weighing judgement in the homeland*"[1].

Another great front in World War I was created in southern Mesopotamia. As early as September 1914 British warships patrolled the Shatt al Arab[2] as in Gallipoli to a quick victory,

1 Liman von Sanders „Fünf Jahre Türkei".

2 Gehrke "Persia in German Oriental Policy during the First World War" p. 72. https://de.wikipedia.org. - Shatt al rab. United river of Euphrates/Fırat and Tigris/Dicle on both sides Basra, plus border river between the then

therefore called the campaign a "*Mesopotamian picnic*". They should be mistaken here too, because the British, after a long tough struggle, finally stood hard south of the oil-rich Mossul for the armistice, then marched into the city afterwards, violating the armistice conditions. From the campaign only a glance at the decisive phase in the period 1916/1917, the time of Ottoman successes and the fall of Baghdad should be taken.

From the beginning, the campaign was characterized by extreme climatic conditions, heat, floods, sandstorms, but also snow and cold, numerous pests such as sand fleas and flies, which led to many diseases and failures among the troops. In addition, lack of drinking water and food for the animals made operations more difficult, and in the south a lack of wood and stone made bridge building more difficult. In addition, there were incalculable Bedouins who were hostile to the Turks, especially in the south, so that even scattered soldiers of the defender were attacked and died. North of Baghdad was the Tigris/*Dicle* generally only navigable with rafts (*Kelek*[1]), the Euphrates only with flat ships (*Schachtur*)[2]. Warships also had to be extremely shallow-moving. Means of transport such as trucks were hardly usable in the area, the railway construction of the British from the south became extremely arduous. The Baghdad Railway had bottlenecks or interruptions in the Taurus and Amanus and a large gap east of the Euphrates to Samara. From there, the German railway engineer in Ottoman service Heinrich August Meißner Paşa[3] had already built a section to Baghdad; during the war, a light railway was also operated between Risvaniye on the Euphrates and Baghdad.

The infrastructure and terrain in Mesopotamia were thus very detrimental to the logistics of the Ottoman troops, but also hindered the advancement and logistics of the British/Indian/Australian troops. The few British planes could not compensate for the logistical weaknesses, Ottoman booty planes and own machines were only available from the beginning of 1916. The floods and already overstretched supply routes of the British were decisive for the defeat of the British in the Battle of *Selman-ı Pak*/Ktesiphon[4] in November 1915 and the next defeat in the 2nd Battle of *Kût'ül-Amare*/Kut el Amara[5] in April 1916, besides serious operational/tactical mistakes of the British leadership. The infantry strength of the Ottoman troops, especially after the influx of the notoriously undemanding and tough Turkish troops under Halil Bey (later Paşa, Kut), together with the predominantly technical support from Germans and Austrians, also represented a considerable increase in fighting strength.

From December 1915 the commanders LTC Süleyman Askeri Bey[6] and later in May 1916 Nureddin Paşa[7] had performed tactical counter-attacks and sabotage operations on the British pipeline to Persia along the Karun River - supported by German and Austrian specialists - within the overall framework of delaying operations to the gates of Baghdad.

The 1st Battle of Kut el Amara, which was more like a hand-off without a fight[8], had been lost on 29.10.1915 and the British General Charles Vere Ferrers Townshend had allegedly been ordered by General John Nixon to proceed further into Baghdad. *"All my study indicated*

Ottoman Empire and Persia (from 1935 called Iran).

1 Raft made of inflated goat skins for about 40 men. Duration from Mossul to Baghdad 1-2 weeks.

2 Double chute for max. 33 men or 12 to. The Tigris at that time navigable from Birecik, as already explored by Moltke and Sven Hedin. Travel time up to Baghdad 3-8 weeks.

3 https://de.wikipedia.org. - Heinrich August Meissner. Previously already successful as "Father of the Hedschas Railway"/*Hicaz Demiryolu.*

4 https://tr.wikipedia.org. – *Seman-ı Pak Muharebesi.*

5 https://tr.wikipedia.org. – *Kût'ül-Amare Kuşatması.*

6 https://tr.wikipedia.org. - Süleyman Askeri.

7 https://tr.wikipedia.org. - Nuredin İbrahim Konyar.

8 Therefore Turkey does not designate this as the 1st battle.

disaster to me. However, the die was cast; my superior had judged otherwise"[1]. Townshend's first mistake was to respond only to a report by British pilot Maj. Reilly

Confident that no Ottoman reinforcements had been sighted in the Baghdad area, Townshend entered the battle on 11.11.1915 with about 25,000 men. The original British intention had also been to avoid the for Sunnis and Shiites important day of the 10th *Muharram*, the *Aşura* day[2] of the 18.11.1915. He should have done some more reconnaissance beforehand, also on the ground, because as is well known the situation can change in a few days. When Reilly ascended again on 21.11.1915, he would probably have made a contrary report, but he could not any more, because he stranded in *Selman-ı Pak*/Ktesiphon[3] and became a prisoner of war. In addition an important map was lost.

Nureddin had occupied the above mentioned positions along the Diyala line[4] with about 19,000 men, but growing up. After hard fighting and losses on both sides of about 20% - 25%, Townshend stopped the battle on 25.11.1915 because of additional sandstorms, logistical problems (water, ammunition, recovery of wounded) and his suspicion or realization that the defender was strengthening. Instead of defending he goes over to the loss-pregnant delay until Kut el Amara: "*If anyone fell behind the rearguard, his throat was at once cut by the Arabs"*.

Townsend also lost his gunboat "Firefly", which the Ottomans were able to use against him because the crew forgot to take the 4.7 inch breech off the gun. Also the British paddle steamers "Comet" and "Shaitan" were captured[5]. British prisoners of war and wounded were handed over to the British for lack of own supply capacity. Kut was reached on 03.12.1915, after marching 140 km in 8 days. However, some British troops like cavalry, parts of the navy and air force moved even further south to Sheikh Sa'ad and Ali Garbi. Kut el Amara is now trapped. According to an old Ottoman custom Nureddin demands the surrender of the city and the Poona Division on 07.12.1915, but Townshend refuses.

The author shares Moukbil's view, in addition to the causes already mentioned, including the inadequate balance of power, that the British and Indians had previously fought against defeated opponents in the colonial wars, but now for the first time against an equal one. Practically at the same time as Gallipoli fights, the misjudgement had been repeated[6]. Again it caused severe losses on both sides.

Due to German directives of 18.10.1915, confirmed by Enver Paşa, the 72 year old von der Goltz Paşa arrives in Aziziye south of Baghdad on 12.12.1915, where he takes over the command of the 6th Army from Nureddin Paşa. However, the order to von der Goltz now fatally includes the extension of operations to Persia, which will eventually lead to a dispersal of forces and an early fall of Baghdad. Von der Goltz gives Nureddin the strict order to besiege the city and monitor the enemy further downstream with cavalry. But Nureddin continues to attack in the absence of von der Goltz and takes Sheikh Sa'ad. This will lead to his later replacement by Halil Bey (from 19.04. 1916 Paşa) in consultation with Enver Paşa[7].

1 Townshend " My Campaign in Mesopotamia" and "Desert Hell: The British Invasion of Mesopotamia". https://de.wikipedia.org. - Charles Vere Ferrers Townshend.
2 For the Shiites, the anniversary of the death of the third Imam Husain. https://de.wikipedia.org. - Ashura.
3 https://tr.wikipedia.org. - Tızpon.
4 https://tr.wikipedia.org. - *Selman-ı Pak Muharebesi.*
5 Nunn „Tigris Gunboats".
6 Moukbil „La campagne de l'Irak".
7 https://tr.wikipedia.org. - Halil Kut.

FROM BASRA TO BAGDAD, BACK TO KUT AL AMARA AND BACK TO BAGDAD

Map 14

Due to the local situation, von der Goltz applied to Enver Paşa for reinforcements on 20.12.1915 and initially refrained from a major operation in Persia towards Afghanistan[1]. In the period 28.12.1915 - 07.01.1916 von der Goltz explores the situation in Persia together with the German Oberst Arthur Bopp, who becomes responsible for the operations there, as far as

1 Kiesling „Mit Feldmarschall von der Goltz in Mesopotamien und Persien".

Kermanschah[1], 320 km away. The then neutral Persia was occupied in the north by Russia, in the south by Great Britain. Germany and the Ottoman Empire, however, also had interests and wanted to take over power in cooperation with local fighters and Persian gendarmes, who had Swedish instructors. Meanwhile a coup by the German embassy secretary Heinrich Prince von Reuß had failed on 15.11.1915, as well as efforts of the German military attaché Georg Emil von Kanitz[2] with his death on 15.01.1916.

Since there were only 6,000 unreliable tribal riders present on the spot, apart from 800 Turks, some German soldiers, about 1,000 gendarmes and some Austrians, a reinforcement by another 4 Turkish battalions took place in February 1916. The primary objective was now first of all to eliminate the Russian flank threat from the direction of Hamadan. After a counterattack under Halil Paşa on 09.05.1916, supported by German pioneers, Kermanschah was reconquered on 01.07.1916, Hamadan was taken on 10.08.1916. Support from the air was available here from Squadron 12, which had only a low level of operational readiness due to a lack of fuel, machinery and spare parts. Nevertheless, the reconnaissance flight to Hamadan on 28.11.1916 with an armed "Albatross" here was a nice success, as again a mixed crew with a Turkish pilot and a German observer managed the risky operation[3].

Turkish pilots also had the courage to fly machines unknown to them, so beside two captured machines another British Caudron G.III, which was forced to land on 16.09.1916 after rifle fire and whose crew had been captured. *"İngilizlerin uçak müfrezesinin bu kayıplarına karşılık, Türk biliklerinin 16 Eylülde ele geçirdikleri Caudron G.III oldukça iyi durumda olup, kullanılabilecek vaziyetteydi".* ("In return for these losses of the English flying squadron, a Caudron G.III could be restored to a good airworthy condition, which had been captured by Turkish units on September 16. Translation by the author).

Moreover, because of the difficult terrain, the British also converted aircraft into seaplanes that could take off and land on the rivers. In the period from January 1916 to May 1918, the two Ottoman flying squadrons of the Mesopotamian/Iranian Front received a total of 64 aircraft, and from April 1916 the first Fokker. In the summer of 1916 even temporary air superiority (*Hareket Üstünlüğü*)[4] could be achieved, until far into 1917 they were at least equal to the attacker.

With the advance of the Russians towards Baghdad Kermanschah fell on 11.03.1917. The union with the British troops in Kızıl Robat west of the Persian border took place on 02.04.1917, but the Russians did not take part in the fighting in Mesopotamia any more. The Russian revolution in March 1917 had created a new situation. The remote XIII Ottoman Corps under Colonel Ali İhsan Sabis (later Paşa) unfortunately came too late to relieve the 6th Army in the fight for Baghdad/Bağdat[5].

When von der Goltz arrived back at Kut el Amara at the beginning of January 1916, after his vehicle had broken down and he had been riding the horse at night, he assessed the situation of a British relief attack, he ordered a gradual retreat along the northern bank of the Tigris, following the marshes there. After the fading attack by the British, a ceasefire is declared on 21.01.1916 at the request of the British. The confinement of Kut has already led

1 https://tr.wikipedia.org. – Kirmanşah (Şehir).

2 https://de.wikipedia.org. - Kanitz

3 Pilot Unteroffizier Konrad, observer First Lieutenent Nüzhet. Kurter "*Türk Hava Kuvvetleri Tarihi" Cilt V Sayfa 95.*

4 Kurter "*Türk Hava Kuvvetleri Tarihi Cilt II Sayfa 165.*

5 https://tr.wikipedia.org. - 13. Kolordu (Osmanlı), https://tr.wikipedia.org. - Ali İhsan Sabis. Commanding General of the Corps February 1916 - October 1917, then commander of the 6th Army until the armistice. https://tr.wikipedia.org. - 13. Kolordu (Osmanlı),

to considerable food shortages, horses have to be slaughtered. The Muslim Indians, however, refuse to eat horse meat despite a fetva, which also leads to desertion. The Sikhs, Hindus and Ghurkas do not cause Townshend these problems. Opium is also given to fight hunger. On 03.02.1916 the British "Chief of the Imperial General Staff" also orders the return of Muslim-Indian troops. Even south of Selman-ı Pak Townshend had already experienced disciplinary problems, because the Muslims considered the area a holy place, but even more so the city of Baghdad as a long-standing caliph city of the Abbasids[1].

THE RUSSIAN AND BRITISH SPHERES OF INFLUENCE IN PERSIA

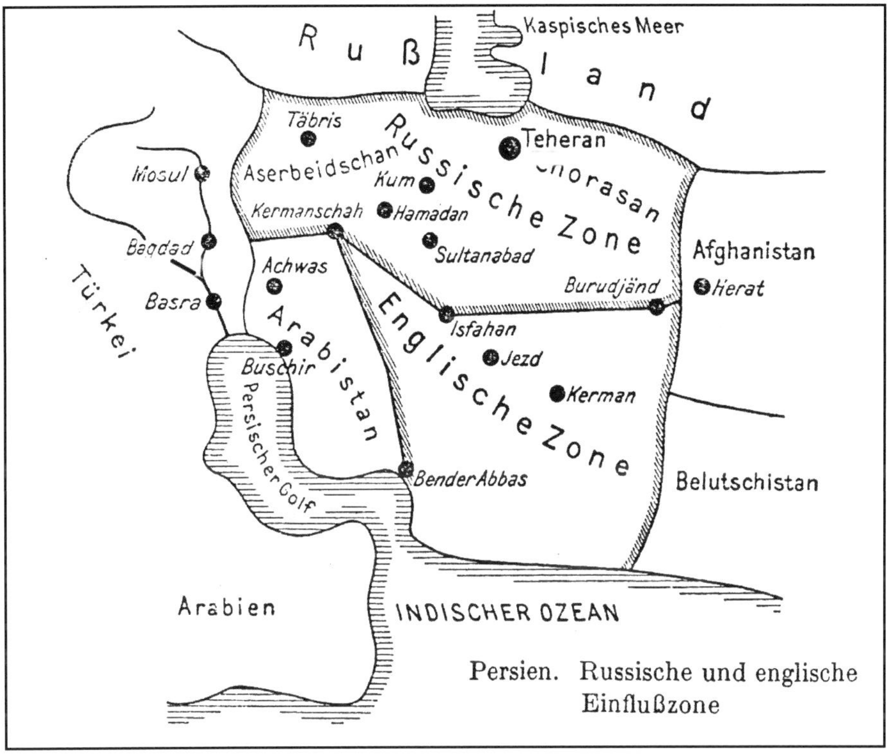

Map 16

Meanwhile Halil Bey replaces Nureddin on 20.01.1916. Von der Goltz leads further from the front, thereafter leaves the local leadership to Halil Bey on 31.03.1916 and returns to Baghdad himself.

The British undertake a last unsuccessful relief attack in the period 12.04.-26.04.1916 on the south bank against flooded terrain and with combat ships on the Tigris, but for weeks they have not been able to nearly ensure the supply from the air with 14 airplanes and 140 flights from 15.04.1916. On 29.04.1916 the surrender takes place; 13.000 go into captivity, among them 1/3 British soldiers and 5 generals. Up to this time the British have lost about 40,000

1 Süleman Pak is said to have been a comrade-in-arms of the Prophet. https://de.wikipedia.org. - Abbasids.

men[1] during the Mesopotamian campaign. Erickson later considers this to be the most serious defeat of Great Britain between 1783 (Yorktown) and 1942 (Singapore)[2].

Von der Goltz had been infected on the ship when returning to Baghdad and died of typhus on 19.04.1916. He was finally buried on the German embassy grounds in Istanbul/Tarabya in June 1916.

Halil Paşa becomes commander of the 6th army. He grants generous treatment to British officers, and even, according to a report by Sven Hedin, gives a farewell or fraternization party without German officers on 11.05.1916. *"The mood at the table was even cheerful; it was a real fraternity celebration and the champagne was flowing in abundance"*[3].

Unfortunately the tensions between Halil Paşa and the Germans after the death of von der Goltz led to frictions in the cooperation, concentrated in Halil's view: *"Osmanlı Ordudir"*. ("It is an Ottoman army" or "The army is Ottoman". Translation by the author).

By this Halil probably meant that the co-determination of the Germans would go too far for him[4]. This was also shown later once again by commander Halil in the dismissal of his German chief of staff in the Army Group East, Oberstleutnant Ernst Paraquin, in September 1918[5], who had already served under Halil in the staff of the 6th Army. In retrospect, the Germans had provided considerable personnel and material support for the 6th Army in a coalition army with machine gun units, artillery, engineers, command vehicles, motor vehicles, medical supplies, aircraft and in the construction of a Tigris flotilla.

General Townshend will have pleasant quarters on one of the Princes' Islands, and later even takes part in the armistice negotiations in Istanbul in October 1918; whereas his soldiers had to undertake a long and painful march on foot to the POW camps.

It took the British three quarters of a year to replenish their human and material resources and to be able to launch a new attack. They started on 13.12.1916 with great superiority under General Frederick Stanley Maude, conquered Kut el Amara again[6] on 25.02.1917, Ktesiphon on 06.03.1917 and Baghdad on 11.03.1917, at the same time as the fall of Kermanshah. The further course of the campaign resembled a long Ottoman delay fight with a temporary lull in the fighting from December 1917 after the fall of Tikrit[7] on 05.11.1917. The British front moved troops to neighbouring Persia/Azerbaijan to support General Lionel Dunsterville in the fight for Baku[8]. From March 1918 the British advanced both on the Euphrates and the Tigris.

On 03.07.1918 the command changed from Halil to İhsan Paşa, whereby the 6th army was reduced to the XIII Corps. For the armistice the front at the Euphrates had advanced to Hit, at the Tigris to Kalat Schergat south of Ninive/Mossul.

Two weeks after the armistice British troops marched into the undefended city of Mossul, citing § 7 of the armistice treaty: *"The Allies to have the Right to occupy any strategical points in the event of a situation arising which threatens the security of the Allies"*[9].

1 https://tr.wikipedia.org. - *Kût'ül Amâre Kuşatması.*
2 Erickson "Ottoman Army Effectiveness in World War I".
3 *Hedin "Baghdad, Babylon, Nineveh."*
4 With this view he did not differ from Mustafa Kemal (Atatürk), who also expressed this clearly on several occasions. The stories about his allegedly good relationship with Liman von Sanders (watch gift) must therefore be viewed with scepticism. With Enver Paşa at the top, however, cohesion was maintained.
5 Lisec „Der Völkermord an den Armeniern – Deutsche Offiziere beteiligt?" p. 145.
6 According to Turkish understanding this is only the 2nd battle for Kut el Amara. https://tr.wikipedia.org. - *İkinci Kut Muharebesi.* In reality it was the third, but the1st wasn't a real battle.
7 https://tr.wikipedia.org. - Tikrit.
8 Dunsterville "The Adventures of Dunsterforce".
9 Moberly "History of the Great War" Volume III p. 323.

However, the city had not offered any occasion of this kind. The text of the Turkish file reads: "*15 Kasım 1918 tarihinde İngiliz askerleri Musul'a asker çıkarıp işgal ettiler".*[1] ("On November 15th 1918, the British soldiers occupied Mossul which had been abandoned by the soldiers". Translation by the author). The Mosul question was only to be “solved” with a decision of the League of Nations[2] in 1925 and a subsequent agreement between Turkey and Great Britain, which had received the mandate over Iraq, on material/financial compensation.

Townshend concluded by praising the Mesopotamian campaign on the Turks, writing that they had committed a total of some 900,000 men of the enemy there during the war *...the Turks should claim the Campaign as a moral Victory*[3]. However, this figure seems excessive in comparison with Churchill's estimate.

At this point, a conclusion about this chapter shall be drawn without examining the other theatres of war of Ottoman troops in World War I, the Hicaz, Yemen and the European theatres of war, into which Enver Paşa had transferred considerable troops. This was certainly a weakening and had a negative influence on the battles especially in Palestine and Mesopotamia. However, his decision to shift the focus towards the Caucasus front towards Baku at the end of the war in pursuit of his Panturanian ideas or to gain a bargaining chip for the expected peace negotiations also contributed to this weakening. According to Turkish information, approximately 2.850 million soldiers were deployed during the First World War[4].

With regard to the basic questions we asked at the beginning, a differentiated judgement can probably be made.

Within the framework of a coalition army, the Ottoman army was only able to fulfil its mission of saving the fatherland in part. Eastern Thrace and Anatolia were not occupied at the time of the armistice, and some troops were still intact. The indirect mission, however, especially in Germany's interest, namely the binding of the Entente's strong forces, was fully accomplished. According to Churchill[5], 480,000 British/Indian troops alone were bound on the fronts in Palestine/Syria and Mesopotamia. A weakening of strength at home was certainly the transfer of 6 Ottoman divisions in the period 1916-1918 to Galicia, Romania and Bulgaria/Saloniki Front[6]. Moreover, the fighting Ottoman troops, which were almost exclusively Turkish/Arabic due to the lack of Armenians and "Rum", including units of the Jandarma, were able to achieve impressive victories before the eyes of the world: In Gallipoli, in Kut el Amara, in two Gaza battles. Once again, it has been shown that the army, when it comes down to it, is capable of great achievements.

The Turkish share of the troops remained loyal to the politicians, represented by the young Turk Enver Paşa as Commander-in-chief, even though the number of deserters increased significantly in the last two years of the war. The Arab portion became less reliable with the events in Mecca in mid 1916 or even became an enemy.

- Besides a growing national consciousness, the Islamic religion still played a major role, also on the side of the Entente. Although the declaration of the Holy War by the Şeyh-ül İslam in November 1914, reinforced by the Sultan and Shiite clergy in Mesopotamia, did not have the hoped-for effect, the faith of the Turkish soldier was still an important motivating factor. Townshend judges the Turks:"*He does not and will not understand patriotism nor does he*

1 https://tr.wikipedia.org. - *Musul Sorunu*.
2 https://de.wikipedia.org. - Mossul.
3 Townshend „Desert Hell“ p. 520.
4 https://wikipedia.org –Türk Silahlı Kuvvetleri.
5 Churchill „Die Weltkrise 1914-1918” II p. 194
6 Uyar & Erickson "A Military History of the Ottomans" p. 264.

care. I believe, for the patrie - but his religion in his life and world, and for that he will fight in the most dogged and tenacious manner"[1].

- Due to the long preceding years of war and the economic conditions, the army could not quite keep up with the necessary renewals. This was evident not only in the lack of large-calibre artillery ammunition or the number of machine guns, but above all in the condition of the navy and air force. However, the deficiencies could be partially compensated by contributions from the allies.

- The so-called brotherhood of arms with Germany in World War I still has a positive effect on the political relationship between Turkey and Germany, but also between their armies in retrospect of the greatest joint and combined military campaign in history.

With the Ottoman Army to the Republic

In the period between the armistice of Mudros/Mondros in 1918 and the peace agreement of Lausanne in 1923 intense military hostilities took place simultaneously in a major political transformation from the Ottoman Empire to the Turkish Republic. Due to internal threats, they temporarily had the character of a civil war, due to external threats as a consequence of the First World War and the negotiations in Sèvres until 1920 as well as the Greek attack in 1919, they had the character of conventional acts of war by regular and irregular forces in various regions of the Ottoman Empire. This complex political situation, in a phase of internal disruption, naturally also had a considerable impact on the army, centred on the question of loyalty under different forms of government.

Mustafa Kemal Paşa, who, in anticipation of his later surname, is now to be called Atatürk for simplification, had been commissioned by the Sultan and the British to enforce the demobilization of the Ottoman army in Anatolia. The deployed forces of the allies in the order of about 200,000[2] men were not sufficient for this. It was recognized too late that Atatürk, still in soldier status, was concerned with the exact opposite, i.e. first of all with the preservation and strengthening of the remaining parts of the army. Whether he already had the vision of the united unoccupied Turkish Republic of 1923 in mind when he landed in Samsun on May 19, 1919 remains open. After all the way there seemed to be nearly impossible, what afterwards almost was to be called a miracle. Probably it was preceded once again by a wrong assessment of the situation by the British, similar to Gallipoli, but above all a complete underestimation of the qualities of Atatürk and the will to live of the Turkish people.

Gallipoli should have realised that Atatürk was a distinguished and outstanding patriotic officer. What was not yet apparent to outsiders was that he had also been a courageous revolutionary against the Sultan at an early stage, detached from the Young Turks. His qualities as a strategically thinking politician only became apparent in the following, whereby he always used the respective situation pragmatically. Thus one had made "the buck a gardener", but could not turn back the wheel of history, neither with attempts to get hold of him or to murder him, by imposing a death penalty and Fetva in April 1920. Already before that, in July 1919, Atatürk had anticipated his dismissal from the army on request. However, this was not a weakening of his position, now without formal military authority, because he lived on his outstanding reputation in the army and many comrades stood by him and protected him. One of them was Kasım Karabekir Paşa, who was still in command of a considerable regular contingent of troops. It was also important that the probably mainly military operating

1 Townshend „My Campaign in Mesopotamia“.

2 Nationwide about 38.000 British, 59.000 French, 17.000 Italians and after invasion 90.000 Greeks. About half of the troops were concentrated in Istanbul.

personnel of the nationwide telegraph system would be loyal to Atatürk, as well as a part of the civilian governors/Vali.

THE TURKISH WAR OF INDEPENDENCE –
EXTERNAL THREATS TO ANATOLIA AND EASTERN THRACE

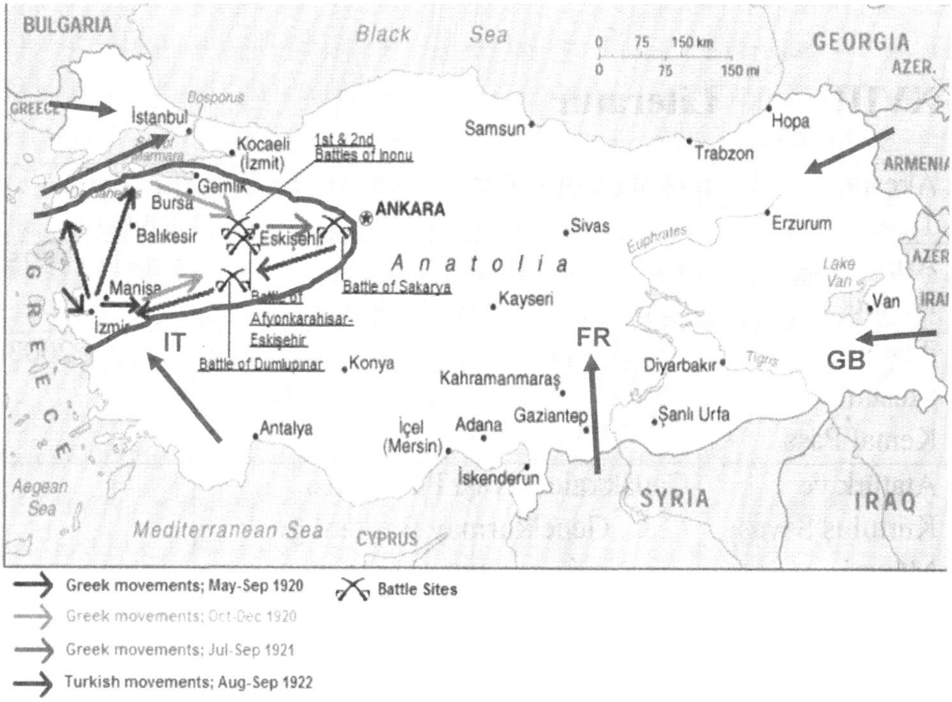

Map 17

According to Özakmann,[1] there were still about 35,000 - 40,000 regular troops and about 400,000 uncontrolled free-corps troops, whose political orientation was unclear or partly even contrary to Atatürk's. The latter troops had been in existence since 1918/1919. They were mainly recruited from dismissed former soldiers, who thus "muddled through" and endangered public safety and order. Since the Jandarma, which had participated with contingents in the World War, was not yet functional again, self-help groups were also formed among the population to close these security gaps. Among them was e.g. the mounted armed partisan group around Kara Fatma Seher (Erden) with about 43 women, who exercised police functions on their own initiative and were integrated into the armed forces in 1921 with most of the other irregular troops. Atatürk had realized that he first had to eliminate the internal threats before he could turn to the external ones. This had to go hand in hand with the revolutionary national political unification process.

1 Özakman "Şu Çılgın Türkler". This factual novel, which to the author's knowledge has not yet been translated, is the standard work on the period covered here, 1919 - 1923. It also formed the basis for documentary and feature films about this period. The author has also drawn on Özakman's in-depth research in his book „Der Unabhängigkeitskrieg und die Gründung der Türkei".

The biggest internal opponent was the Sultan and Caliph Mehmet VI, who hoped with his cabinet to be able to save as much of the old order as possible in cooperation especially with the Brits, but sacrificed national interests of unity and independence in the process. The Sultan had even in his capacity as Caliph, with the support of a fetva of the *Şeikh- ül İslam* and with British material/financial help against the growing *Kuva-yı Milliye*[1] troops of Atatürk, set up his own troops, the *Kuvâ-yı İnzibatiye,*[2] also called *Hilafet Ordusu*/Caliphate Army, in the order of 4,000 men. This unit existed only between April and June 1920, was commanded by the Circassian Ahmet Anzuvur and was under the command of the War Minister of Sultan Süleyman Şefik Paşa.[3] A confrontation broke out in the Izmit area, among others, when national troops tried to take control of it.

"Hilafet ordusu birlikleri Nisan ve Mayıs aylarında İzmit bölgesinde yığınaklanmalarını bitirdiler. Britanya birlikerli de Hilfat ordusunun arkasında konuşlandı. İzmit limanına demirleyen Britanya savaş gemileri mevzileri top ateşi iledestekleyebilecek bir konum aldılar". ("Units of the Caliphate Army suppressed concentrations in the area İsmit in the months of April and May. Units of the British and the Caliphate Army had previously made arrangements. The British warships anchored off İzmit "cleaned up the situation" by supporting artillery fire on the positions. Translation by the author).

At the end of June 1920, Ali Fuat Cebesoy Paşa, Commandıng General of XX Corps and irregular troops/Freikorps succeeded in destroying the Caliphate Army. He had been appointed by the congress in Sivas on 11.09.1919 and became formal commander of the Wesern Front on 18.06.1920.

By the way it should be mentioned that Izmit had to mourn about 300 dead on 24.06.1921 in the context of the later Greek advance. The British writer Toynbee[4] has reported about this.

It should be noted that the British in particular did not remain neutral in the fight for independence and intervened on the side of the Greeks, not only in June 1920. 15 limited skirmishes with British troops took place after Özakman, whereby the last confrontation at the end of September 1922 in Çanakkale was without bloodshed due to the agreement of British General Charles Harington and contrary to the instructions from London.[5]

Another internal threat to Atatürk were the free corps troops of the defector Çerkez Ethem,[6] the *Kuvâ-yı Seyyâre*[7] in strength of initially about 4,600 men. This unit had changed sides at the end of 1920, also because the British paid well, but were then crushed in January 1921.

Atatürk was now able to turn to the external threats, even if as seen, internal and external threats could not always be clearly separated. This also applies e.g. to the Ottoman citizens of Greek descent, the so-called "Rum", who provided support, either covertly or openly, during the invasion of the Greek division in Izmir[8] on 15 May 1919. The Greek Orthodox Patriarchate in Istanbul openly sided with the invaders. It remains unclear how many Rum were in the service of the Greek army, as soldiers or as civilians. According to statements by the Greek General Anastasios Papoulas in July 1921 and the Metropolitan of Izmir in June 1922 probably 100,000 men, including a larger contingent from the Black Sea region around Trabzon and the Mediterranean coast, must be assumed. This estimate is certainly still

1 https://tr.wikipedia.org . – *Kuvâ-yı Milliye.*
2 https://tr.wikipedia.org. - *Kuvâ-yı İnzibâtiye.*
3 https://tr.wikipedia.org. - Süleyman Şefik Paşa.
4 https://tr.wikipedia.org. - İzmit Katliamı. Toynbee "The Western Question in Greece and Turkey".
5 Harington „Tim Harington looks back".
6 https://tr.wikipedia.org. – Çerkez Ethem.
7 https://tr.wikipedia.org. – *Kuvâ-yı Seyyâre.*
8 https://de.wikipedia.org. – Besetzung von Izmir. https://tr.wikipedia.org. – *İzmir'in İşgalı.*

conservative in view of the approximately 1.25 million Rum that had to leave the country in 1923 with the population exchange agreement of Lausanne.

Before discussing the Greek-Turkish war of 1919-1923, however, the other nations and interest groups should first be considered. These parties had been negotiating a peace agreement in Sèvres since January 1919, which ultimately failed in August 1920, because Atatürk's military successes made their decisions a waste of paper. Although signed by Grand Vizier Damat Ferit Paşa as head of the Sultan's delegation, the paper was never ratified by any Ottoman or even Turkish parliament.

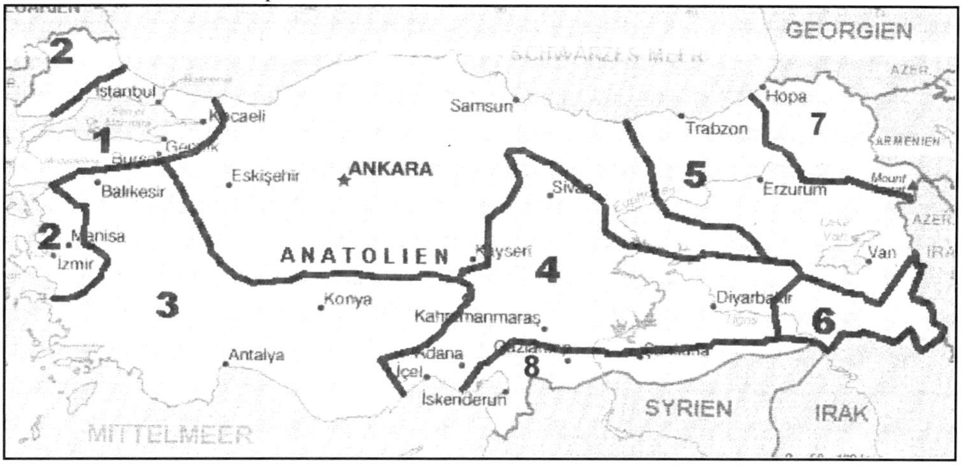

Map 18 The Treaty of Sèvres 1920

The Sèvres Agreement[1] provided for zones of influence (see map above) for the victorious powers in a secret supplementary agreement, as well as possible claims by the Kurds in south-east Anatolia (Region 6), represented by Great Britain, and the Armenians in the northeast (Region 5). Region 7 north of it belonged since 1878 to Russia. France's zone of influence in the south (Region 4) stretched as far as Sivas, that of the Italians in the southwest (Region 3) as far as Bursa and Konya, that of the Greeks covered eastern Thrace and a region around Izmir (Region 2), the waterways were to be demilitarised under Allied administration (Region 1). Region 8 foreseen for Syria. This would have brought the Ottoman Empire down to a small core area from Ankara to Samsun, in accordance with various pre-war plans of the victorious powers.

Atatürk was initially unaware of these plans. In addition to political work, he now concentrated on military operations on the fronts, but did not address the main threat from the Greeks until other sections of the front were under control. His strategy was thus that of pragmatic serial political and military action. After skilful negotiations and military successes in the south and north-east, he reached agreements with Italy, France and Russia.[2] Italy withdrew until July 1921, after which it even supported Atatürk with deliveries of "non-military goods". With France he concluded the Franklin-Bouillon[3] secret treaty on 20.10.1921

1 https://www.lib.byu.edu/index.php/Section I Articles 1-260. https://de.wikipedia.org. – Vertrag von Sèvres (Osmanisches Reich).https://tr. wikipedia.org. – *Sevr Antlaşması..*

2 The treaty with Russia on 16.03.1921 was to be followed by others in the years 1925, 1929 and 1931, but it was not until 1945 that a separation from Russia took place.

3 https://de.wikipedia.org. – Vertrag von Ankara (19219. www.hri.org/docs/FT 1921/Franco-Turkish.

to the wrath of the British. France and the Armenian voluntary troops withdrew from Cilicia/Çukurova until the beginning of January 1922. France then supported Atatürk, also by deliveries of military goods, so in 1922 alone by supplying 10 modern airplanes. In the northeast Karabekir Paşa pushed back the Armenians until 18.11.1920. In the negotiations with the Armenians and Russians, the Treaty of Kars[1] of 13.10.1921 not only restored the old Ottoman eastern border, but also agreed on a cooperation with Iljitsch Lenin.

The supply of military goods from Russia was a decisive factor in the happy course of the war with Greece. In combination with smuggled Ottoman weapons and ammunition from the depots guarded by the Allies, especially from the Istanbul area, and by skilfully reworking unsuitable calibres of artillery ammunition, Atatürk finally had the resources for a Blitzkrieg lasting only a few days in the summer of 1922.

The climax of the conflict, however, was the repulsion of the Greek invasion in several phases, the destruction of their "Megali Idea".[2] From the Ottoman point of view, the Greeks took advantage of the initial Ottoman territorial losses around Izmir, after that fought the battles of Inönü I and II, attacked up to the Sakarya with the decisive Greek defeat there. At the end Atatürk achieved the final victory at Dumlupınar, followed by the reconquest of Izmir and the last operation in this war, the unsuccessful British uprising around Çanakkale on 28.09.1922.

The author[3] has described the individual phases with sketches in the book mentioned below. Some elements from this war and the reasons for the victory should be emphasized again. First of all, these are the lack of a uniform political/military and continuous leadership of the Greeks, the unclear intention of their war goal, their renewed underestimation of the Turkish army, their lack of resources, their military resignation or lethargy after the defeat at the Sakarya until the battle at Dumlupınar. In addition, Greece lost the support of the Italians and the French at an early stage, later also that of the Brits. The Greeks had trusted them for too long, especially the British Prime Minister David Lloyd George,[4] and felt encouraged to the invasion into Izmir.

On the Ottoman side the causes were partly on the opposite side, first of all based on the outstanding personality of Atatürk as the real saviour and founder of his new fatherland. By putting on his uniform again he united political and military power as commander-in-chief in the decisive months. The unity in the military leadership was also maintained by his extremely capable comrades-in-arms İsmet İnönü Paşa[5] as commander of the Western Front and Fevzi Çakmak Paşa[6] as chief of the general staff. Atatürk's orders of 08.08.1921 on the national requisitioning conditions (*Tekâlif-i Miliye Emirleri*),[7] which practically provided for a total exhaustion of the national human and material resources, were also decisive. In this respect, the transition to a "total war", although not with an expansion of saturated warfare contrary to international law. Thus e.g., women bore the main burden in logistics, while men fought at the front. The women are immortalized in stone at the national monument on Taksim Square in Istanbul. Atatürk's strategic and operational foresight also played a major role in the success of the operation. During the long delaying operations he made it clear to the impatient parliament several times that the time needed to gain strength could only be gained by

1 https://tr.wikipedia.org. – *Kars Antlaşması*. http://groong.usc.edu/treaties/kars.html.
2 https://en.wikipedia.org. – Megali Idea.
3 Lisec „Der Unabhängigkeitskrieg und die Gründung der Türkei“.
4 https://en.wikipedia.org. – David Lloyd George.
5 https:de.wikipedia.org. – Ismet Inönü.
6 https://tr.wikipedia.org. – Fevzi Çakmak.
7 Atatürk Nutuk or Söylev Vol. II.

temporarily giving up space, while the Greeks became vulnerable due to their overlong supply routes. A historical example of this is Napoleon's failure before Moscow in 1812.

Atatürk set an example by demanding mobile command and control not only on a large scale but also tactically in defense. "*Hatt-ı müdafaa yoktur, Saht-ı müdafaa vardir. O satıh bütün Vatandır*".[1] (The fight does not take place on a line/trench, but in an area. And this is the whole fatherland". Translation by the author).

This was implemented by the troops in the Battle of Sakarya in that they prepared a 2nd, sometimes even a 3rd trench line, to which they could go back, only to stop or throw the opponent back again by using operational reserves. In the last decisive battle Atatürk led again from the front, also a psychological means of good leadership, sought success in surprise and speed especially with the intense use of cavalry and by massive artillery fire. He did not give the enemy a chance in a powerful operation by splitting and enclosing them.

Although the political events can only be touched upon marginally, the core of his will and political heritage should not remain unmentioned: The National Pact/*Misak-ı Milli* is the political manifesto of the independence movement under Atatürk. It was still ratified by the Ottoman Parliament on 28.01.1920 in the 6 point version (compared to the previous 8 point version) and subsequently formed the basis of all relevant treaties for Atatürk - also for Lausanne treaty 1923 - and for Turkish constitutions. The core concepts are the unity of the nation and its independence.

NATIONAL PACT/MISAK-I MILLI

§ 1 *Osmanlı İslam çoğunluğuyla meskûn bulunan kısımlarının tamamı hakilaten veya hükmen hiçbir ayrılma kabul etmez bir bütündür.*

The entirety of the parts inhabited by an Ottoman-Islamic majority forms a unit whose actual or decreed division is not permitted.

§ 6 *tam bağımsızlık ve serbestiye mazhar olmaz ...*

...we enjoy complete independence and freedom..

(Translation by the author).

The geographical boundaries were not defined until the Lausanne Peace Treaty of 1923. Atatürk still had to give up Western Thrace, the Vilayet Musul/Mossul, Cyprus and some islands in the Aegean Sea. Changes still occurred in 1939 with the accession of the province of Hatay[2] and the regulation of the waterways in the Montreux Agreement[3] of 1936. The war of independence ended almost simultaneously with the foundation of the Turkish Republic on 29.10.1923. Its first president was Atatürk. (Fig. 27) Already one year before the Sultanate had been abolished, in 1924 the last caliph was also deprived of power.

Still to be seen in connection with the revolutionary events is the new constitution[4] of 24.05.1924 and subsequent amendments. Some articles of this will also have an impact on the army and its leadership, and Atatürk's army is even seen as the protector of some fundamental principles.

1 Atatürk Nutuk Vol. II. In modern Turkish in Söylev: *"Savunma hattı yoktur. Savunma alanı vardır. O alan bütün yurttur"*.

2 https://de.wikipedia.org. - Hatay (Province) https://tr.wikipedia.org. - *Hatay Devleti.*

3 https://de.wikipedia.org. – Vertrag von Montreux.

4 www.verfassungen.eu/tr/tuerkei24.htm.

In article 2 of the constitution Islam is still stated as state religion, but this passage is deleted without replacement on 10.04.1928. This applies equally to the statement about the Sharia/Şeriat in article 26 and the mention of Allah in article 38. The renewed substantial change of the article on 05.02.1937, among other things with the imperative of Laicism, will be discussed later in the context of Kemalism.

Article 5 assigns the executive power (*İcra Kudreti*), to the core of the Great National Assembly (*Büyük Millet Meclisi*), even though further executive rights in the exercise of this power lie with the President and the "Council of Executive Officers", the predecessor of the Cabinet. For the army, this means that, to this day, it is a parliamentary army similar to the German Bundeswehr. In essence, therefore, it is the Parliament that decides on the deployment of the army, with some exceptions. These are laid down in the constitution.

Article 40 stipulates:

"Başkumandanlık Türkiye Büyük Millet Meclisinin şahsiyeti maneviyesinde mündemiç olup Reisicumhur tarafından temsil olunur. Kuvayı Harbiyenin emir ve kumandası hazarda kanunu mahsusuna tevfikan Erkânı Harbiyei Umumiye Riyasetine ve seferde İcra Vekilleri Heyetinin inhası üzerine Reisicumhur tarafından nasbedilecek zate tevdi olunur" ("The supreme command of the army is vested in the Grand National Assembly of Turkey as the legal authority and is represented by the President of the Republic. In peacetime, the command of the Army shall be given to the Chief of the General Staff in accordance with a special law, and in wartime to a person to be appointed by the President of the Republic upon the proposal of the Council of Executive Officers. Translation by the author). Here the character of a parliamentary army is emphasized once again.

With the new state form of the Republic, a modern constitution, which has not yet completely established the separation of powers between the legislative and executive branches, the subsequent constitutional changes until 1928 and the staffing of the highest state offices, a new era of external peace also begins for the army after seemingly endless years of war. The normalisation of political relations with the other states is also accompanied by a normalisation of military relations, the exchange of military attachés, cooperation in training and armament. It therefore seems appropriate at this point to take stock again of the important years immediately after the First World War in the sense of the questions we formulated at the beginning.

The official mission of the Rest of the Ottoman Army was actually the further disarmament on the instructions of the victorious powers and the Sultan. The orders from the revolutionary Atatürk towards a re-growing regular army with the irregular/Freikorps troops to be integrated was in the opposite direction: He wanted to clear up the internal situation and expel all occupying forces.

The issue of the army's loyalty to "the sovereign" must therefore also be differentiated. While regular troops are increasingly unwilling to follow the Sultan, they are convinced by Atatürk's liberal/nationalist/republican ideas and become the guarantors of the realization of his vision. The people had to learn that in a Republic "the sovereign" is no longer a person, but they themselves, represented by the parliament. The army now occupies a special position in the state for Atatürk, in that he sees it as the guardian of Kemalism, among others.

- The army's relationship to religion, specifically to the caliph, increasingly gave way to the idea of a Turkish national consciousness. Aware of this fact, Atatürk also acted cautiously by abolishing the caliphate and religious institutions only after the Republic had become a reality in 1923. Atatürk was also aware, however, that Islam could again develop a new reactionary or even revolutionary force, which is why the separation of religion and state, laicism or secularism, will be so important.

- The above mentioned years have shown that the Turkish army, which was bled dry in the struggle for independence against Greece and the fight against other occupying forces, once again showed amazing personnel qualities. Due to the occupation situation, the material prerequisites for the early victory were only given by its own strength with the help of Russia, later Italy and France. According to the author's conviction, however, Atatürk would have achieved his goal without outside help, albeit later. The war-weariness of the victorious powers and Greece's strategic mistakes were to his advantage.

FROM THE CREATION OF THE REPUBLIC TO THE PRESENT DAY

The Army under Atatürk and Inönü

Since Atatürk died in 1938 he did not live to see the Second World War, but the international dangers that have become visible on the horizon have already been identified. As President, he continued to determine, together with the Cabinet and the party, the *Cumhuriyet Halk Partisi (CHP)*, the fate of the nation politically while he was no longer an active soldier. For him the separation of both functions is extremely important to ensure the principle of command and not to dilute obedience, even if in a national emergency such as the independence fight in his case seemed to have been an exception and he had been a stroke of luck. Atatürk has therefore also insisted that officers in parliament one side or the other would have to decide, because for him party affiliation and at the same time military status is incompatible. In September 1909. he already said at the congress of the party *İttihat ve Terakki* in Selanik:

"Ordu mensupları Cemiyet içinde kaldıkça hem fırka kuramıyacağız, hem de ordumuz olmıyacaktır. Mensuplarının pek çoğu Cemiyet âzası olan Üçüncü Ordu günün mânasile modern bir ordu sayılamaz,"[1] ("We members of the Army, who are currently on the committee, can't do both to the Party as well as to our army. Since quite a few members' relations with the committee, the 3rd Army, which is still significant today, can no longer be a modern army." Translation by the author).

This has been reflected in later constitutions. Nevertheless has been running through Atatürk's thinking since the above-mentioned dissonance with the Young Turks before the First World War an ambivalence in the relationship between the military and politics - i.e. abstinence versus interference - which repeatedly leads to frictions. So it is to be expressed to Celal Bayar again on 01.03.1924:

"...the separation of army and politics is a fundamental point of view that the Republic has always kept in mind. Thanks to this conception, which we have followed, the armies of the Republic, which are the true and steadfast guardians of our beloved country, have permanently achieved a position of prestige and strength."

Already the second Chief of the General Staff in the new Republic, Marshal Fevzi Çakmak (1922-1944 !), was no longer a member of the cabinet[2] from 1924. In February 1931 Atatürk is said to have clarified that the army was the spearhead of the realization of national ideals and in the officers' messes a saying of him is said to have hung on the walls with the sentence that the army had always been the leader in the progress of the people. This sentence was contained in the textbooks for the training of the general staff.[3]

The party program of the ruling CHP from 1935, adopted at the fourth party congress, contains a passage in § 72 that clearly assigns a political role to the republican army with the formulation: "*...ve ulusal ülküyü, ulusal varlığı ve devremi kollayan ve koruyan...*".[4] ("...and the national ideal of preserving and protecting the national heritage and revolution...". Translation by the author).

---

1 *Bayar „Atatürk'ten Hatıralar" p.18 ; https://de.wikipedia.org – Komitee für Einheit und Fortschritt.*

2 Ministry of Defence By law of 03.03.1924 the General Staff was established under the name *Erkân-ı Harbiye-i Umûmiye Reisliği or Riyaseti* independently, i.e. separate from the political institutions of the Council of Ministers. In 1935 it was given the current name *Genelkurmay Başkanlığı*. See homepage *Türk Silahlı Kuvvetleri Genelkurmay Başkanlığı.*

3 Vgl. Birand „Shirts of Steel: The Military Academy".

4 TBMM - *Kütüphane ve Arşiv Hizmetleri Başkanlığı* - CHP Programı 1935.

The army, represented by the general staff, always saw itself in a guard role of Kemalism, supported by large parts of the population and the CHP. In the one-party state until 1950, control was given by the Senate and the Grand National Assembly, and later additionally by the cabinet and by the National Security Council (MGK - *Milli Güvenlik Kurulu).* As long as the selection of personnel for top military functions and careers remained largely in military hands, continuity in the thinking of the officer corps was ensured. In the judgment of most experts and authors there was no doubt about this. Nye, for example, judges:

"The Guardian role of the military was institutionalized by Atatürk in the 1920's."[1]

In his speeches, Atatürk has also repeatedly seen the youth in a similar watchdog or testamentary role,[2] since they would determine the politics of the future. The guardian role assigned to the military has certainly justified the later interventions. The attempted coup of 2016 seems to be out of the question, especially since it was not carried out by the top of the army with the clear goal of preserving Kemalist principles. The term Kemalism is not easy to grasp. It is usually shortened with an explanation of the six principles (*Altı Ok* = literally six arrows, also on the emblem of the CHP since 1931), which as a part of the party program of the CHP 1935 subsequently found their way into the constitution. The law of 05.02.1937 revised article 2 of the constitution, which contains the six principles/characteristics in the first sentence:

"Türkiye Devleti, Cümhuriyetçi, milliyetçi, halkçı, devletçi, lâik ve inkılâpçıdır. Resmî dili Türkçedir. Makarrı Ankara şehridir."

("The Turkish state is republican, nationalist, popular, interventionist, laical and revolutionary. Its official language is Turkish. Its capital is the city of Ankara." Translation by the author).

A central concern of Atatürk was the separation of religion and state, i.e. Laicism, which Anglican authors rather describe with the term Secularism. Among other reasons the violation of this principle was in each case one cause of the interventions from 1960 to 2007. It should be remembered that the National Pact, the reforms and Atatürk's actions during his lifetime revealed other principles, e.g. his demand for state independence and unity, his love of peace, his egalitarian thinking on women's suffrage, his orientation towards the West. Often overlooked is his pragmatic principle of *İnkılâpçılık*, sometimes also called *Devrimcilik*, i.e. the evolutionary or even revolutionary principle of reformism. Atatürk was not a static ideologist, but a pragmatic man of progress and modernization. As in any hierarchy of goals, there can be competing objectives on a case-by-case basis, e.g. between the independence of the nation and the orientation towards the West. His successor, the Kemalist president İsmet İnönü, clearly answered the question after the Second World War by turning to the UN, NATO and the USA - knowing that this would be accompanied by a partial loss of state sovereignty. An even more serious decision concerns the ongoing question of membership in the EU, which overrides the national parliaments in many respects through majority decisions, or through their supranational jurisdiction.

For the army, the decades after 1922 could have been a period of calm and consolidation, but this was only partly achieved. Domestic unrest again demanded it, and tensions with neighbouring states such as Greece always demanded readiness for battle, not to mention the unclear situation and critical years of the Second World War. It led to the necessary

1 Nye "The Military in Turkish Military Politics" p. 248.

2 Atatürk's speech of several days, called NUTUK, with the statement of 20.10.1927: *"Turkish Youth! Your first duty is to always preserve and defend the national independence, the Turkish Republic".*

mobilisation and increase in the military presence to 1.5 million men, which once again resulted in major civilian casualties by suffering.[1]

A first major crisis within the country was the Kurdish uprising of 1925, after Kurds had already caused the Sultan difficulties in the area of Homs, Aleppo and Arbil from 1832 onwards, as reported by Moltke in 1839. Other examples are the Kurdish uprisings of 1879 under Sheikh Ubeydallah with about 900 men, who were exterminated by the army, or those of 1887 in the Erzurum and Van[2] area. Abdülhamid II had not only set up his Hamidiye regiments against the Armenians, but he also wanted to keep the Kurds in check, among other things through balanced contributions and appointments. The political weakness of the Sultan around 1908 provoked the founding of Kurdish organisations and actions up to their striving for independence, which were also suppressed by the army.[3] In 1920/1921 there were again riots in the Dersim (Tunceli from 1937) and Sivas area by Alevi Kurds, while about 2/3 of the Kurds are Sunni-Safiite[4] oriented. The core of the 1921 unrest is also known as the Koçgiri uprising. It was crushed in June 1921[5]. Due to cultural heterogeneity and the resulting lack of unity among the Kurds, their uprisings have been bloody but not really successful until today.

In June 1920, Atatürk is said to have given the commander of the southern front Nihat Anılmış Paşa the order: *"As for areas inhabited by Kurds, we consider it a necessity both of our domestic and of our foreign policy to set up a local government gradually"*. Later still: *"...to prepare gradually for the establishment of local government bodies and thus win for us the hearts of the Kurds and to strengthen the links which bind Kurdish leaders to us by appointing them to civil and military positions"*[6].

In order to restore public order (*toplumsal düzen*), the parliament enacted Law No. 578 *Takrir-i Sükûn Kanunu* on March 4, 1924, to stop the fighting and to have perpetrators tried by independence courts *(İstiklal Mahkemesi)*[7]. There was no appeal body above this. However, the subsequent Kurdish uprising of 1925 exceeded the previous actions. The Sheikh Sait/Sex Seid rebelled after a previous congress in 1924 with many officers in the area west of Lake Van. The reasons were a mixture of conservative protest against the new political secular course after the abolition of the caliphate, Turkish nationalist restrictions on the Kurdish languages and cultures, access to offices, restrictions on land ownership (Law No. 1505) up to the official abolition of the term "Kurdistan[8]". Of course it was also about autonomy or independence. The Kurds attacked the Ottoman troops in Diyarbakır with the tried and tested trick of attaching small Qur'ans to the bayonets of the rifles to stop enemy rifle fire. İsmet Paşa as Prime Minister "cleaned up" the situation in March 1925 with about 35,000 men and the use of the air force. The Sheikh and many of his comrades-in-arms were captured, sentenced to death by the above mentioned special courts, Kurdish villages were destroyed. In 1928 an amnesty was issued in this regard.

In 1926, 1927 and 1930 the Kurdish uprisings continued with the centre around Ağrı Dağı/Ararat, partly supported by Armenians and Iranian Kurds[9]. The total number of insurgents is said to have been 5,000-8,000. While the first two insurrections by Turkish

1 Kreiser „Kleine Geschichte der Türkei" p. 393.
2 https://de.wikipedia.org. - Sheik Ubeydallah. Cf. Arfa "The Kurds". p. 22 ff.
3 Cf. Van Bruinessen "Agha, Sheikh and State" p. 337.
4 The Turkish religious authority *DIYANET* primarily supports Hanafi Sunni Islam in contrast to the Shafiite school of law. https://de.wikipedia.org. - Shafi'ites.
5 https://tr.wikipedia.org. - *Koçgiri İsyanı.*
6 See Mango in Kedourie "75 Years of the Turkish Republic" p. 13.
7 Cf. Gülbeyaz " Mustafa Kemal Atatürk".
8 Ibidem. pp. 541 ff. p. 572. p. 586. https://de.wikipedia.org. - Sheikh Said. https://tr.wikipedia.org. - *Şeyh Said İsyanı.*
9 https://de.wikipedia.org. – Ararat Aufstand.

Jandarma and Turkish troops could not yet be completely eliminated, this was achieved in 1930 with the help of the air force. The proclamation of a "Republic of Ararat" remained wishful thinking, (Fig. 28). The second attempt to found a Kurdish state in 1946 in Mahabad in northwest Iran remained an eleven-month episode[1]. The resettlement law of 1934 was another reason for unrest, as it gave the Minister of the Interior a free hand for internal resettlements in Turkey, including the Kurds[2].

The biggest and bloodiest uprising of the Kurds, however, occurred again in the Dersim area in 1937/1938[3] and Atatürk expressed his deep concern before the parliament:

"Mustafa Kemal Ataturk, 1 Kasım 1936 tarihinde yatığı TBMM konuşmasında Dersim'deki ağalık düzeni sorununuTürkiye'nin en önemli iç sorunu olarak tanımladı." ("Mustafa Kemal Atatürk, in a scheduled parliamentary session on November 1, 1936, described the Dersim problem as the most important domestic political problem of Turkey in terms of rank. Translation by the author). Also in this case Atatürk proved his far-reaching visionary ability.

Once again, the causes were of various kinds, including the 1936 Settlement Law *(Tunceli Kanunu No. 2884)*, which in turn caused unrest among the population and demands for local autonomy. The Turkish army carried out a final operation under the name *"Tedip ve Tenkil"* ("Punishment and Deportation". Translation by the author) with about 50,000 men and 40 airplanes, deported about 12,000-50,000 inhabitants, supposedly used poison gas and had ringleaders sentenced. About 13,800 insurgents are said to have died. In 1964 there was another amnesty.

On 01.01.1995 the female Prime Minister Tansu Çiller tried in vain to promote the growing together of the different ethnic groups by a modern modification of the famous sentence of Atatürk, by not focusing on Turkishness but on Citizenship:

"Ne mutlu Türkiye'nin Vatandaşıyım diyene[4]." ("Happy is he who can say of himself that he is a citizen of Turkey." Translation by the author).

When the terrorist organisation PKK[5] again operated in this region in 1980, evacuations or deportations took place again. In 2011, the Turkish Prime Minister Recep Erdoğan apologised for the events of 1937/1938 with the words:

"Eğer devlet adına özür dilenecekse, böyle bir literatür varsa, ben özür dilerim, diliyorum." ("If an apology is to be made on behalf of the state, and if the literature is right, then I would like to express this apology." Translation by the author). The former state's action had certainly been disproportionate.

Nevertheless, since then the spiral of Kurdish and state violence has continued - with interruptions - without any current hope for pacification. Of course, the situation certainly leads to strong tensions in the army between Kurds and Turks, undermining the reliability and thus the operational capability of the armed forces.

Law No. 2590 of 1934[6] abolished the Ottoman titles - such as *Paşa* -, on the other hand, the rank designations for generals and admirals were redefined. For the Army and Air Force in descending order: *Mareşal,* then the general ranks *Birinci Ferik, Ferik and Liva*; for the Navy the admirals ranks again *Birinci Ferik, Ferik and Liva.*

1 https://de.wikipedia.org. - Republic of Ararat. https://tr.wikipedia.org. - *Ağrı ayaklanmaları.* https://de.wikipedia.org. - Mahabad. Above mentioned van Bruinessen p. 549 ff.

2 Law 2510 of 14.06.1934 or Resmi Gazete No. 2733 of 21.06.1934 *İskan kanunu.*

3 https://de.wikipedia.org. – Dersim Aufstand. https://tr.wikipedia.org. – *Dersim İsyanı.*

4 *See Poulton "Top Hat, Grey Wulf and Crescent".*

5 https://de.wikipedia.org. - Labour Party of Kurdistan.

6 Legal title: "*Efendi, Bey, Paşa gibi lakap ve unvanların kaldırılmasına dair kanun*".

THE KURDISH UPRISINGS 1925 – 1937

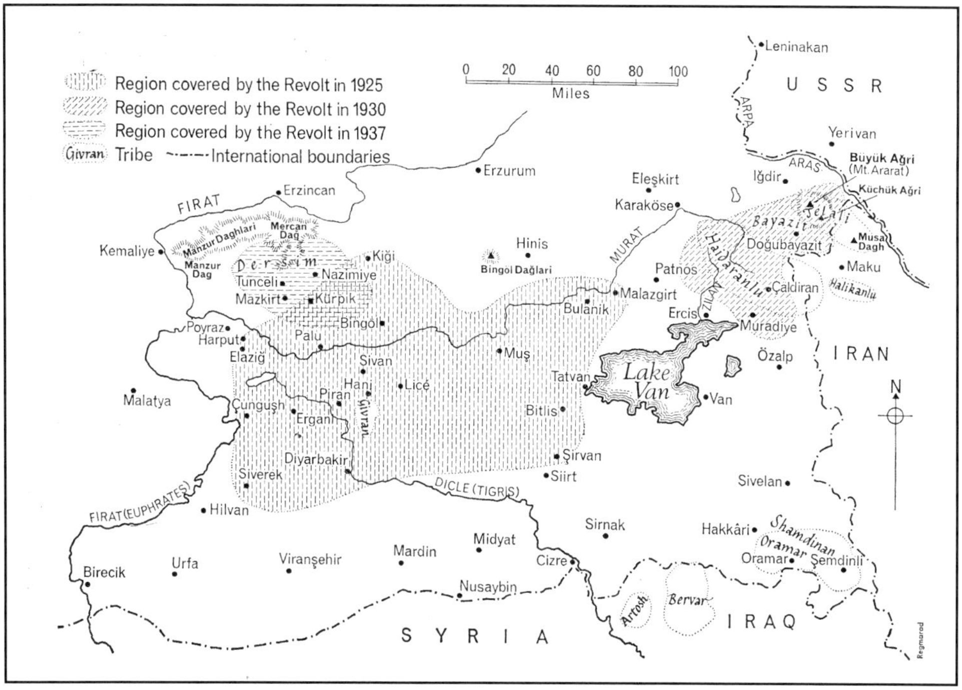

Map 19 *(Hassan Arfa „The Kurds" p. 35)*

For the army it was actually necessary to consolidate in the years after 1923 and, despite financial and economic problems, to catch up with the West in terms of armaments. Such a milestone was the installation of the first tank company in Lüleburgaz in 1934, the establishment of airborne troops after 1939, a comprehensive repair programme for the navy, the readmission of the cruiser *Hamidiye,* returned from the British in September 1924 and its re-commissioning, the acquisition of two Ro III A Rodra long-range reconnaissance flying boats from the German company Rohrbach in the period 1926-1936.

However, the greatest progress was made in civil aviation and in the Turkish Air Force, which became a separate service of the Turkish Armed Forces in 1944 (although its date of foundation was set at 1911). In addition to extensive procurements in Germany, Italy, Great Britain, Poland, the USA and France, it was possible to manufacture numerous aircraft under licence and acquire technical know-how at the Kayseri aircraft factory (KTF- *Kayseri Tayyare Fabrikası)* from 1932 onwards. During the 2nd world war, Germany continued deliveries to neutral Turkey until April 1944, while the USA and Great Britain imposed an embargo in this respect. Deliveries from Germany ended with the breaking off the diplomatic relations in August 1944, a forced concession by Turkey in favour of an imminent accession to the United Nations. Turkey had already agreed the training of its pilots with France before 1935, and later also with Great Britain and the USA. Thus, in 1945, with approximately 26,000 men,

Figs. 18, 19 The coat of arms of the Turkish Air Force and the Air Force School

Fig. 20 Bleriot XI

(http://www.tayyareci.com. – Blériotxi.asp)

Plate X

Fig. 21 Sultan Mehmed V. endeavours to keep pace with the German

(https://commons.wikimedia – Deutsche Militärmission Türkei Kladderadatsch) (1909).

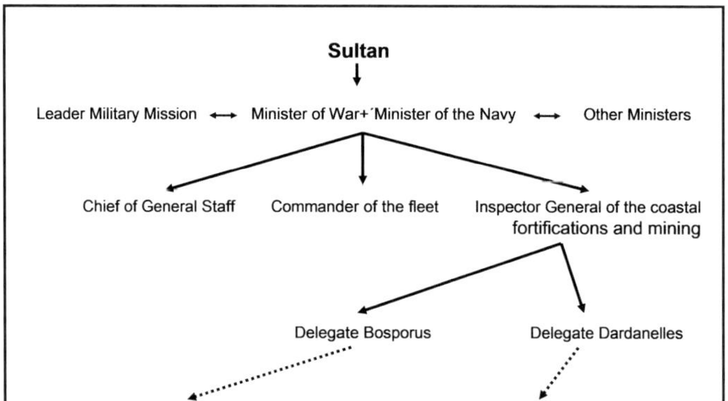

Fig. 22 The Top Military Structure in Istanbul

Fig. 23 Minelayer Nusret
(https://commons.wikimedia.org. – Ottoman minelayer Nusret)

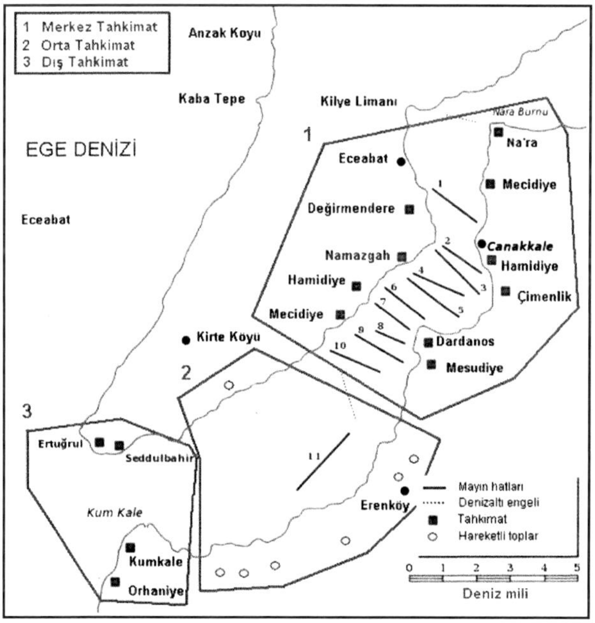

Fig. 24 The Mine Fields
(https://commons.wikimedia.org.- Çanakkale Deniz Savaşları Tahkimat)

Plate XII

Fig. 25 A Machine Gun (MG)

Fig. 26 Telephone switchboard amd field telephone

(https://commons.wikipedia.org – Turkish Field Telephone)

1922 Commander in Chief
Marshall Gazi

1923 President

Fig. 27 Mustafa Kemal Astatürk
(Atatürk ve Kurtuluş Savaş Müzesi)

Fig. 28 (Inscription: "Here lies the Dream of Kurdistan buried (Newspaper Cumhuriyet from 19.09.1930)

Plate XIV

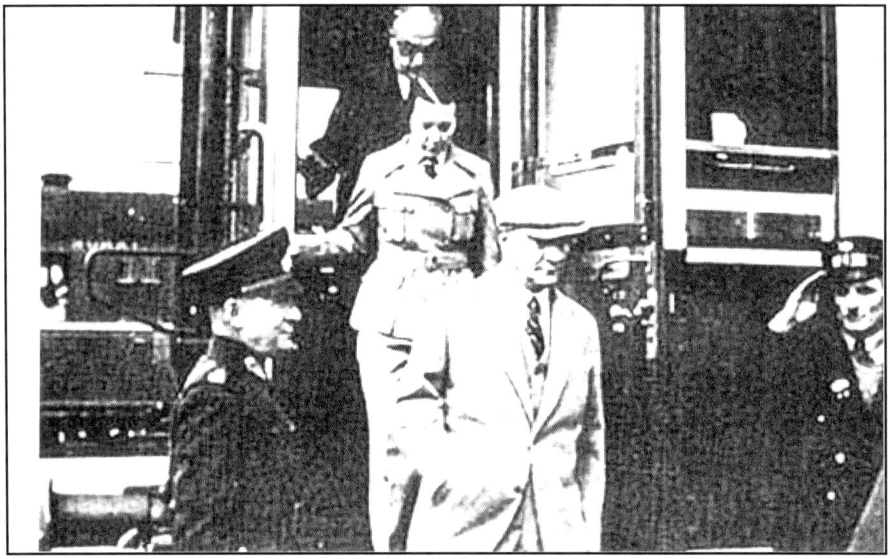

Fig. 29 Aratürk and Sabiha Gökcen - The first female fihghter pilot

(http:///www.ctie.monash.edu.auhargrave/images/goken 4500 jpg)

Fig. 30 T-129 Atak

(https://de.wikipedia.org. – TAI T- 129)

Fig. 31 Battle Tank Altay

(https://tr.wikipedia.org. – Altay Tank.jpg)

Fig. 32 Korvette F - 511

(https://commons.wikimedia.org. – Korvette Heybeliada (F 511)

Plate XVI

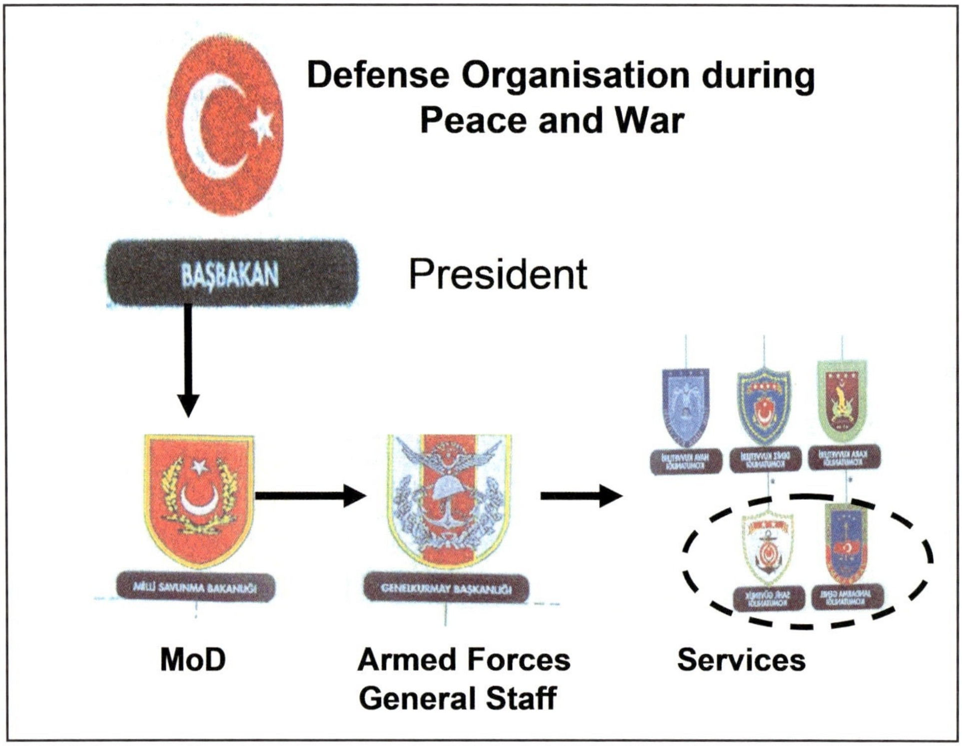

Fig. 33

Fig.34 Armed Drone Bayraktar

including 1,000 pilots, and 749 aircraft, it had an impressive capacity, although it was still dependent on supplies of special spare parts and aviation fuel[1].

Another famous example of Atatürk's promotion of women's emancipation is the first female fighter pilot in Turkey, probably even in the world, Sabiha Gökçen[2]. (Fig. 29) After all, she had about 8,000 flying hours and 32 combat missions, including those against the Kurds in 1937/1938. She flew 22 types of aircraft, learned to parachute and took part in the Korean War. Atatürk had adopted her as an adolescent and encouraged her. As is well known, the airfield on the Anatolian side of İstanbul is named after her.

President İsmet İnönü had been able to keep Turkey out of the 2nd World War by means of a clever foreign policy and treaties with the war opponents, for the benefit of the Republic. In 1945, he led Turkey as a founding member of the UNO, after membership of the League of Nations had already existed since 1932. Although Turkey was not a victorious power in the War, this time - unlike after the First World War - it took part in the UNO conferences as an invited member with equal rights. İnönü temporarily ended his political career in 1950 as president and representative of the old Kemalist guard, which he will only continue as prime minister after the military coup in 1961-1965. İnönü had supported the introduction of the multi-party system after two failed attempts under Atatürk, which led to the Democratic Party (DP) winning the elections in 1950. The Kemalist CHP to the present day never again has been able to form the government alone. The year 1950 thus represented a turning point for the still young Republic, which would be followed by further stormy years, including for the army.

The conclusion for the time under the two state presidents Atatürk and İnönü 1923-1950 in the sense of our question is also this time mixed:

The army's mission did not include operations against an external enemy, but several operations against the Kurds. However, the army could not and cannot achieve a real and final calming of the situation; this is left to politics. Unfortunately, internal operations and serious political disagreements always affect the cohesion of the army and jeopardise the loyalty of the troops.

The units of the army and air force deployed against the Kurds have obviously been loyal to the political principals, represented by parliament and the executive.

- The Kemalist principle of Laicism demanded not only the separation of religion - to remain purely a private issue - from the army in daily military service, but far beyond that, its advocacy of the state's stated goal in a guardian function. In this way, the conflict between the army and politics was settled if Kemalist principles or the general internal security situation appeared to be endangered.

- The economic situation after 1923 allowed the army to catch up with the West only slowly. With the onset of industrialisation in the 1950s, the necessary civilian infrastructure was created. Out of necessity, Atatürk had advocated the principle of "*Devletçilik*", also known as "*Etatism*", i.e. that of a dirigiste planned economy. Over the years, resources were pooled by the state to implement priority projects. With the later transition to a largely free market economy, the principle disappeared, also from the constitution.

1 See EADS „100 Jahre Deutsch/Türkische Zusammenarbeit in der Militärischen Luftfahrt".

2 https://de.wikipedia.org. - Sabiha Gökçen. https://tr.wikipedia.org. - Sabiha Gökçen. Before her there was already a female Turkish civilian pilot.

Domestic operations of the army 1950 - 2007

The following decades brought several tensile tests for the army as a result of military interventions at home, including new requirements in the context of national and international operations. The latter will only be dealt with in the next chapter. The years 1950-2007 were marked by great political instability. During this time the cabinet changed almost every 3 years, whereas the periods before and therafter were charcterized by a certain stability due to the presidents Atatürk, İnönü and Erdoğan, the last two also serving many years as prime minister. Military coups against the government to uphold Kemalist principles would have been fruitless before 1950, because the Kemalists, represented by the CHP, provided the governments and the presidents. After 1950, the transition to a multi-party system created a new situation due to some governments which, according to the military, disregarded Kemalist principles. The military saw itself repeatedly forced to intervene, but also for other reasons.

These were mostly a mixture of:

- Islamization or violation of the principle of Laicism
- Violations of the Constitution or Laws
- Suppression of the parliamentary or extra-parliamentary opposition
- Separatism Efforts
- Left- or right-wing extremism
- Violence on the streets, numerous murders and approaches to anarchy
- Actions following the declaration of a state of emergency
- Danger of civil war
- Loss of state authority
- Social and economic problems, inflation
- Corruption
- Press censorship
- Muslim orientation of a presidential candidate (2007).

The larger interventions up to 2007 were either bloody from the beginning or in the aftermath (1960, 1980) or bloodless (1971, 1997, 2007) and, with the exception of those of 1960, including the smaller preceding ones, were carried out from the top of the general staff. They were successful in terms of the actors (1960, 1971, 1980, 1997) or unsuccessful (2007). Common to all successful interventions before 2007 is that the army made it possible to form a civilian government again after a temporary assumption of power. The first three major coups were accompanied by new constitutions or at least constitutional amendments. This is the reason why parts of the population perceived the army as a stabilizing factor for the republic or developing democracy and why foreign countries regarded the army's conduct as mild[1]. After all, Turkey had been an important member of NATO since 1952 and had also confirmed its ties with the West by participating in the Korean War in 1950. By the end of the 1950s, even American medium-range ballistic ground-to-ground missiles of the Jupiter i.e. Redstone type[2] were stationed in Turkey, which could also be equipped with nuclear warheads. This is another trustworthy step in military bilateral cooperation which, within the framework of NATO's nuclear deterrence, has remained fundamentally valid to the present day.

With the formation of the cabinets of Prime Minister Adnan Menderes[3] in 1950-1960 with the Democratic Party (*DP-Democrat Parti*) and the CHP, political resistance arose, reinforced

1 https://de.wikipedia.org. – Militärputsch in der Türkei. https://tr.wikipedia.org. – *27 Mayıs Darbesi.*

2 https://de.wikipedia.org. – Redstone (Rakete). See also Robins „Suits and Uniforms".

3 https://de.wikipedia.org. - Adnan Menderes. https://tr.wikipedia.org. - Adnan Menderes.

by Menderes' authoritarian leadership. Among other things, Menderes had demanded that the Turkish state remain Muslim. Already at the beginning of his reign, the call to prayer had to resound again in Arabic, after having resounded in Turkish since 1932.

Samuel Huntington generalizes that in the countries with Muslim population in the 1970s - i.e. almost at the same time - an "Islamic Resurgence" had taken place. Here he considers the capitalization of the term appropriate because of the importance of the development. In 1969 the laicist state Turkey joined the OIC (Organisation of Islamic Cooperation) as founding member, after an accession to the predecessor organization, the Congress of Islamic States, had not yet succeeded in 1964[1].

In the military it rumbled, so that the head of government Menderes let replace the chief of staff Nafiz Gürman with further 14 generals and 150 officers because of preparation of a coup already on 06.06.1950[2]. In 1957 there was another coup attempt[3].

From 1948 onwards, US training aid began to take effect, controlled by JAMMA (Joint American Military Aid Mission to Turkey), which led to considerable modernization steps. However, tensions with the USA arose due to the presence and controversial status of the trainers and military advisors on site and the implementation of infrastructure measures within the framework of stationing. To this day, the question of the competent jurisdiction for the stationed soldiers remains a controversial issue. Another temporary focus was the use of Turkish ports by the US Navy. On 03.07.1969, a bilateral cooperation and stationing agreement with the USA on the use of US bases in Turkey and regulations on the military presence[4] was concluded. In the meantime such procedures have become established at least between the NATO states. At the beginning of deployments on foreign soil a "Status of Forces Agreement" (SoFA) is concluded with the necessary additional agreements. Turkey joined NATO in 1952. With this measure the orientation towards the West was underpinned. From 1955 the first female cadets were also trained[5]. Since then women have occupied an important place in the entire army.

The coup of May 27, 1960 was started by the just resigned commander of the land forces General Cemal Gürsel, companion of Atatürk, who became prime minister and commander-in-chief of the army after the coup and president until 1966[6]. However, on the day of the coup, he stayed at İzmir, while about 38 younger officers under the right-wing extremist Pantürkist Colonel Alparslan Türkeş[7] were acting on site, which reminded a little bit of the "Young Turks". President Celâl Bayar, Prime Minister Adnan Menderes and Chief of General Staff Rüştü Erdelhun were arrested, his successor Ragıp Gümüşpala was forced to resign. Menderes and two other ministers were executed in 1961, but all three were rehabilitated in 1990 in an act of state. The army was subjected to extensive purges[8]. It was no longer homogeneous behind the Atatürk party CHP - the majority of which subsequently welcomed the coup - but partly behind the overthrown DP (*Democrat Parti*) of Menderes. From now on, diversity in the heterogeneous party landscape also left its mark on the army. In justifying the coup, the putschists - who got off lightly - were able to rely on Law No. 2771, which had been passed

1 Cf. Huntington „Kampf der Kulturen" p. 170.
2 https://tr.wikipedia.org. - Nafiz Gürman. Cf. Gülbeyaz "Musta Kemal Atatürk".
3 Cf. Firuz "The Turkish Experiment in Democracy".
4 Weiher „Militär und Entwicklung in der Türkei, 1945-1973" p. 104.
5 Cf. Robinson "The First Turkish Republic".
6 https://tr.wikipedia.org. - Cemal Gürsel. https://de.wikipedia.org. - Cemal Gürsel.
7 https://de.wikipedia.org. - Alparslan Türkeş. https://tr.wikipedia.org. - Alparslan Türkeş. The officer and politician was imprisoned several times, but also held ministerial posts from 1975-1978. In 1969 he founded the nationalist MHP (*Milliyetçi Harekat Partisi*) and the extreme right-wing subgroup of the Grey Wolves (*Bozkurtlar*), who are blamed for over 600 murders.
8 See Weiher "Military and Development in Turkey" p. 157.

in 1935 under the responsibility of İnönü and Atatürk, although only the army as a whole was mentioned here:

***Ordu Dahili Hizmet Kanunu* - Law for the service of the Turkish Armed Forces within the Interior**, No. 2771 (as of 18.06.1935)

§ 34

"Ordunun vazifesi; Türk yurdunun ve teşkilâtı esasiye kanunile tayin edilmiş olan Türk Cümhuriyetini kollamak ve korumaktır." ("The duty of the army: To protect and defend Turkish territory and the Turkish Republic established by the constitution." Translation by the author).

Thus, it was not only about the defence of a territory, but also about the protection of a form of state, i.e. "Republic", possibly against everyone. After the coup, the law was revised in 1961 and adopted with a new title. In other words, the mission of the army - now contained in the first sentence of § 35 - basically said the same thing as the previous law.

***Türk Silahlı Kuvvetleri İç Hizmet Kanunu* - Law for the service of the Turkish Armed Forces within the Interior,** No. 211 (as of 04.01.1961)

§ 35

"Silahlı Kuvvetleri vazifesi; Türk yurdunu ve Anayasa ile tayin edilmiş olan Türkiye Cumhuriyeti kollamak ve korumaktır."

("The duty of the armed forces: To protect and defend Turkish territory and the Turkish Republic anchored in the constitution. Translation by the author).

The EU still noted much later in the Commission report on Turkey of 10.10.2012:

"No change was made to the Internal Service Law for the Turkish Armed Forces, which defines the duties of the military and contains an article leaving the military significant potential scope for intervention in politics."

In the meantime, Turkey has implemented the requested changes. The currently valid version of § 35 from 2013 no longer contains this justification for the coup[1]. The newer wording includes foreign deployments and once again emphasizes the central role of parliament. This formulation is now in line with the ideas of NATO and the EU, who do not grant the army as part of the executive a special undemocratic role:

§ 35 (Law 211 as of 13.07.2013 and still as of 25.06.2019)

"Silahlı Kuvvetler'in vazifesi, yurt dışından gelecek tehdit ve tehlikelere karşı Türk vatanını savunmak, caydırıcılık sağlayacak şekilde askeri gücün muhafazasını ve güçlendirilmesini sağlamak, TBMM kararıyla yurtdışında verilen görevleri yapmak ve uluslararası barışın sağlanmasına yardımcı olmaktır."

("The duty of the armed forces is to prevent threats or dangers to the fatherland from outside, to enable them to guarantee military power for protection and maintenance of power, to carry out parliamentary decisions for missions abroad and to ensure the maintenance of international peace. Translation by the author).

§ 38 of the above-mentioned law states that troops of the Army, Air Force and Navy may also be assigned to a county/province/*sancak*, i.e. for internal use. The limited authority of the General Staff vis-à-vis the Minister of the Interior with overall responsibility or a receiving Governor (*Vali*) of a province (outdated "*vilaye*t "or "*sancak*", more recently *"il"*) must be taken into account.

1 http://www.mevzuat.gov.tr. (See Act No 211 with amendments).

In the current constitution as of 16.04.2017, there is still no article dedicated solely to the mission of the armed forces. In Article 5, the state (*Devlet*) is generally required to protect the independence and unity of the Turkish nation, the unity of the people, the republic and democracy. Indirectly, the mission of the army is only mentioned in article 117 concerning the supreme command:

"Milli güvenliğinin sağlanmasından ve Silahlı Kuvvetlerin yurt savunmasına hazırlanmasından, Türkiye Büyük Millet Meclisine karşı, Cumhurbaşkanı sorumludur." ("The President of the Republic is responsible to the Turkish Grand National Assembly for ensuring national security and the readiness of the armed forces to defend the fatherland. Translation by the author). This passage e.g. does not contain any statement about operations abroad.

One consequence of the coup was the constitution of 1962 following a previous referendum[1]. A glance at this constitution[2] also reveals other important articles on the armed forces: "In principle", all citizens have the right to vote and to stand for election in accordance with the law (Art. 55); however, the right to stand for election was subject to completion of military service (Art. 68). This is a general duty according to Art. 60; officers and non-commissioned officers (NCO) must retire from active service before they are eligible for election (Art. 68). A restriction on the right to vote for soldiers was a 1961 amendment to Electoral Law No. 298, which now allowed officers to exercise the right to vote, but not non-commissioned officers and enlisted[3]:

The essential unequal treatment was later also anchored in the constitution as of 23.07.1995. Art. 67 stipulated that enlisted and non-commissioned officers (*Er ve Onbaşlar*) under arms do not have the right to vote or stand for election.

Art. 138 regulated the military criminal proceedings, Art. 141 established the Military Court of Cassation as an appeal instance, Art. 145 established a Constitutional Court.

Also important is the establishment of the National Security Council (MGK - *Milli Güvenlik Kurulu)*[4], which had predecessors under other names. The presidency is incumbent on the president. Its members were ministers designated by law, the Chief of General Staff and representatives of the armed forces. The MGK had to support the executive branch with decisions concerning national security. In the constitution of 1961, Article 111, paragraph 3, second half-sentence states:

"...kararlarin alınmasında ve koordinasyonun sağlanmasında yardımcılık etmek üzere gereklı temel görüşleri Bakanlar Kuruluna bildirir." ("... for making decisions and ensuring coordination, to support the cabinet by providing information on the necessary basic viewpoint". Translation by the author).

The 1971 constitution granted the MGK more extensive powers. The corresponding passage now reads

"...kararlarin alınmasında ve koordinasyonun sağlanmasında gereklı temel görüşleri Bakanlar Kuruluna tavsiye eder." ("...to give the Cabinet a recommendation on the necessary basic viewpoint for taking decisions and ensuring coordination." Translation by the author).

Opinions on the power of this institution differed widely, partly because little came out of the MGK meetings. They ranged from a literal interpretation of the later wording "recommendation" to a de facto shadow cabinet as an instructional body. Udo Steinbach [5] formulated in 2003:

1 https://tr.wikipedia.org. - *Türkiye anayasa referandumu.*
2 http://www.verfassungen.eu/tr/verf61.htm.
3 See (Election) Law No 298 of 26.04.1961 § 7 *(Seçimleri temel hükümleri ve seçmen kütükleri hakkında kanun).*
4 https://tr.wikipedia.org. - Milli Güvenlik Kurulu.
5 Steinbach „Geschichte der Türkei" p. 46 und p. 61.

"Up to the present it became a powerful < watchdog >, who often displaced the cabinet as the center of governmental power."

Udo Steinbach later mentions an example of the exertion of influence in 1997 - which is actually irrelevant according to the statute - by "decree of a school reform" to the detriment of the religiously oriented *İmam Hatip* schools in the context of a major military coup, which was carried out without bloodshed. The MGK, which was dominated by the military in 1997, obviously still saw itself as an advocate of Kemalism and its central concern, Laicism.

After the current constitutional amendment of Article 118 by referendum in 2017, the recommendations of the MGK to the President of the Republic will now be made after the Prime Minister's office has ceased to exist. After the abolition of the representation of the Jandarma, the inclusion of the Minister of Justice and an unspecified number of deputies of the President, the staffing of the committee ensures that the civilian portion is predominant by at least 6:4. The committee is thus clearly limited to the function of consultation while military influence is reduced.

The military coup of 1960 was followed by further coup attempts in 1962 and 1963 under the ringleader Colonel Talât Aydemir, who was executed in 1964. They reflected the still ongoing dissension in the officer corps between the still dissatisfied radicals and the moderates, the younger and the older ones[1].

The second successful military coup on March 12, 1971[2] - which was now carried out by the incumbent General Staff in a united manner - was essentially bloodless, after the Chief of General Staff Memduh Tağmaç had handed over a demand for resignation to President Cevdet Sunay, which concerned the cabinet of Süleyman Demirel. In Turkish, the more harmless term "*Muhtıra*" (memorandum) is therefore also used instead of the word "*Darbe*" (coup, coup d'état). The memorandum was read out on the radio and discussed in parliament. The reasons for the demand for resignation were as above: Again the danger of civil war, anarchy on the streets and various social and economic unrests. The memorandum referred to Atatürk. As a result, there was further unrest, mass arrests and deaths on the streets. On 26.03.1971 already Nihat Erim formed a new coalition government.

Also this time extensive purges in the army followed the coup. The losers were again the "radical" officers or the "revolutionarily infected". In addition, a law is said to have been passed on April 27, 1972, "which provided for five years in prison for officers who joined a political party, held political meetings, wrote or signed political articles or manifestos[3]. The author could not research any further details on this, not even a date of repeal of the law. In the context of the second military coup d'état in 1971, a number of constitutional amendments were adopted, but no new constitution. This came into being again in 1982 after another referendum in the context of the 3rd major military coup.

On September 12th 1980 - parallel to a NATO exercise in Turkey with about 3,000 men - the biggest and subsequently bloodiest military coup to date - now directed against the cabinet of Süleyman Demirel - started, initiated by the Chief of General Staff Kenan Evren[4]. This was preceded by a memorandum to the President of the Republic, Fahri Korutürk, on December 27, 1979, referring to the army's duty to protect the Republic according to § 35 of the above-mentioned law. The reasons fall again into the familiar pattern, this time accompanied by at least 3,000 murders, caused by left and right-wing extremists and Islamists. Inflation rose to

1 Özbudan „The Role of the Military in recent Turkish Politics" p. 34. Der Spiegel 29/1964. https://tr.wikipedia.org. – Talat Aydemir. Weiher „Militär und Entwicklung in der Türkei, 1945-1973" p. 157 f.

2 https://de.wikipedia.org. – Militärputsch in der Türkei 1971. https://tr.wikipedia.org. – *12 Mart Muhtırası.*

3 Weiher „Militär und Entwicklung in der Türkei, 1945-1973" p. 157.

4 https://de.wikipedia.org. – Militärputsch in der Türkei 1980. https://tr.wikipedia.org. – *12 Eylül Darbesi.*

100 %: 15% unemployment, high foreign debts, 115 unsuccessful election attempts to appoint a new president, a state authority lying on the ground. The army with the Jandarma is involved in restoring security and order. General Evren appoints a cabinet under military control of the General Staff and the MGK with the former commander of the Navy and new Prime Minister Bülent Ulusu, which is only transferred to the elected Prime Minister Turgut Özal after the 1983 elections. There were mass arrests and mass trials, often resulting in death.

Evren is elected president of the state for seven years in 1982. In the same year, after a referendum in which no public discussions were allowed, a new constitution was enacted, which is still valid despite many subsequent amendments. In the transitional article 15, those responsible for the coup agree to go unpunished. The electoral law sets a 10% threshold for the parties, which is still valid[1].

With a constitutional amendment on 13.05. 2010, the above-mentioned transitional article and thus the immunity of the members of the military junta is lifted, allowing the prosecution of criminal offences. Kenan Evren (96) and former Air Force Chief Tahsin Şahinkaya (89) were indicted in 2012 and sentenced to life imprisonment in 2014, but did not have to serve their terms due to old age. Both generals died in 2015.

Below are other relevant articles concerning the army, including the current constitution as of 2017. Kemalism and Atatürk's objectives remain formally enshrined in the current Constitution, as stated in the preamble, Articles 1, 2, 3, 42, 58, 81, 103, 134, etc. However, official current policy is increasingly diluting these objectives in practice, especially Laicism and the principle of separation of powers mentioned in the preamble. Obviously, opinions differ on the term "*democratic*", which is also mentioned in Article 2. One obstacle to the elimination of references to Kemalism, apart from tactical considerations, is certainly the prohibition of the introduction of relevant amendments in Articles 1 to 3, as laid down in Article 4. However, in the opinion of many observers, as Joseph Croitoru has said, "*Islamisation has overtaken Kemalism*"[2]. Perhaps the army could have relied on Article 4 of the Constitution, if necessary, with renewed intervention and broad interpretation, although it remains unclear to what extent the term "state" (*devlet)* also meant and if it still means the army. In fact, the Constitution still lacks an article on the mission of the army in the sense of the new wording of the above-mentioned Internal Service Act for the Armed Forces, laid down in Law 211 as amended on 13.07.2013 and still valid as of 25.06.2019.

Current Constitution Article V

"Devletin temel amaç ve görevleri, Türk Milletinin bağımsızlığını ve bütünlüğünü, ülkenin bölünmezliğini, Cumhuriyeti ve demokrasiyi korumak, ..."

("The basic aims and tasks of the state are to protect the independence and unity of the Turkish people, the indivisibility of the country, the republic and democracy ...") Translation by the author).

However, after a continuous process of disempowerment since 2003, the army currently no longer has the ability to implement the Kemalist goals against Islamizing tendencies, because the AKP's election successes have meant that the loyalty of a part of the army to any military adventure is not guaranteed. This became clear even before the attempted coup in 2016. Art. 38 of the Constitution forbids the death penalty since 2004, which also applies to wartime conditions. However, the discussion about this has flared up again. Members of the army are

1 Act No 2839 of 10.06.1983 § 33. *Milletvekilli Seçimi Kanunu.*
2 Cf. Joseph Croituru in "Bonner Generalanzeiger" of 15.10.2016.

not allowed to join political parties, but according to the latest legal situation their commander-in-chief, the president, is.

Art. 76 allows that eligibility for election to a member of parliament is now possible from the age of 18 instead of 25. The exclusion from eligibility for election has also been changed. In the previous version, those who had not completed compulsory military service *(yükümlü olduğu askerlik hizmetini yapmamış olanlar)* were excluded, while the current version now excludes those who are related to military service (*askerlikle ilişiği olanlar*). At the same time, the discussion has flared up again and again as to whether general conscription is still appropriate or necessary. At the very least, the percentage of volunteers should now be significantly increased, thus strengthening professionalism.

Art. 92 on the proclamation of the event of war and the permission to use armed force remain unchanged. In principle, the right lies with the parliament, but if the parliament is not available, if the country is attacked with armed force and an immediate decision has to be made, the president of the state can decide on the use of the army.

Article 104 on the duties and powers of the President of the State continues an old passage. He represents the armed forces on behalf of the Turkish Grand National Assembly as commander-in-chief. He decides on the deployment of the army after the basic parliamentary decision. The original sentence reads: *"Türk Silahlı Kuvvetlerin kullanınmasına karar verir."* There seems to be a contradiction here with Article 92, which in principle gives Parliament the right to declare war and the right to send the armed forces abroad. The above-mentioned vague Turkish word "*kullanınmasına*" probably requires more precise translation or interpretation. The author understands it in such a way that - as always practised under the form of government of the Republic - the deployment of armed forces must in principle first be approved by parliament, but then the president decides on the details of implementation, in consultation with the Defence Minister and other ministers. The general staff would contribute.

However, there is no wording there on domestic deployment. On the other hand, the new comprehensive Article 118 contains the right of the president to declare a state of emergency for up to six months and the right to govern by presidential decrees (*Cumhurbaşkanlığı Kararnamesi, Decrees*). The scenarios are described cover a wide range. Of course, it can be assumed that armed forces will be deployed if necessary. The role of the Parliament is emphasised in the revised Article 104, especially the character of a parliamentary army. Article 117, which is unchanged on this point, also states that the supreme command cannot be separated from the "spiritual/adoptive (*manevi)* existence" of Parliament.

The previous formulation of the right to appoint the Chief of General Staff was explicitly not reinstated in Art. 104, but was already enshrined in Art. 117 with the current omission of the formulation "upon the proposal of the Council of Ministers". What remains unchanged there is that the function of commander-in-chief in war is exercised by the Chief of General Staff on behalf of the President of the Republic; now, after the structural change in the competence of the General Staff, certainly also controlled by the Minister of Defence. Extensive changes have been adopted in the jurisdiction of the courts, with the trend towards the curtailment of the competences of the military and the corresponding courts, the elimination of parallel jurisdictions with competences that are not always clear and their general civilisation:

- No more existance of military courts in peace, only disciplinary courts (Art. 142, Art. 145). In war, however, members of the military may be brought before military courts in the event of criminal offences.

- Art. 148 now excludes the commander of the Jandarma from criminal proceedings before the State Court (*Yüce Divan*), while this continues to apply to the top military officials. This takes into account the demilitarisation of the Jandarma through closer ties to the Minister of the Interior.

- The Military Cassation Court (*Askeri Yargıtay*) is also repealed by Article 156 as a consequence of the above-mentioned Articles 142, 145. It was the last instance above the military courts.

- According to Article 157, the Military Administrative Court (*Askeri Yüksek İdare Mahkemesi)* is abolished. It was the last instance in administrative court proceedings against military persons.

- Article 125 on decisions of the High Military Council (*YAŞ - Yüksek Askeri Şuranı*), to which no appeal could be lodged, now states since 2017: *"All decisions of the High Military Council concerning the promotion of personnel and, apart from suspension from service and retirement due to lack of posts, termination of service shall be subject to legal remedy".*

- Already on 25.07.2016 the members of the above-mentioned YAŞ had been redefined in Law 1612[1], now as of 09.11.2016. The President chairs whereas the other members are his deputies, the Ministers of Defence, Justice, Foreign Affairs and the Interior, as well as the Chief of General Staff and the commanders of the 3 services. In § 6 the office of the Secretary was assigned to the Ministry of Defence. Thus, in YAŞ as in the MGK, a "civilizing" of the body has taken place with a weakening of the military influence in both bodies.

The year 1982, however, brought another important change for the structure of the armed forces, namely the foundation of the Coast Guard (*Sahil Güvenlik*) with Law No. 2692[2], which also had predecessors in the Ottoman Empire since the middle of the 19th century with the main task of collecting customs duties..

With the law as of 02.07.2018, the Coast Guard's task is to maintain safety and order in the coastal area, including rescue at sea, police operations (*Kolluk Görevleri*), etc. With regard to the various insinuations, it is now stated that the Coast Guard is in the following command, comparable to Jandarma:

"Bu Komutanlık İçişleri Bakanlığına bağlıdır. Seferberlik ve savaş hallerinde, Sahil Güvenlik Komutanlığının Bakanlar Kurulu kararıyla belirlenecek bölümleri Deniz Kuvvetleri Kommutanlığı emrine girer, kalan bölümü normal görevlerine devam eder. ("This command is under the Ministry of the Interior. During (military) operations or in war, the Coast Guard Command is subordinated to the Naval Command, while the remaining units continue to perform their normal duties". Translation by the author). §2 of the law states that if necessary, the president can subordinate the command of the coast guard to the navy. To carry out its tasks, the coast guard contains about 6,000 men, 106 ships, helicopters and aeroplanes.

In 2017, the homepage of the General Staff still showed the former structure with the three services or five organizational elements, marked with a star and a footnote regarding the different insinuations of Jandarma and Coast Guard in peace and war. For war, the pictures would apply if the coast guard or parts of it were subordinated to the navy as shown, i.e. did not remain independent, and if the Jandarma were completely or partially subordinated to the army. Such an integration of additional elements would not change the number of army services:

1 Yüksek Askeri Şuranın kuruluş ve görevleri hakkında kanun.

2 https://tr.wikipedia.org. – *Sahil Güvenlik (Türkiye).* https://de.wikipedia.org. – Türkische Küstenwache. Law 2692 „*Sahil Güvenlik Komutanlığı Kanunu*" as of 02.07.2018.

"Türk Silahlı Kuvvetleri; Kara Kuvvetleri, Hava Kuvvetleri ve Deniz Kuvvetleri olmak üzere ana kuvvetten oluşur". ("The Army, Air Force and Navy form the main part of the Turkish Armed Forces." Translation by the author).[1]

The defence organisation (*Savunma Organizasyonu*) is headed by the President; subordinated is the Ministry of Defence with nowadays far reaching powers, below the armed forces, led by the General Staff, then the 3 services with the special arrangements for the Jandarma and the Coast Guard for Peace and War. This new organisation abolishes the former dual-track system, now with the General Staff in the single-track hierarchy, while strengthening the ministry. From the author's point of view further questions remain whether the associated 2 commands are completely subordinated when only parts of their troops transfer to the armed forces and to what extent the MoD could still influence the training of the non - organic personnel during peace. The transition to the new organization was connected with the transfer of the Chief of General Staff Hulusi Akar to the civil office of the Minister of Defence; he was followed in the office of the Chief of General Staff by another 4-star general.

The former homepages of the General Staff used to show the strengths of the individual branches of the armed forces. It is clear that the Jandarma with about 195,000 men (2017) and the coast guard with about 6,000 men could provide considerable reinforcements. The traditional services in 2017 ontained about 390.000 personnel, 350.000 soldiers and 40.000 civilians: Land Forces 250.000, airforce 90.000 and navy 50.000. Speciel Forces *(Özel kuvvetleri)* with about 45.000 are not included therein.

Thus Turkey continues to provide the second largest contingent in NATO after the USA. It remains to be seen to what extent the conversion of the armed forces, which started in 2019, to a higher proportion of volunteers will affect the overall strength. In any case, it is also evident that Turkey will continue to be able to draw on a large pool of personnel while maintaining compulsory military service with short periods of military service, from 1 - 6 (12) months, while maintaining the principle of fairness in conscription. It also continues to include the traditional possibility, to a limited extent, of reducing military service in return for payment.

The next major domestic political event was a successful 20-point MGK memorandum of 28 February 1997 against Islamist Prime Minister Necmettin Erbakan[2]. Erbakan, who had already been arrested after the 1980 coup d'état and was temporarily banned from politics, had been targeted by the military at an early stage. In a speech in Konya on 6 September 1980 he had demanded a new "just order" (*Adil Düzen*)[3] or "just economic order" (*Adil Ekonomik Düzen*), but in reality meant a "İslamic order" (*İslami Nizam*). He was just not well advised to pronounce the term. Erbakan, as founder of the movement "*Milli Görüş*"[4] (National View), demanded in principle the return to a state with a Muslim constitution. This meanwhile international movement was and is essentially Islamist, anti-Semitic and nationalist. Erbakan resigned on 30.06.1997, Mesut Yılmaz became his successor.

For a while Recep Erdoğan was Erbakan's political companion, but then became co-founder of the AKP (*Adalet ve Kalkınma Partisi* - Justice and Progress Party). During Recep Erdoğan's reign in 2012 hundreds of people involved in a pretended coup, including 30

1 https://tr.wikipedia.org. – *Türk Silahlı Kuvvetleri Genelkurmay Başkanı.*
2 https://tr.wikipedia.org. – Necmettin Erbakan.
3 Bekaroğlu „*Siyasetin Sonu*" p. 362.
4 https://tr.wikipdia.org. - *Milli Görüs*. Erbakan's book of the same name "*Milli Görüş*" was published as early as 1973. Today, the Saadet Party represents this view.

officers and retired General Çevik Bir[1], were arrested and charged under the criminal code[2]. Bir had been deputy commander of the army at that time. In 2013, however, he was released subject to conditions. Parallel to these arrests, an even greater wave of criminal proceedings ran from 2007 to 2016, this time not because of an attempted coup, but because of alleged coup attempts or a major coordinated attempt. The indictments of hundreds of people, including more than 50 active and retired generals and admirals, officers and civilians - many of them journalists - have been reported in the media under the names of *Ergenekon*[3], *Balyoz* (forge hammer), *Sarıkız (hashish)* and others. Ergenekon was later used as a generic term for all proceedings. In 2013, life and long prison sentences were pronounced.

This was triggered by a report in the later banned magazine "*Nokta*" in 2007 about a diary of Admiral Özden Örnek[4], from which plans for a coup had been "revealed". In the same year 27 hand grenades were found at a retired NCO in Istanbul, allegedly further proof of an upcoming conspiracy. Örnek was commander of the navy from 2003 to 2005. He denied the charges, while "witnesses" and "evidence" incriminated him. The then Chief of General Staff Hilmi Özkök[5] (2002-2006) allegedly wanted to have stopped the rumour-based attempt in 2003, but his investigations remained without result[6] (*sonuçsuz*). Özkök then avoided normal food for fear of poisoning.

At the end of 2009, Örnek as former Navy Commander and General Aytaç Yalman[7], who had been caught up in the maelstrom, were taken into custody as former Army Commander and General İbrahim Fırtına[8] as former Air Force Commander. In July 2012, Yalman and Fırtına were acquitted: Örnek was sentenced to a reduced 20 years imprisonment for involvement in the other trial named Balyoz in July 2012, but was later acquitted as well.

In January 2012, the former Chief of General Staff İlker Başbuğ[9] (2008-2010) was arrested in the Ergenekon affair and sentenced to life imprisonment in August 2013. Başbuğ has always asserted his innocence, but on the other hand confirmed the existence of certain compromising papers, which were later exposed as forgeries. He was released in March 2014. Strangely enough, during his term in office in 2008, he had still demanded that the military interventions of 1971, 1980 and 1997 be removed from the school books. These three interventions had started from the top of the general staff, in contrast to the one of 1960. Now "democratic - conformist" texts were to be inserted as a substitute. The measure, intended for "eight-year-old pupils", was announced by the media[10] on 04.10.2008. The same restrictions in textbooks should be applied to the Gulf War 1990/1991 and to texts about Abdullah Öcalan.

The commander of the 1st Army in İstanbul, General Çetin Doğan[11], had been accused in 2010 after a publication of the daily newspaper "*Taraf*" of having planned a coup d'état with many participants in a planning exercise called Balyoz in March 2003. After a trial starting in December 2010 with many more accused, Doğan was sentenced to 20 years in prison in 2012.

---

1 https://en.wikipedia.org. – Çevik Bir.

2 Law no. 5237: *Türk Ceza Kanunu* § 312.

3 Actually the term for a mystical country or valley of origin of the Turks from the grey prehistoric times, later the collective term for different procedures. https://de.wikipedia.org. - *Ergenekon* process. https://tr.wikipedia.org. - Ergenekon (örgüt). https://tr.wikipedia.org. - Ergenekon davaları. https://de.wikipedia.org. - *Ergenekon* (chronology).

4 https://de.wikipedia.org. – Özden Örnek. https:tr.wikipedia.org. – Özden Örnek.

5 https://de.wikipedia.org. – Hilmi Özkök. https://tr.wikipedia.org. – Hilmi Özkök.

6 http://www.todayszaman.com. from 04.11.2014.

7 https://tr.wikipeda.org. – Aytaç Yalman.

8 https://tr.wikipedia.org. – İbrahim Fırtına.

9 https://tr.wikipedia.org. – İlker Başbuğ.

10 www.turkishdailynews.com.tr.

11 https://en.wikipedia.org. – Çetin Doğan. https://tr.wikipedia.org. - Çetin Doğan.

After forgery of documents had been uncovered here too, he was released in June 2014 following a ruling by the Constitutional Court (AYM - *Ana Yasa Mahkemesi*) due to considerable previous procedural errors. In the meantime, an individual citizen was granted the right to appeal to the Constitutional Court after going through all instances, and possibly later to the European Court of Human Rights (ECtHR).

Another procedure also came to nothing. In this case the commander of the 3rd Army, General Saldıray, should have conducted a compromising seminar in Erzincan.

A third major case dealt with publications on the Internet in 2009, where 42 pages of propaganda against the AKP were used, probably to overthrow the government. At the same time action plans against the PKK and Christian minorities were disseminated. Başbuğ confirmed the existence of the web pages, described the contents as partly false and closed most of the pages. In December 2011 charges were brought against the parties involved, in April 2012 the trial was merged with the trial of Balyoz.

Because of many inconsistencies, falsifications, dubious witnesses and evidence, the Istanbul Court of Appeal overturned the verdicts against 275 defendants[1] on April 21, 2016. The proceedings were discontinued, 73 officers were reinstated in the army[2] according to statements by the Minister of Defence İsmet Yılmaz. Erdoğan said that he had been deceived, thereby rehabilitating the army in turn[3].

A scandal was the joint resignation on 29.07.2011 of the Chief of General Staff Işık Koşaner and the commanders of the three services, with the exception of the commander of the Jandarma, Necdet Özel[4]. On the same day he became commander of the army and on 04.08.2011 Chief of General Staff. According to old tradition, in his new position he should have commanded the land forces before. Koşaner explained in connection with the ongoing processes:

"Tutuklamaların evrensel hukuk kaidelerine, hakka, adalete ve vicdani değerlere uygun olarak yapıldığını kabul etmek birçok hukukçunun da ifade ettiği gibi mümkün değildir." According to the norms of international law, in accordance with the law, justice and the values of conscience, even according to the explanations of many lawyers, the approval of the arrests is not possible". Translation by the author). This declaration and the measure of resignation honours those concerned.

After about ten years, five indictments, three waves of arrests, the replacement of judges and prosecutors, acquittals brought the trials to an end in 2016. From the author's personal and military point of view, a commentary on these events seems necessary, although much remains in the dark. However, the events have certainly affected the army deeply, not only the defendants. Unfortunately, senior officers have accused each other[5] in court, thereby driving a further wedge into the army's solidarity. Those who had to serve prison sentences have - if they were innocent - suffered mentally, as have their families. Reductions in pay and failure to promote were also connected with this. From the "distant viewpoint" of the author - who has no original knowledge of his own and is not familiar with all the publications on this highly complex and extensive subject - there is little evidence to support the assumption that coup plans were planned by the army leadership or only parts of the army. Actions on the Internet from the general staff only confirm the general mood, but cannot be interpreted as real

1 http://www.hurryetdailynews.com. from April 21, 2016.
2 http://www.hurriyetdailynews.com. from 5-15-2015.
3 Cf. Today's Zaman, Turkish Daily News, 20.03.2015.
4 https://tr.wikipedia.org. - Işık Koşaner. https://de.wikipedia.org. - Necdet Özel. https://tr.wikipedia.org. - *Türk Silahlı Kuvvetleri 29 Temmuz 2011 Krizi.*
5 http://www.hurriyetdailynews.com. Dtd. 15.12.2014 „Former comrades in Turkish army accuse each other of delivering false statements“.

coup preparation, rather as a warning. When the AKP presented the prime minister to the military at the end of 2002, it became clear to the military that there was a danger of Re-Islamization. It intensified with the by-election of Recep Erdoğan in 2003 and his assumption of the office of prime minister. Another coup therefore would have been in the historical continuity of the army leadership.

However, all other indications and evidence available since 2003 speak against this; they tend to indicate a poor staging, which did not, however, fail to have its effect. The mastermind or masterminds of the coup still remain hidden. Erdoğan, perhaps initially still in cooperation with Fethulla Gülen[1], wanted to return the role of the army to the normal level in a democracy, but then turned in a power struggle from 2012 at the latest after dissent in foreign policy (relations with Israel, secret negotiations with the PKK) and a corruption scandal in 2013 against Gülen that was not pursued further. Looking back from 2020, it must now be assumed that Gülen was at least partly responsible for the Ergenekon affair.

The disempowerment of the army took place in many smaller and some larger steps, via amendments to the constitution and simple laws or via mere orders, as already mentioned in part:

- 2003 the exchange of the military secretary in the National Security Council, the further personnel "civilization" of the MGK, no more membership from the Commander of the Jandarma, the lifting of important secret MGK papers in 2010, which remained hidden from the public and also from the author before[2],

- 2003 stronger control of the defence budget and thus of the expenditure of the General Staff, stronger involvement of the Court of Auditors[3], reinforced by President Abdullah Gül in a "Report on Defence[4]" in 2014

- 2004 the removal of military representatives from the Supreme Radio Council (*RTÜK - Radyo ve Televizyon Üst Kurulu*) and the University Council (*YÖK - Yüksek Öğretim Kurulu),*

- 2004 the trial of former Admiral İlhami Erdil, now before a civil court[5],

- In 2008, the establishment of an Under-Secretariat for Internal Security under the Minister of the Interior,

- 2009 Restrictions in military jurisdiction,

- In 2010, unusual intervention in promotion matters below the level of the General Staff through the intervention of the Minister of Defence, and later also greater political influence on the occupation of top military posts,

- 2010 "walking the front" by the presidential wives Mrs. Hayrünnisa Gül with headscarf together with the German Mrs. Bettina Wulff, the two presidents in advance,

- In 2011 a shift of tasks to the police, e.g. the previous 91-year-old symbolic guarding of the parliament building in Ankara,

- 2011 the transfer of intelligence competencies from the army to the secret service MIT under the supervision of the prime minister, from 2017 on the president,

- 2012 the intervention of the Minister of Culture and Tourism Ertuğrul Günay in the playing of the funeral march by a military band for the deceased Sergeant Osman Çelik in Antalya and request to speak the "*Tekbir*", the Islamic prayer formula "*Allahu ekber*"[6],

1 https://de.wikipedia.org. – Fethulla Gülen.
2 Law No. 2945 of the MGK. https://tr.wikipedia.org. *Milli Güvenlik Kurulu (Türkiye).*
3 http://www.hurriyetdailynews.com from 20.11.2012.
4 http://www.hurriyet daily news.com from 23.08.2014.
5 https://tr.wikpipedia.org. - İlhami Erdil.
6 http://www.hurriyetdailynews.com. of 08/25/2012.

- 2013 Replacement of the so-called Emasya Protocol from 1997 (agreed between the Minister of the Interior and the General Staff) by a new agreement, according to which the General Staff now requires the approval of civil authorities[1] before domestic deployment,

- In 2013, the assignment of the lead role for military industrial procurement to the office of Secretary of State to the Minister of Defence[2] (SSM - *Savunma Sanayii Müsteşarlığı*),

- 2004 Erdoğan's approval of the Annan Plan for Cyprus,

- 2014 the non-involvement of the military in negotiations with the Kurds.

In an intact democracy e.g. the last three points are normal processes within the framework of the primacy of politics. Incidentally, the General Staff even held a public debate on who was allowed to make official political statements at all.

From the author's point of view, the accusations concerning the seminars with the 1st and 3rd armies in particular were completely implausible. Coup plans are not discussed - even with reversed omens[3] - in planning exercises of large groups with younger officers. This should be done in small groups or private discussions without leaving any documents behind. A good example of the development of a military operation plan, although not a coup plan, is a major planning exercise in preparation for the German Wehrmacht's May 1940 campaign to the west. Although a copy of the plan had secretly survived, the operation plan only existed in the minds of the most important commanders days later. Another example is the almost successful putsch of Colonel Claus Schenk Graf von Stauffenberg on July 20, 1944 against Adolf Hitler, which was almost perfectly prepared in an extremely difficult environment.

A further and initially penultimate action was the futile attempt by the Chief of General Staff Yaşar Büyükanıt (2006-2008) to prevent the election of Abdullah Gül[4] as President of the Republic on 27.04.2007 with a longer - self-written - statement on his homepage. Right in the first sentence the "main concern" is formulated, the character of a possibly binding "memorandum" later denied by General Yaşar Büyükanit:

"*Türkiye Cumhuriyeti devletinin başta laiklik olarak olmak üzere, temel değerlerini aşındırmak için bitmez tükenmez bir çaba içinde olan bir kısım çevrelerin bu gayretlerini son dönemde artıdikları müşahede edilmektedir.*"

("It has been observed that some circles that are making never-ending efforts to destroy the fundamental values of the Turkish Republic, especially laicism, have recently increased their efforts. Translation by the author)[5].

After an invalid first parliamentary vote in April and a ruling by the Constitutional Court, the Chief of General Staff and the CHP at least managed to force new presidential elections, even if the latter was then won in Gül's third round on 28 July 2007. Even before this last round of elections, Büyükanıt had again warned that the armed forces were determined to defend democracy and the separation of state and religion. Already on 04.05.2007 there had been a four-eye discussion between Büyükanıt and the Prime Minister Erdoğan in the Dolmabahce Palace in İstanbul[6], about which almost nothing got out, but which was evaluated

1 http://www.todayszaman.com. of 29/06/2013.

2 http://www.huriyetdailynews.com. of 13.08.2013.

3 For example, there are no plans for a surprise attack on a TV broadcasting station in the context of a coup, but rather the (alleged) liberation of this institution from putschists. Many planning elements in both scenarios are very similar, up to a pre-formulated announcement via broadcasting.

4 https://de.wikipedia.org. - Abdullah Gül.

5 The text recorded from the screen is difficult to read. https://upload.wikimedia.org. – E-Memorandum.jpg. A more detailed text at: http://news.bbc.co.uk/l/world/europe/6602775.stm. Excerpts of Turkish armv statement.

6 http://www.hurriyetdailynews.com - Turkish court summons former top commander to testify over 2007 E-Memorandum. http://www.todayszaman.com on 15.12.2015.

as a standstill agreement. Only in 2012, parallel to the above mentioned charges, a lawsuit was filed against the pensioner Büyükanıt, which, however, had no consequences.

The wide time span between 1950 and the near past contains a wealth of serious military-political events with considerable effects on the army. Before making an overall assessment of this time span, it is therefore necessary to take a look at the Armed Forces' operations abroad, in the national or international context, which again bring military operations and the respective state of the Armed Forces more to the fore.

Military operations abroad and the fight against the PKK

Of the numerous Turkish assignments abroad only the most important ones will be described from the author's perspective. For example, an overview of 33 operations of various types and sizes is contained in the German-language file on the Turkish armed forces.[1]

The first major foreign military operation for Turkey after World War II was the Korean War [2] 1950-1953, when North Korea, supported by China and the Soviet Union, attacked North Korea in 1950. Turkey defended South Korea under the leadership of the USA and with the support of numerous other nations, sanctioned by UN Security Council Resolution No. 85.

A Turkish brigade arrived in Pusan in October 1950 with 5,090 men under the command of Brigadier General Tahsin Yazıcı. Soon it was involved in a loss-making delaying operation at Kundri as a reserve of the IX US Corps, which was under the command of the 8th US Army. After difficulties in the transmission of orders by the IXth US Corps, the Turkish Brigade was late and almost surrounded by the enemy. In this battle, including the prisoners, it suffered more than 1,000 men lost and more than 2,000 wounded, but with the time gained by fighting, it enabled the other allied troops (2nd US Div., IX. US Corps, 8th US Army) to escape a larger embrace and to deploy in an orderly manner.

General Yazıcı was honored by US General Walton Walker, Commander of the 8th US Army, with a medal and the words:"*The heroic soldiers of a heroic nation, you have saved the 8th Army and the IX Army Corps from encirclement and the 2nd Division from destruction. I came here today to thank you on behalf of the United Nations Army.*"

UN Commander-in-Chief Douglas MacArthur said: "*The Turks are the hero of the Heroes. There is no impossibility for the Turkish Brigade.*"

The brigade was replaced three times during the war, which resulted to an establihment of more than 20.000 personnel, until the Turkish troops were able to return home in July 1953. As is well known, only a ceasefire has been maintained to date; North and South Korea are separated basically along the 38th latitude as a demarcation line. The tensions between the two states continue. Other major tensions have emerged in recent years, especially between the USA and North Korea, as this state appears to be developing long-range missiles with nuclear warheads.

The next major trouble spot developed in Cyprus.[3] This island had once belonged to the Ottoman Empire from 1571-1878, went to Great Britain in 1914 and became independent in 1960 (with the exception of two British military bases), contractually regulated in two agreements signed by the three signatory powers Greece, Great Britain and Turkey. After a coup d'état by Cypriot-Greek officers on 15.07.1974 under the leadership of General Dimitrios Joannidis - with the support of Greece against the Cypriot President Michael Christodoulos

1 https://de.wikipedia.org. – Türkische Streitkräfte.

2 https://de.wikipedia.org. – Koreakrieg. ttps://tr.wikipedia.org. – Kore Savaşı. https://tr.wikipedia.org. – Türk Tugayı. http:/www.korean-war.com/turkey.html. – The Turkish Brigade.

3 https://de.wikipedia.org. – Zypernkonflikt. https://tr.wikipedia.org. – *Kıbrıs Harekâtı*. https://en.wikipedia.org. – Cyprus.

Makarios III, who was able to flee - with the aim of unification with Greece (Enosis), Turkey intervened militarily on 20.07.1974 to protect the Turkish-born population, who mainly lived in the north. On 16.08.1974 a ceasefire was agreed under the leadership of the UNO, which is still valid today, and a buffer zone around the ceasefire line (Green Line, Attila Line) was established, which also shares the capital Nicosia/Lefkosa.

THE PARTITION OF KOREA

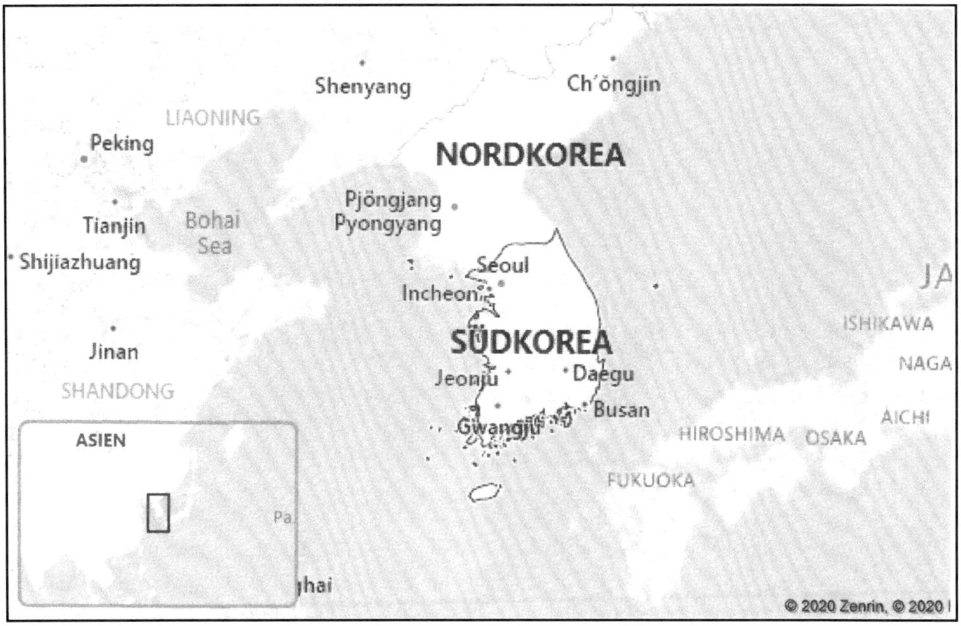

Map 20

On November 15, 1983, the northern part declared itself independent as the Turkish Republic of Northern Cyprus[1] (*Kuzey Kıbrıs Türk Cumhuriyeti*), which has so far only been recognized by Turkey - contrary to UN Resolution 541. After the failure of the Annan Plan[2] in 2004 due to rejection by the Greek-born population, Cyprus as a whole became a member of the EU on 01.05.2004.

As a sign of Turkey's close ties with Northern Cyprus, shown in the same red colour as Turkey itself, the Turkish General Staff showed a map on its homepage, which however disappeared again with the change of the Chief of General Staff on 28.08.2008. Similar pictures could be seen on mountain slopes in Northern Cyprus with the famous Atatürk lettering: "*Ne mutlu Türküm diyene*" ("How happy that I am allowed to call myself a Turk.") Translation by the author). Turkey's nationalist aspirations are reinforced by the similarity of the North Cypriot flag to that of Turkey and by the common national anthem, i.e. the Independence March (*İstiklâl Marşı*). Turkey emphasizes the independence of Northern Cyprus, but intensifies the ties through resettlement of mainland Turks, economic support

1 https://de.wikipedia.org. – Türkische Republik Nordzypern. https://tr.wikipedia.org. – *Kuzey Kıbrıs Türk Cumhuriyeti*.

2 Kofi Annan, UN General Secretary 1997 - 2006.

(water and electricity) and permanent stationing of troops. New disputes with Greece over oil and gas exploration near the island since 2019 create additional international tensions.

TURKEY AND NORTHERN CYPRUS

Map 21 (Homepage Turkish General Staff in August 2008)

After thoroughly planned invasion of Turkish troops on 20.07.1974 of initially approx. 6,000 men with participation of all services, supported by Turkish-Cypriot fighters (*Serdalı*)[1] and after fighting against the initially superior Greek-Cypriot National Guard of approx. 10,000 men, supported by Greek Junta troops,[2] a temporary ceasefire on 22.07.1974 and negotiations in Geneva took place. During the fragile ceasefire, Turkey provided further reinforcements during the still ongoing fighting and reached a troops' strength of about 30,000 men, now a military superiority. In the course of the following weeks until 16.08.1974 Northern Cyprus extended its area of influence with the help of Turkey up to the Attila line mentioned above.

1 Northern Cyprus had been maintaining its own troops since 1958 against the Greek organization EOKA of 1955. https://tr.wikipedia.org. - *Türk Muhavemet Teşkikatı*. https://tr.wikipedia.org. - EOKA. See Birand „30 Heisse Tage".

2 Official title *"Kıbrıs Barış Harekâtı"* - "Cyprus Peace Operation" https://de.wikipedia.org. - Ailla. https://tr.wikipedia.org. - *Kıbrıs Harekatı*. https://de. wikipedia.org wikipedia.org. – Türkische Besatzungstruppe in Zypern. https://tr.wikipedia.org. – *Kıbrıs Türk Barış Kuvvetleri*. https://de.wikipedia.org. – Streitkräfte der Türkischen Republik Nordzypern. https://tr.wikipedia.org. – *KKTC Güvenlik Kuvvetleri Komutanlığı*.

Altogether there were casualties of about 600 men on the "Turkish" and 2,000 on the "Greek" side, in addition also many civilians. The UN Security Council Resolution 550, which in 1984 qualified the whereabouts of Turkish troops as "occupation", later caused great and long disgruntlement on the Turkish side. Looking back at the military-political situation, parallels can be drawn with the Greek invasion of the Ottoman Empire in 1919 in that Greece, motivated by the attitude of the Western powers, underestimated Turkey's reaction, whose strong resistance was not considered likely. In addition, there was again an internal political and military disruption in Greece, which led to the overthrow of the Junta regime during the war on July 23, 1974. Also after this war there were subsequent relocations of population groups, although not to the same extent as in 1923.

A multi-year arms embargo imposed by the USA in February 1975 led on the Turkish side to the closure of US facilities, blocking access to Turkish infrastructure and a prolonged period of resentment.[1] This only came to an end with a bilateral treaty in March 1980 and extensive US military aid.

In 2017, the USA apparently imposed a "covert embargo" on high-tech weapons again because of differences of opinion regarding military action in Syria. Thus, after 22 years, a similar situation seems to be repeating itself and the danger remains that Turkey will drift away as a NATO partner and make itself dependent on Russia or China not only economically but also in terms of armament. In the background there is also a smouldering disagreement regarding the action against the Gülen movement after the attempted coup on 15.07.2016. [2]

After 1974 and failed negotiations in 2017, Turkish troops will remain stationed on the island with a corps staff in the port city of Girne/Kyrenia[3] and about 36,000 men in addition to about 5,000 men from the army of Northern Cyprus who are under the command of the Turkish corps.[4] In addition, there is the coast guard of Northern Cyprus. Furthermore, there are about 1,000 UN blue helmet soldiers stationed to monitor the ceasefire agreement, the UNFICYP (United Nations Pecekeeping Force in Cyprus) and British troops on their military bases.

The next military challenges were the so-called three Iraq/Gulf wars in the period 1980-2003 in the crisis region of Iraq and Iran, later extended to Kuwait, Saudi Arabia and Israel. While Turkey remained neutral in the first Iraq war 1980-1988,[5] in the second Iraq war in 1991 it supported militarily the coalition troops: Over 30 nations, a coalition of the willing, supported by UN mandates under the leadership of the USA against Iraq in the operation "Desert Storm".[6] Turkey allowed the US forces to use Turkish bases and even marched up itself to the Iraqi border with 180,000 troops with the aim to bind Iraqi troops.

First of all, the Turkish Chief of General Staff Necip Torumtay[7] (1987-1990) resigned on 03.12.1990, because he did not want to open a second front against Iraq, i.e. to invade, contrary to US President George Bush (the elder) and President Turgut Özal, but supported by the Prime Minister Yıldırım, Foreign Minister Ali Bozer and Defence Minister Safa Giray.

1 Cf. Der Spiegel 13/1977. Cf. Robin's "Suits and Uniforms".

2 http://www.eurasianews.de - Covert embargo of the USA against Turkey: Is Russia now becoming a strategic military partner?

3 https://de.wikipedia.org. - Kyrenia.

4 Such a construction does not necessarily have to be seen as a partial renunciation of sovereignty, but can be appropriate from a military point of view. There are similar examples among various NATO states, even sometimes understood as building blocks of a future European Army.

5 https://de.wikipedia.org. -. First Gulf War. https://tr.wikipedia.org. – *İran- Iraq Savaşı.*

6 http://www.u-s-history.com. - Desert Storm. https://de.wikipedia.org. - Gulf War II. https://tr.wikipedia.org. - *Kuveyt'in İşgalı.*

7 https://tr.wikipedia.org. – Necip Torumtay.

The following account gives a slightly different justification, whereby this war is referred to here as the first Gulf War:

NO-FLY ZONES (NFZ) IN IRAQ

Map 22 *(https://commons.wikimedia.org. – Iraq No Fly Zones.png.*

"Görevden ayrılmasına sebep olarak I. Körfez Savaşı'ında hükümetin tutumuna tepki olduğu öne sürüldü. Ordunun teçhizatının yetersiz olduğu içi, zamanın cumhhurbaşkanı Turgut Özal tarafından Irak'a karşı ABD ile beraber hareket edilmesine uymak istemediği ileri sürüldü." ("He cited as the reason for his leaving the service that he could not approve of the government's position on the First Gulf War. He also said that the army's equipment was inadequate and that he did not consider it appropriate for Acting President Turgut Özal to conduct the operation against Iraq together with the US. Translation by the author). The successor in the office of the Chief of General Staff, Doğan an(1990-1994) did not approve of an attack, but agreed to US support.

For the USA, the war will be the biggest mission after the Vietnam War. With their superior strength, growing to 340,000 men, and the coalition with a total of about 660,000 men, Iraki President Sadam Hussein is driven back after his attack on Kuwait on August 2, 1990 and is devastatingly defeated by his enemy's using the most modern weapons and means such as GPS (Global Positioning System). Already on 02.03.1991 a ceasefire is reached under UN-Resolution 686. With losses on the coalition side of less than 1.500 the number of victims on the Iraqi side is at least 25.000. Alledgedly about 1,5 million Kurds from Iraq take refuge in Turkey. In order to protect the remaining Shiites and Kurds against Sadam Hussein's Arab-Sunni regime, no-fly zones are being established, with controversial reference to UN Resolution 688.

Twelve years later, the conflict was to flare up again in 2003 as the third Gulf or Iraq War.[1] This war lasted only from 20.03.2003 to 01.05.2003, ended with a defeat of Iraq and the fall of Hussein. The latter was sentenced to death by an Iraqi court in 2006. The invasion of the coalition troops from the south was preceded by a controversy whether the UN Resolution 1441 allowed an attack of the USA and allied states, since in Iraq still weapons of mass destruction were suspected - which was not confirmed afterwards.

In Turkey there was again disagreement on the approach to be taken. Even before the parliamentary elections of 03.11.2002, Prime Minister Bülent Ecevit had shown restraint, President Ahmet Necdet Sezer - lawyer and former president of the Constitutional Court - and the new Prime Minister Abdullah Gül had equally strong reservations about opening an "active" second front with the USA, while the Chief of General Staff Hilmi Özkök simply saw parliament as having a duty to make a decision. This rejected on 01.03.2003 an active commitment with reference to the UN Charta. It was about the justification of a preventive war, likewise a stationing of foreign troops on Turkish soil. The UN Security Council did not take a decision to justify intervention.

With assumption of office of Erdoğan as Prime Minister starting from 14.03.2003 this promised the USA concessions. After further debates in parliament, the latter agreed even before the war began that the USA could use military bases in Turkey and modernize them with an initial stay of only three months. On March 20, 2003, i.e. the beginning of the attack, Parliament now permitted the use of airspace for six months and authorized the government to send troops to northern Iraq.[2] However, according to official statements, only troop reinforcements were instead transferred to the province of Hakkari in south-eastern Turkey. NATO had already decided on 19 February 2003 to transfer AWACS aircraft, Patriot defence missiles and NBC detection equipment to Turkey.[3]

After the end of the war on 01.05.2003 US troops remained stationed in Iraq until 2011. Therefore the Turkish parliament allowed the USA to use the air force base İncirlik and the ports of Mersin and İskenderun for another year on 23.06.2003. On 07.10.2003, it again approved the deployment of Turkish troops in Iraq in accordance with the Turkish government's instructions, but this was no longer possible due to objections from the Iraqi government and the US head of the interim administration in Iraq Paul Bremer (2003-2004). This plan was abandoned on 23.10.2003. Reliable overall figures on military and civilian losses in the Iraq wars are not available; estimates vary widely. Once again, the civilian population seems to have suffered particularly, also in the context of many post-war unrest events.

---

1 https://tr.wikipedia.org. – *Irak Savaşı*. https://de.wikipedia.org. – Irakkrieg. http://www.blz.bayern.de – Die Drei Golfkriege.

2 http://www.linksnet.de. – Artikel 18992 – Die Türkei und der Irakkrieg.

3 http://www.daily mail.co.uk. – Patriot missiles deployed by NATO on Turkey's border with Syria.

Since then, both the globally operating terrorist organization Al Qaeda[1] and especially the so-called Islamic State (IS)[2] - which initially operated under various names regionally in Iraq and Syria - have terrorized Iraq for a long time. In 2014, the so-called IS proclaimed a caliphate and thus pronounced a supra-regional claim as a Muslim-Sunni leading power. From a military point of view, however, the IS is in retreat in the Iraqi-Syrian region, while it is shifting geographically and opening up new threat fronts. This also affects Turkey in its own country, which is fighting against a wide variety of terrorist organizations both domestically and abroad.

Because of Turkey's operations in northern Iraq against the PKK, Turkey's obvious interests in the war described above and the continuing historical dispute over the oil-rich former Ottoman province of Mosul - which was actually settled as early as 1926 - bilateral relations with Iraq remain tense. Further areas of tension are the oil pipeline from the autonomous region of Kurdistan in northern Iraq, which has been in operation since 2013 due to the non-participation of the Iraqi government, the dispute over the water of the Tigris, Turkish protection interests of "their Türkmen" and the Shiite majority of about 60% of the population in Iraq. The independence efforts of the autonomous region of Northern Iraq, rekindled by a clear referendum on 25.09.2017, are also a thorn in the side of the Turks,. Mutual economic interests with Turkey and Iran have initally been able to prevent the outbreak of a further military conflict and leave it at economic sanctions, such as the ban on the use of Erbil airport. At present, however, tensions have increased again due to Iran's support for Syria. This will be discussed later.

Another major trouble spot was the Balkans, where Turkey is also involved militarily. After the disintegration of the multi-ethnic state of Yugoslavia from 1990 onwards, the Yugoslav wars or the so-called Bosnian War from 1992-1996, began including a high number of victims and expulsions. In July 1995, the Srebenica massacre[3] under Serbian responsibility took place. Almost at the same time as the Bosnian war, UN forces were stationed in Croatia and Bosnia-Herzegovina under the name "United Nations Protection Force" (UNPROFOR) to monitor a ceasefire. These forces consisted of approximately 32,000 military observers including police and civilian observers. Turkey provided about 1,464 men[4] and committed itself by supplying weapons and material:

"*Hollanda raporlarına göre, Türkiye Bosna'da bulunan İslamcı Birliklere silah verilmesine yardım etti.*" (According to reports from the Netherlands, Turkey has provided arms supplies through the Organisation for Islamic Cooperation (OIC), (*İslam Konferansı Örgütü*).[5] This influential organisation with over 55 member states was founded in 1969 and was led e.g. by the Turkish Islamic scholar Ekmeleddin İhsanoğlu[6] in the period 2005-2013.

A "No Fly Zone" (NFZ) was established during the Bosnian war and operated by NATO as part of Operation "Deny Flight" from April 1993 to December 1995 to protect the surveillance forces, but also the population. To this end, additional close-air support and air

1 https://de.wikipedia.org. – Al Qaida.

2 https://de.wikipedia.org. – Islamischer Staat (Organisation).

3 https://de.wikipedia.org. – Massaker von Srebenica.

4 http://www.un.org/en/peacekeeping /missions - UNPROFOR. Cf. magazine Fahrzeugprofile No. 10, 1977 p. 29 "IFOR-The Sword of NATO in Bosnia".

5 https://de.wikipedia.org.–Bosnienkrieg. https://tr.wikipedia.org. – *Bosna Savaşı*. https://de.wikipedia.org. - United Nations Protection Force. http://web.archive.org. – 148268 – *Hollanda Raporu Türkiye Bosna'ya Silah sağladın.*

6 https://de.wikipedia.org. - Organization for Islamic Cooperation.

interdiction operations[1] were carried out from August 1993. Turkey also participated in the operation with about 4,500 men, using F16 fighter aircraft from a base in Italy to monitor the NFZ.

BOSNIA-HERZEGOVINA

Map 23

With the Dayton Agreement[2] of 14.12.1995, the Bosnian war was transferred under UN supervision to the NATO-led Operation "Implementation Force" (IFOR).[3] The IFOR troops with approx. 57,000 men in Bosnia-Herzegovina/Bosna-Hersek included all services of the armed forces under the name "Joint Endeavour", including Russian troops deployed in the US sector. In the south-western British sector the Multinational Division South West - MND SW was stationed with a 1,500 strong Turkish brigade with its HQ in Zenica,[4] in the map below in the centre. This Bosniak-Muslim region had of course also been part of the Ottoman Empire from 1463 until Bosnia-Herzegovina was annexed by Austria-Hungary in 1878. There also exist two Turkish city partnerships with the town.

On 20 December 1996 IFOR became part of the Stabilization Force (SFOR)[5] (*İstikrar Gücü*). The NATO Force SFOR operated in Bosnia-Herzegovina until December 2004 with the mandate to enforce the Dayton Peace Agreement and to support the civil reconstruction of the country within the framework of "Civil Military Cooperation" (CIMIC). The country was again divided into sectors, with the number of troops being reduced compared to IFOR. key kept its HQ in Zenica, this time in the US sector of the Multinational Task Force-North (MNTF-N). While in the beginning a Turkish company still performed guarding duties of the

1 https://de.wikipedia.org. – Operation Deny Flight. https://tr.wikipedia.org.–Uçus Yasağı Harekâtı. https://web.archive.org. – www.afsouth.natoint/archives/operations/Deny Flight.
2 https://de.wikipedia.org. – Dayton (Ohio).
3 https://de.wikipedia.org. – Implementation Force. https://tr.wikipedia.org. – IFOR.
4 https://tr.wikipedia.org. - Zenica. Cf. Europa Militaria No. 22, 1996 "IFOR: Allied Forces in Bosnia" p. 44.
5 https://de.wikipedia.org. – SFOR. https://tr.wikipedia.org. – SFOR.

SFOR HQ in Sarajevo, the main forces in strength of a battalion stayed in Zenica and performed various tasks there.[1]They included collecting and destroying weapons, patrolling, but also informing the population about the danger of mines. Additional support resulted from the construction of a bridge. Practicing cooperation with the other nations to achieve interoperability, i.e. the ability to operate together, is always part of joint military training, e.g. in the medical field.

At the end of 2004, the EU task was taken over from NATO under the name "European Force" (EUFOR) "Althea".[2] The basis was formed by several resolutions of the UN Security Council within the framework of the UN Charter Chapter VII. The command structure for Althea is progressive in that it represents close cooperation between NATO and the EU. Militarily; the operation is led by the EU Military Committee (EU-MC) in Brussels. The next lower level of command, that of the "Operational Commander" or Operational HQ (OHQ) , is led by the Deputy NATO Supreme Commander (Deputy SACEUR, D-SACEUR) in Mons/Belgium,[3] who in turn can draw on the working capacity of SHAPE (Supreme Headquarters Allied Powers in Europe) staff. The tactical level of the "Force Commander" in Sarajevo is provided by a leading nation, since 2008 performed by Austria. With the lowering of the threat and the reduction of the tasks the number of troops has been reduced to currently about 600 men, from which Turkey provides 150 personnel. There are planning measures in place for rapid reinforcements in case of need. [4] The nature of the tasks, i.e. implementation of the Dayton Agreement, training assistance for the armed forces of Bosnia-Herzegovina, cooperation with the police, etc., are essentially unchanged.

Turkey, although not a member of the EU, had been an associate member of the now dissolved WEU (Western European Union) since 1992. In 2014, Turkey made official contact with the "EU Military Committee" (EU-MC) in Brussels.[5] In general, it can already be stated here that Turkey participates in EU military operations on a case-by-case basis, such as the establishment of rapid EU intervention forces, the "EU Battle Groups". Inter alia, under the leading nation Italy and with the participation of Romania, a trinational battle group with at least 1,500 men had been formed, which was already available with OHQ in Rome[6] in the second half of 2010. This group has been in charge during the first half of the year 2020.

.[7] As an integral part of NATO Force planning, Turkey is of course also participating in the NATO Response Force (NRF), a high readiness intervention force, which was created in 2012. It is considerably larger than an EU battlegroup, as it also includes air and naval forces besides land forces. Therefore, operational command and control lies with the two NATO HQs in Brunssum and Naples. The duration of operational readiness period is 1 year. In 2021 Turkey will take over the leadership of the NRF Another trouble spot in the Balkans is the Republic of Kosovo/Kosova, which declared independence in February 2008. Kosovo is now

1 http://www.nato.int/sfor/nations/turkey.htm.

2 https://de.wikipedia.org. – Operation Althea. https://en.wikipedia.org. – EUFOR Althea. https://tr.wikipedia.org. – EUFOR Althea. http://www.euforbih.org.eufor. – European Union Force in Bosnia and Herzegovina.

3 Normally a British 4-star general.

4 https//:en.wikipedia.org/wiki/operation Althea.

5 http://www.todayszaman.com. – news detail 3367 – „Turkish Military establishes contact with EU military body" on 15.01.2014.

6 https://de.wikipedia.org. – Westeuropäische Union. https://tr.wikipedia.org. – *Avrupa Birliği Savaş Grupları.* https://en.wikipedia.org. – Military of the European Union. https://en.wikipedia.org. – EU Battlegroup.

7 https://jfcbs.nato.int.

THE REPUBLIC OF KOSOVO

Map 24

recognised by most states and now even had to be accepted as a fact by the former war opponent Serbia. The Serbian President Aleksandar Vucic expressed himself in this sense.[1] In the Kosovo war[2] 28.02.1998 -10.06.1999, which had preceded the above declaration, NATO took part from 24.03.1999 with an air war under the designation "Allied Force" against Serbia. On 10.06.1999 the war ended with the withdrawal of the Serbs from Kosovo and the adoption of UN Resolution 1244. On this legal basis NATO then stationed the "Kosovo Force" (KFOR) with HQ in Pristina, which since then has supported the protection of Kosovo and the establishment of stable political conditions, including the return of refugees, under the name "Joint Guardian". This has been done in cooperation with other organisations and forces and the Kosovo Security Forces (*Kosova Güvenlik Gücüler).* From an original strength of about 50,000 men from 39 nations,[3] KFOR has now reached a scope of about 6,000 after the situation has calmed down.

The German NATO commander General Klaus Reinhardt visited the Turkish battalion on 31.10.1999 in the Dragash area, which was under the command of the MNB(S) (Multi National Brigade South) led by Germany, and judged:

"The Turkish soldiers make a first-class impression. They are very disciplined and excellently equipped with modern facilities".[4]

1 See FAZ of 04.08.2017 "Criticism of the coffee house table heroes".

2 https://de.wikipedia.org. - Kosovo war. https://de.wikipedia.org. - Kosovo. https://de.wikipedia.org. - History of Kosovo. https://de.wikipedia.org. - Kosovo war. https://tr.wikipedia.org. - *Kosova Savaşı.*

3 Reinhardt „KFOR Streitkräfte für den Frieden“ S. p 549.

4 *ibid. p. 163.*

For historical and religious reasons, Turkey feels connected to Kosovo/Kosova,[1] especially since the region belonged to the Ottoman Empire since the battle of the Blackbird Field/*Kosovo Meydan Muharebesi* in 1389, belonged to it from 1455 and had to be ceded to the Austro-Hungarian Empire in 1878.

Turkey continues to participate in a restructured KFOR contingent with battalion strength in a "Battle Group", the "Multi National Battlegroup East" (MNBG-E). The Turkish Colonel Mustafa İhsan Tavazar e.g. headed the "Joint Regional Detachment South" (JRD-S) from Prizren since 2016 including all Turkish troops in Kosovo. The detachment currently includes Austrians, Poles, Swiss and US-Americans. The main task is not combat, but rather the monitoring of the situation by "Liaison and Monitoring Teams" (LMT).[2] In the Balkans, following the death of Broz Tito and the disintegration of Yugoslavia, other wars have taken place, mainly civil wars, which are not dealt with here. Among other things, this file provides an overview.[3]

Attention should now be drawn to the ongoing international trouble spot Afghanistan, where Turkey has been engaged for many years. This is also a matter of supporting Muslim brothers in faith, since the mass of the Afghan population also consists of Hanafi Sunnis. As a direct consequence of the attack on the World Trade Center on September 11, 2001, the United States forces invaded Afghanistan where the mastermind of Al Qaeda, Saudi Osama Bin Laden, was cooperating with the radical Islamist Taliban.[4] Bin Laden had already opened an office in Peshawar (Pakistan) in 1984. He was caught and shot by the Americans in Pakistan in May 2011. Since the withdrawal of the Russians in 1989 with the occupation of the city of Kandahar in 1994, the Taliban had increasingly taken power in Afghanistan, occupied Kabul on 2 September 1996 and exercised a regime of terror.

On 07.10.2001 the Americans started the national "Operation Enduring Freedom" (OEF),[5] which was conceived in various regions of the world as a fight against terror. In Afghanistan, this large-scale operation ran in parallel in terms of time and location to an operation led by NATO from 22.12.2001 onwards, with the stationing of the "International Security Assistance Force" (ISAF). On 12 September 2001, the NATO Council proclaimed for the first time that the Alliance would be subject to Article V[6] of the NATO Agreement.

Both operations were merged in June 2008 under the leadership of a US general. The ISAF mission followed UN Resolution 1386 and was a peace enforcement operation. By November 2001, Kabul had already been liberated from the Taliban, with other parts of the country following. The first three ISAF operations were still conducted according to the "Lead Nation Principle", i.e. under a national commander in Kabul who was subordinate to a NATO commander. From ISAF IV of 11.08.2003, there was a transition to a purely NATO structure with a NATO commander on the ground. Here it should not be misunderstood that every NATO commander is still attached to the umbilical cord of his home country. However, this kind of double subordination has been a practice for many years and is regulated for the commanders and their troops with a clear NATO terminology and agreed procedures.

1 https://tr.wikipedia.org. – *Kosova Türkleri.*
2 https://jfcnaples.nato.int/kfor/-NATO KFOR Home. https://de. Wikipedia.org.–KFOR. https://tr.wikipedia.org. – KFOR. https://tr.wikipedia.org. – *Kosova Güvenlik Gücü.*
3 https://de.wikipedia.org. – Jugoslawienkriege.
4 https://de.wikipedia.org.– Afghanistan. https://de.wikipedia.org.– Al-Qaida. https://de.wikipedia.org. – Taliban. https://de.wikipedia.org. – Osama bin Laden.
5 https://de.wikipedia.org. – Operation Enduring Freedom.
6 https://de.wikipedia.org. - Alliance case.

AFGHANISTAN

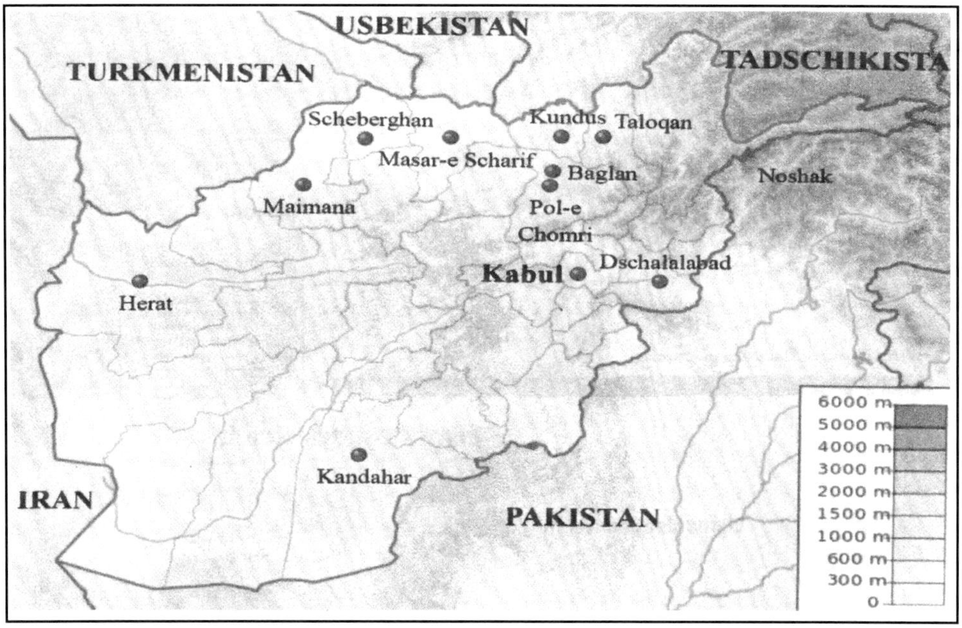

Map 25

The stationed foreign troops from about 50 countries, including non-NATO states, reached a maximum of about 131,000 by 2010, while Afghanistan was able to provide its own land forces of about 170,000 men, supplemented by about 135,000 police officers. Very soon the foreign troop strength and the number of nations had decreased significantly until termination of ISAF at the end of 2014. In addition, many foreign civilian forces and organizations are still in the country today to help rebuild the country.

In the case of Turkey, the first provision of a Turkish national commander with ISAF II took place from June 2002 to February 2003 under General Hilmi Akın Zorlu.[1] In addition to the troops of the other participating nations, he was also in charge of the approximately 1,800 Turkish soldiers who were deployed mainly in the Kabul area, i.a. to protect the airport. The number of Turkish troops was then reduced in line with the reductions of the other nations to about 500 soldiers in 2018.

The first Turkish NATO commander was General Ethem Erdağı, the previous Commanding General of the NATO Corps Staff in Istanbul (NRDC-T - NATO Rapid Deployable Corps-Turkey).[2] He took the majority of the NATO personnel of his staff from

1 https://de.wikipedia.org. - International Security Assistance Force. https://tr.wikipedia.org. - *Uluslararası Güvenlik Destek Gücü.* https://tr.wikipedia.org. - *Afganistan Savaşı* (2001-2014). https://de.wikipedia.org. - War in Afghanistan since 2001. https://de.wikipedia.org. - Operation Enduring Freedom.

2 The author has served in this NATO HQ at İstanbul from 2002-2005. Already in peacetime, it comprises, in addition to the staff, a Turkish supply- and a telecommunications regiment with a total strength of about 2,500 men. In wartime, divisions of different NATO states could be subordinated. NATO already "owns" a number of corps staffs of a similar kind, which are mostly supported by a "Lead Nation".

İstanbul and integrated himself into the given structure of the NATO HQ in Kabul. Additionally required material was carried from Turkey.

The last ISAF contingents were always under US command within the NATO umbrella until 31.12.2014 when ISAF was transferred to the "Resolute Support" (RS)[1] mission, still with an operational - in theatre US commander on top. The US call it "Operation Freedom's Sentinel". In addition to the original and still ongoing threat from the Taliban, the above mentioned globally operating terrorist organization Al Qaeda remains active. Since 2015, the above-mentioned so-called "Islamic State" (IS) has been operating as a third transnational terrorist organization with a previous focus on Iraq and Syria, here now from the border area with Pakistan.

Resolute Support under the leadership of NATO with 40 states, including non-NATO states, has had a pure training and support mission since the beginning of 2015, in order to bring the Afghan security forces to a modern state. With a scope of approximately 20,000 men - grown by recent US reinforcements in 2017 due to increasing threats - the trainers are deployed in various regions. They train the land and air forces of the Afghan army as well as the police. Turkey is still participating in RS by leading TAAC Capital (Train Advise Assist Command, Capital) in the Kabul area to train the army and police there. At the same time Turkey supports TAAC North under German leadership in the Masar-e Scharif area. As of 2018 Turkey provides about 500 personell for the 2 TAA's, whereas the overall strength in 2019 is about 16.000.

In February 2020, the US government and the Taliban concluded an agreement in Doha following bilateral negotiations. I.a., they agreed on the withdrawal of all foreign troops from Afghanistan within 14 months and an exchange of prisoners with subsequent peace negotiations under the premise that the Taliban would behave peacefully. Immediately afterwards the Taliban spoke of a victory. Third parties such as Afghan President Ashraf Ghani and the other nations are getting involved as well.

However, the biggest security policy problem for the Republic of Turkey since its foundation in 1923 and thus for its security services is not the military coups and coup attempts until 2016, nor loss-making foreign deployments, but rather the prevention of the Kurdish groups' [2] attempts at autonomy or the fight against the armed arm of the PKK at home, in northern Iraq and its sister organizations in neighboring countries. The core of the problem has long been the Kurds' aspirations for a transnational autonomy in Turkey, Iran,[3] Iraq[4] and Syria,[5] possibly even leading to a Kurdish state. The proportion of Kurds in Turkey is estimated at about 20%, the Kurdish proportion in Syria at 10%. The situation is further complicated by internal political upheavals in the neighbouring countries of Iraq and Syria,[6] an ongoing civil war in Syria and by international terrorism, especially the so-called IS. In the author's view, however, this overall problem cannot be solved by the security forces alone. The core of the solution can only be a political one involving neighbouring states, the major powers and the UN. Even the erection of walls along the 144 km border with Iran with stationary surveillance balloons[7] or drones and the 828 km border with Syria will not deter the

1 https://de.wikipedia.org. - Resolute Support. http://www.rs.nato.int/Resolute Support Mission.
2 https://de.wikipedia.org. – Kurden in der Türkei.
3 https://de.wikipedia.org. – Mahabad.
4 https://de.wikipedia.org. – Autonome Region Kurdistan.
5 http://www.hurriyetdailynews.com. – „Syria Kurds will declare self-rule in all Kurdish regions within a week" from 23.01.2014.
6 https://de.wikipedia.org. – Bürgerkrieg in Syrien.
7 http://www.hurriyetdailynews.com. dtd. 24.07.2015 „Turkey to fly surveillance balloons, build new fence and moat for border security".

rebellious Kurds from cross-border operations.[1] With Law No. 3497 as of 25.04.2013 the army has already been obliged to take over the border security tasks from the Jandarma:

"*Kara sınırlarını korumak ve güvenliğini sağlamak görevi Kara Kuvvetleri Komutanlığına ait olup, bü görev sınır birliklerince; ...*". ("With regard to the protection of national borders and ensuring their security, this task at the border for the command of the land forces includes the following; ...". *Translation by the author*).

The transitional paragraph 2 of this Law obliges Jandarma and the army to cooperate. This means that the army had been assigned a new task. This mission is meanwhile listed on the homepage of the General Staff as of 10.06.2017 under Tasks.[2]

SETTLEMENT AREAS OF THE KURDS

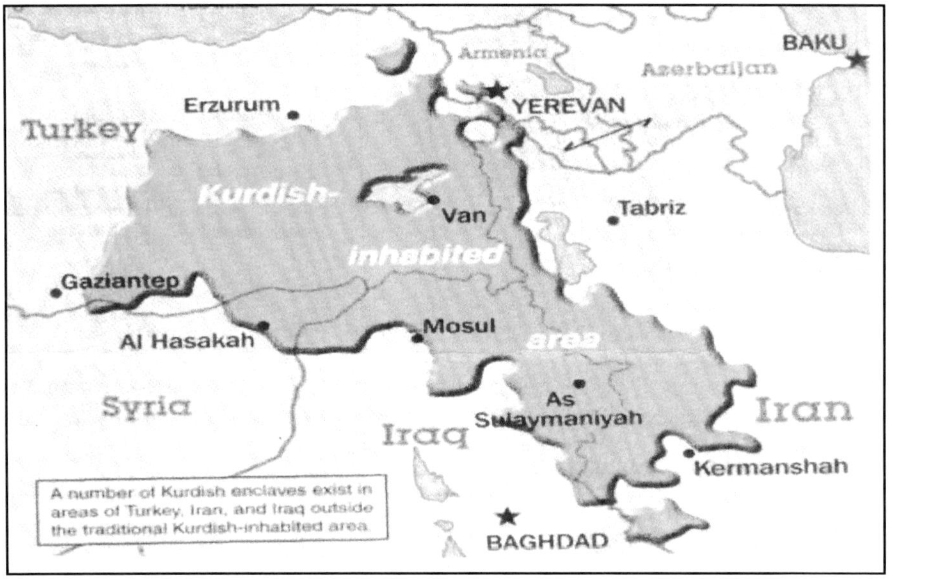

Map 26 *(https://commons.wikimedia.org.- Kurdish inhabited area by CIA (2002)*

The main security forces at Turkey's disposal are the armed services, in addition the Jandarma, the coast guard, the police, the secret services[3] and the system of paramilitary village guards (*Koruculuk Sistemi*) recruited since 1985. These armed forces, originally established under Law 442 (*Köy Kanunu* - Village Law) of 1924 and set up in 1985, reached a total of 95,000 men in 2002, whereas by then some 3,000 villages and over 380,000 Kurds had been evacuated. By 2015, the number of voluntary (*Gönüllü*) and mainly paid (*Maaşlı*) temporary (*Geçici*) village guards is expected to have fallen to 57,000. They are deployed in about 35 of Turkey's 81 provinces and are subordinate to the Minister of the Interior, with

1 ttp://www.t-online.de from 02.06.2017 Erdogan: mauern an tuerkischen grenzen bauen. http://www.hürriyetdailynews.comfrom 10.08.2017 Turkey starts building security wall on Iran border. http://www.hurriyetdailynews.com. from 23.09.2017.

2 http://www.tsk.tr/TskHakkinda/Tsk Görevi Türk Silahlı Kuvvetleri Genelkurmay Başkanlığı.

3 The most important secret service MIT - *Milli İstihbarat Teşkilatı* reports to the president. He is also responsible for domestic intelligence. http://www.hurriyetdailynews.com. dated 26.08.2017 - New turkish state of emergency decrees ties intelligence agency to president.

cooperation between the local authorities and the Jandarma. The general staff has also been involved in the training of village guards.[1]

However, the focus in this book should remain on the army and its role in the fight against the PKK (*Partiyen Karkeren Kurdistane* - Kurdistan Workers' Party) and its "People's Defence Forces,"[2] at home and abroad. In Germany, in general language use, no distinction is made between the PKK party and its fighters; one speaks only of the fight against the PKK. In 1993, the German Office for the Protection of the Constitution classified the PKK as a terrorist organisation and banned it.[3] In Turkey, too, there is general talk of the fight against the PKK since 1978[4] and no longer distinguishes between the party and its military arm. The accusations of terrorism sometimes include individual members of the Kurdish oriented party HDP (*Halkların Demokratik Partisi* - Democratic People's Party),[5] which is represented in parliament. Nor is there a term "Kurdistan" in current official Turkish usage, which only needs to be mentioned for translation reasons from Kurdish.

The Turkish descriptions of the topic are extremely extensive and detailed. They describe the numerous name changes of the organizations, name the sub- and sister organizations[6] at home and abroad, list the actions of the PKK. Numerous Internet files provide an overview despite the sometimes tendentious and incomplete representations, as well as the publications mentioned in the bibliography. However, the following brief description attempts to simplify the complex political-military situation for the reader without losing sight of the Turkish army.

The PKK was founded in 1978 under its leader Abdullah Öcalan in the province of Diyarbakır. After the military coup in Turkey in 1980 and the arrest of PKK supporters, Öcalan fled to Damascus, from where he directed the training of his fled fighters in the Bekaa plain[7] in Lebanon. From this region, the struggle was to be carried back to Turkey in 1984 by means of guerrilla tactics. The unacceptable situation from Turkey's point of view and the associated bilateral crisis with Syria was settled in 1999 with the Adana Agreement,[8] which, however, could not prevent recent tensions, not even with the USA. They e.g. do not fully share the view of Turkey in its fight against the Kurds in Syria. Today, the Turkish struggle in Northern Syria is primarily directed against the Kurdish YPG as the military arm of the PYD.[9]

Öcalan was arrested again in 1999 - after a first arrest for a leaflet distribution campaign in 1972 - and sentenced to death, but in 2003 he was subsequently sentenced to life imprisonment with the abolition of the death penalty. Öcalan remains the secret leader of the PKK to this day and communicates with his supporters. The PKK cooperates with its sister parties PCDK in Iraq, PYD in Syria and PJAK in Iran under an umbrella organisation that meets mostly in the Kandil Mountains[10] in the north-east of Iraq.

The armed struggle of the PKK is sometimes referred to as the fifth major Kurdish uprising, starting with the Koçgiri uprising in 1920/1921, but in reality, the still ongoing civil

1 https://de.wikipedia.org. – Dorfschützersystem. See. Ünal „Counterterrorism in Turkey“ p. 51 ff.
2 https://de.wikipedia.org. – Arbeiterpartei Kurdistans. https://de.wikipedia.org. – *Hezen Parastina Gel.* https://de.wikipedia.org. – Geschichte der Arbeiterpartei Kurdistans.
3 Cf. Bundesamt für Verfassungsschutz „Die Arbeiterpartei Kurdistans (PKK).“
4 https://tr.wikipedia.org. – *Türkiye-PKK çatışması.*
5 https;//tr.wikipedia.org. – *Halkların Demokratik Partisi.*
6 https://tr.wikipedia.org. – *PKK saldırıları ve çatışmaları kronolojisi.*
7 https://de.wikipedia.org. – Bekaa Ebene .
8 Cf. Brauns & Kiechle „PKK“.
9 Volksverteidigungseinheiten. „*Yekîneyen Parastina Gel*“ (YPG) - Volksverteidigungseinheiten. https://de.wikipedia.org. – *Partiya Yekitiya Demokrat.* „Partei der Demokratischen Union“.
10 https://de.wikipedia.org. - Kandil Mountains. These are located in the northeast of Iraq parallel to the Iranian border between the two ZAB rivers northeast of Arbil/Erbil.

war at home exceeds all previous dimensions in terms of duration and victims. The civil war started covertly on the part of the PKK against other groups and authorities soon after its foundation, but in 1984 it also took place openly against the security forces of Turkey. Despite repeated ceasefires and interruptions, the bloody struggle continues and has so far claimed thousands of victims on both sides. Numerous measures such as the imposition of states of emergency, the establishment of security zones and restricted areas, numerous forced relocations of Kurds, including complete evacuation of villages with village guards stationed there, have tended to create further tensions but have not solved the problem.[1]

After Öcalan's second arrest, most PKK fighters, in the order of several thousand, withdrew to northern Iraq, from where they operate, but where they are also fought by the Turkish army. These cross-border operations of the army into northern Iraq with land and air forces have been taking place since 1984 with at least 400 killed Turkish soldiers and about 14,000 killed PKK "militants" (*militanlar*).[2] The operations have lasted from one day (e.g. air attacks) to several months (e.g. with land forces). According to one source, 25 attacks were carried out before 2008, with one major attack in 2008 involving approximately 10,000 soldiers.[3] Remarkable is the high percentage of women among the Kurdish fighters, also the result of a clever PKK propaganda in the context of the alleged emancipation of women.

At times, cross-border actions from Turkey to Syria since 2015[4] or to northern Iraq[5] have been justified by selfprotection of Turkey or the fight against the "IS" IAW the UN-Charter or the need to protect local Sunni "Türkmen" (*Öz Kardeş* - inseparable brothers). For the most part these are ethnic groups that remained after the collapse of the Ottoman Empire in 1923, who had also sought protection in Turkey during the wars in Iraq and Syria.[6] With interventions to Syria Turkey refers also to the Adana - agreement from 1999.

A major operation of the Turkish army with about 3,000 men to northern Syria took place in August 2016 - March 2017 under the name "Operation Euphrates Shield" (*Fırat Kalkanı Operasyonu)*[7] with the main goal of preventing a continuous Kurdish corridor or supply belt along the border by the YPG/SDF while simoultanesly repelling the IS. The operation was again based on Article 51 of the UN Charter and was carried out in cooperation with the US Airforce and the FSA (Free Syrian Army) towards Manbij[8] area, by making use of main battle tanks, artillery and Turkish air force. The number of Turkish casualties was 70,[9] whereas about 300 PKK fighters were killed.[10] At the end of March 2017, Turkey declared the operation a success. It had pushed back the IS, but had not achieved a continuous controlled corridor along the Syrian border against the YPG.

1 https://de.wikipedia.org. – Dorfschützersystem.

2 https://tr.wikipedia.org. – *Türk Silahlı Kuvvetleri Kuzey Irak'ta yaptığı operasyonlar listesi.*

3 https://de.wikipedia.org. – Konflikt zwischen der Republik Türkei und der PKK.

4 As early as October 2012, Parliament had approved cross-border operations to Syria, but made this dependent on demands being made of the USA and NATO. http://www.hurriyet dailynews. From 04.10.2012., 28.08.2013 and 10.09.2014. De facto the operations did not start until 2015.

5 Another reason was the holding of the referendum in the Kurdistan Autonomous Region on 25.09.2017.

6 https://de.wikipedia.org. – Turkmenen (Irak). https://de.wikipedia.org. – Turkmenen (Syrien). https://tr.wikipedia.org. – *Irak İç Savaşı* (2014 – *günümüz*).

7 *https://tr.wikipedia.org. – Fırat Kalkanı Operasyonu.*

8 https://de.wikipedia.org. – Manbidsch.

9 https://de.wikipedia.org. – Türkische Militäroffensive in Nordsyrien.

10 Hurriyet Daily News dtd. 10 October 2019. https://wikipedia.org/wiki/Türkische Militäroffensive in Nordsyrien 2016/17.

SYRIA

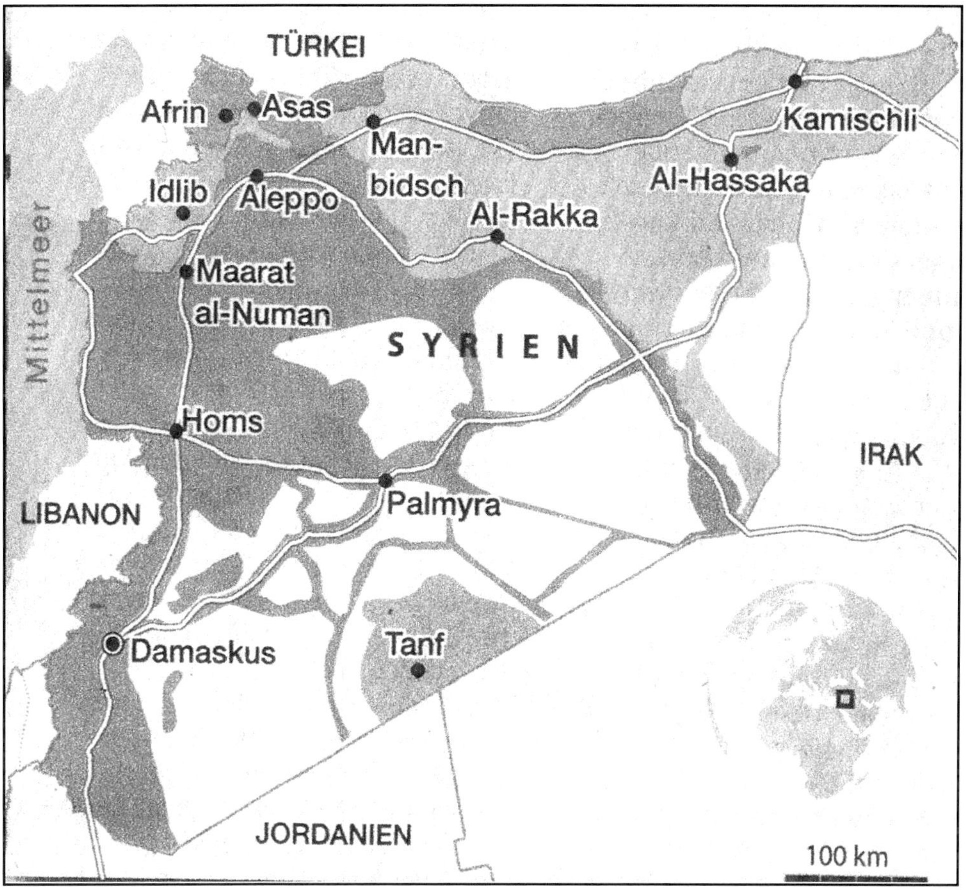

Map 27

A Turkish follow-up operation called "Olive Branch" (*Zeytin Dalı*) towards Idlib in northwest Syria started on 12 October 2017.[1] The aim of the operation was to establish a de-escalation zone and prevent the flow of refugees across the Turkish border. Once again, the parties to the conflict were basically the same. Turkey managed to set up 12 "observation posts" by January 2018, from which the region was to be controlled. President Baschar al Assad from Syria, of course, could not accept the result.

Still in January 2018 the Turkish army started again in the direction towards Afrin.[2] With the same parties to the conflict again, Turkey was supported by local Turkmen. Once again, the YPG was to be pushed back further and a security zone was to be established. In March

1 https://de.wikipedia.org. – Türkische Militäroffensive im Gouvernement Idlib.
2 https://de.wikipedia.org - Türkische Militäroffensive auf Afrin.

2018, undefended Afrin was occupied. The Turks suffered losses of less than 80 men with a contingent of about 6400 men.

At the end of April 2019 Syrian troops loyal to the government and Russian air forces started an offensive on the rebel-held government of Idlib.

On October 9, 2019, a Turkish counter -offensive was launched in this region after US troops were to be withdrawn and the Kurds turned to the Syrian government for help. This operation was called "Operation Peace Spring"[1] (*Barış Pınarı Harekatı).* This time the Turkish troops faced Syrian troops while the USA did not intervene. The Turkish aim was again to establish a security zone west of the Euphrates, which from the Turkish point of view was only partially achieved against the YPG (the Kurds). In October 2019, Russia and Turkey agreed on a future regional distribution of power, and in March 2020 even on joint patrols. A ceasefire was already agreed upon in October 2019 and repeated in March 2020, which is however unstable. US troops nevertheless remained in the country to secure the oil wells. The prison camps with IS fighters also had to be secured or relocated.

In this operation Turkey has used about 15,000 forces.. The Turkish losses by March 2020 are about 50 soldiers; the bulk of them died during an hostile air attack. Measures were taken to hold back about 3 million refugees. It is estimated that in the 9-year-long conflicts in Syria so far, approximately 500,000 people have lost their lives by March 2020.

During operations within Turkey against the PKK, the state suffered numerous casualties in the army, including the Jandarma, in the police, in the village guards and in the civilian population, and of course also among the "*militants*".[2] The Minister for Culture and Tourism Mahir Ünal (2015 - 2016) puts the total number of deaths from 1984 to 2012 at about 35,650, 25,000 of which were among the terrorists, 5,850 among the Turkish security forces and 4,800 among the civilian population. He sees above all religious and national motives in the struggle of the PKK, also as a counterbalance to Turkish secularism and in the corresponding step to Turkish nationalism. Erdoğan considers the PKK to be as great a threat as the so-called IS. He has therefore recently intensified the struggle against the PKK.[3]

The overall balance of the long period since 1950, as described above in the sense of our initial questions about the Turkish army, is very complex and differentiated because of the turbulent political events. The army inevitably followed the partly revolutionary and chaotic conditions at home, while it gave the usual reliable picture during operations abroad. For the soldier, a coup basically raised the question of obedience and the content of his military oath (*Askerlik Andı*). In it he swears in the valid version, shortened by the author:[4]

"Barışta ve savaşta, karada, denizde ve havada, her zaman ve her yerde milettime ve Cumhuriyetime doğruluk ve muhabetle hizmet ve kanunlara ve nizamlara ve amirlerime itaat edeceğime ve ...ant içerim."

("I vow to serve my nation and my state with sincerity and affection, obedient to the laws, regulations and my superiors, in peace and war, on land, on water and in the air, at any time and in any place. Translation of the author).

This vague oath leaves somewhat unclear, to whom exactly the soldier has to be obedient in case of doubt. The educated soldier should know that the parliament is the decisive authority for him and cannot be ignored, except in special cases provided for in the constitution. But how does he behave if the parliament is still silent when the superior gives

1 https://de.wikipedia.org - Türkische Militäroffensive in Nordsyrien 2019.
2 Cf. Ünal "Counterterterrorism in Turkey" p. 4.
3 https://de.wikipedia.org. – Türkische Offensive gegen die PKK seit 2015.
4 https://tr.wikipedia.org. - *ant*. Cf. law no. 211 § 37.

him an order, the coup character of which he cannot recognize at first. Is leaving the barracks with combat vehicles an exercise or e.g. a genuine legitimate operation to protect an important institution ? How should the soldier behave towards the civilian population if they prevent him from carrying out his mission? What is the situation when orders clearly violate the law? What has priority? After all, the soldier fears that he will be severely punished if the order is not carried out. The situation is different if a pilot is given the order to bomb the parliament building. There is no doubt about this. Of course, the problem of obedience described here is not a specifical Turkish problem; however, it has occurred frequently in recent Turkish history and has involved many sacrifices. The common soldier, the lower ranks could hardly be able to assess the overall situation; so in case of doubt they will follow the instructions of their superiors. After all, trust in the legality of their superiors' orders is an important basis for the duty of obedience.

Thus, the following balance could perhaps be drawn for the periods under discussion here:

- The mission of the armed forces, determined by parliament and by law, remained basically unchanged, for operations both at home and abroad. Parliament and government remained largely intact. However, if the army leadership or a sub-grouping was of the opinion that a case had arisen according to the above-mentioned law § 35, in which the "protection of the Republic" in the Kemalist sense was at stake - not meant territorially here - and that the situation could only be mastered by means of military violent or non-violent intervention with the threat of violence, in this case the army acted in accordance with its understood mission, restored the desired political conditions and in individual cases received subsequent approval by a constitutional referendum.

- The relationship between the army and politics was severely disrupted on several occasions as far as actions at home were concerned; the army was repeatedly in a serious conflict of loyalties. No similar conflicts of loyalty or conscience have been reported in foreign operations, not even in operations against terrorist Kurdish compatriots in the Kandil mountain range. The tensions will certainly have existed in this conscription army when Kurds had to fight Kurds.

- In the army's relationship to religion, political phases of distancing from strict Laicism were soon discernible, increasingly from 2002 onwards with the AKP taking over government power. Political majorities and attitudes were ultimately reflected in a conscription army, as was increasing Islamization. This means that the military leadership can not be sure about the unconditional loyalty of the entire army any longer.

- As a result of conscription, the army was naturally well staffed in terms of numbers, while the quality of conscripts in particular was and is a direct consequence of the education and training they had previously received at home and at school or university. With regard to the material condition, a large army cannot be broadband modern when budgetary resources are scarce; it must be gradually upgraded. The ability to produce complex systems of the most modern technology in one's own country is not primarily the responsibility of the army. The purchase of state-of-the-art systems or the co-production of systems with other countries will remain necessary for Turkey for some time to come. In the NATO alliance, only the USA actually has the desirable self-sufficiency in armaments technology.

The Coup Attempt of 2016 and the Further Development of the Army

The failed coup attempt of 16 July 2016 has revealed a new dimension in that for the first time the Fethullah Gülen movement[1] is to be the primary perpetrator, supported by parts of the

1 The journalist Ahmet Şık had already written a book about the Gülen movement in 2011 entitled "*Imam*

security services, the civil service and the civilian population. The files listed below, as of July/August 2017, provide a detailed overview.[1] The map shows the focal points with the probable command center at Akıncı airfield (*Akıncı Hava Üssü*) near Ankara, meanwhile renamed again to the former name "*Mürted Hava Üssü*).[2]

The previously unknown and responsible civil-military group called itself "Council of Peace" (*Yurtta Sulh Konseyi*"),[3] with about 38 members, which was probably meant to remind of Atatürk's famous saying that "*Yurtta Sulh - Cihanda Sulh*", i.e. "Peace at home and in the world", was demanded. But "peace-moving" people do not bomb a parliament.

The motives of the military putschists, who obviously came from all three services, as well as from the Jandarma and the police, were obviously different: A renewed attempt to preserve the secular Kemalism as in earlier coups, but possibly also sympathy with the Gülen movement, perhaps also with the anticipation of an impending arrest in the processing of the existing "black lists"[4] by the government. A Kemalist core demand is the functioning of the state form "Republic", thus no development towards a degenerated democracy with an overpowering autocrat at the top. So there were probably some opposition members to Erdoğan's policy of power concentration. Perhaps they were also people dissatisfied with their career so far, who saw their new chance if the coup succeeded.

Apparently the army leadership, the secret service MIT (*Milli İstihbarat Teşkilâtı*), the military national security council MGK and the government had been aware of the activities for weeks in principle, but more concrete only hours before the coup. The putschists had brought the coup forward to the evening of 15.07.2016 and thereby considerably disturbed their own course of events. It must be stated that the Chief of General Staff Hulusi Akar[5] was not replaced by the President of the Republic. Akar, nowadays Defence Minister, who was released from the rebels after his short arrest, said on 30.05.2017 that they were all surprised that "this organisation" had actually taken the risk of the coup, which caused at least 248 deaths on the side of the defender and 58 on the side of the attacker.[6] Rather, General Akar was subsequently re-confirmed in office at the meeting of the High Military Council (YAŞ) in August 2017.[7] The head of the secret service, Hakan Fidan,[8] also remained in office. The president in Marmaris was warned just in time, the flight to İstanbul survived unharmed. The media enabled him to make an immediate speech, which fell on fertile ground with the population. Allegedly, about 80% of the Imams supported him through appeals, headed by the head of the religious authority *Diyanet İşleri Başkanlığı,* Prof. Dr. Mehmet Görmez. The invulnerability myth of Erdoğan was thus strengthened.

Ordusu" (The Army of the Imam). Also called "Hizmet" movement.

1 https://de.wikipedia.org. – Putschversuch in der Türkei 2016. https://tr.wikipedia.org. – 2016 *Türkiye askeri darbe girişimi.*

2 https://de.wikipedia.org. – Militärflugplatz Akıncı.

3 https://tr.wikipedia.org. – *Yurtta Sulh Konseyi.*

4 Cf. Daily Sabah, 12.07.2017.

5 https://tr.wikipedia.org. - Hulusi Akar.

6 http://www.hurriyetdailynews.com. dated 05.30.2017.

7 The author had the opportunity to get to know General Hulusi Akar, at that time still as Lieutenant General of the NRDC-T or III Corps in Istanbul, in 2011 during an evening table discussion. Turkish table neighbours who already knew him had reported that he was a "very apolitical general".

8 https://de.wikipedia.org. - Hakan Fidan.

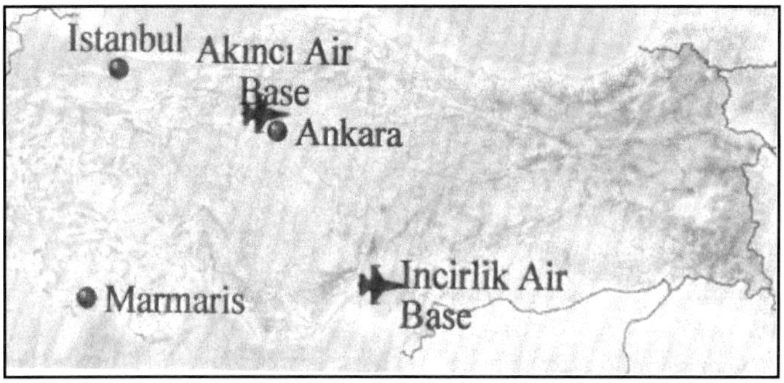

Map28

On 20.07.2016 the state of emergency was declared, which had been extended seven times and gave the state leadership more powers. It was lifted again in July 2018, thus denying the President to pass further emergency legislation any more. However, important aspects are now covered by other laws.

The Turkish Daily News of October 6, 2016 reports of 201 dismissed generals and admirals out of a total of 358, further 29.434 officers. At the head of the affected soldiers are e.g. the four-star generals Akın Öztürk and Adem Huduti.[1] The overall military strength of the army had fallen from 518.166 to 351.376, but primarily because of the removal of the Jandarma with 160.148 and now clear subordination under the Minister of the Interior. Also dismissed were 586 colonels of the 3 services. Even if some of the soldiers were later reinstated, this wave of dismissals must be regarded as a blood-letting in the armed forces and the army leadership, at least temporarily. Worse still, however, is the loss of confidence in the army on the part of the population and politicians, which has led to further steps towards disempowerment. This includes the intended reduction of the competence of the General Staff in their new subordination to the Minister of Defence. Law No. 1324 as of 09.11.2016 on the reduced competence of the General Staff already states in § 2, while anticipating the development:

"*Genelkurmay Başkanı, Milli Savunma Bakanlığının görevleri saklı kalmak kaydıyla; Silahlı Kuvvetlerinin savaşa hazırlanmasında personel, istihbarat, harekat,,, teşkilatve eğitim hizmetlerine ait ilke ve öncelikler ile ana programları tespit eder.*" ("Subject to the fact that the General Staff is part of the National Defence Ministry, its tasks are to provide services to the armed forces in preparation for war in the areas of personnel, intelligence, operations, organisation and training by means of initial and preparatory main programmes. *Translation by the author).(*Fig. 33).

Since 2017, the secret service MIT has been placed under the authority of the President[2] of the Republic with the power to provide information in the field of defence. The MIT can thus more easily detect a coup d'état from the army, starting from the Gülen movement or another grouping. Of course, it can also warn in time and thus exercise a protective function for persons at risk. Further steps of the simplified legislative practice under a state of emergency (*Olağanüstü hal*) were the dissolution of the cadet schools, military schools, military

1 Öztürk was commander of the air force, Huduti commander of the 2nd army in Malatya.
2 Law 2937 as of 15.08.2007 *Devlet İstihbarat Hizmetleri ve Milli İstihbarat Teşkilatı Kanunu.*

academies and their transfer to a new system under the Minister of Defence.[1] The law 4566 as of 15.08.2017 determines in § 3 paragraph d):

"Harp okulu: Kara Harp Okulu, Deniz Harp Okulu ve Hava Harp Okulu olup, Milli Savunma Bakanlığı kuruluşunda, Atatürk ilkerlerine bağlı ve askeri değerleri haiz muvazzaf subay yetiştiren...eğitim ve öğretim, bilimsel araştırma, yayın ve danışmanlık yapan, bilimsel özerkliğe sahip bir yükseköğretim kurumudur." ("War School: The Army War School, the Naval War School and the Air Force War School are assigned to the Ministry of Defence to train professional officers according to the maxims of Atatürk and military ethics.....An organisation is created for training and education, for scientific research, for the dissemination of its results and for information/consultation, for the attainment of scientific autonomy in higher education. Translation of the author). However, the reassurance of the reference to Atatürk's principles thus deprives the army of further powers to politically influence the minds and thoughts of professional officers. In the unquoted paragraph c) of § 3, an association with the highest civilian educational institutions is also indicated. Consequently, the law on higher education (*Yükseköğretim kanunu*) No. 4566 in § 2 obliges the Minister of Defence and the Minister of the Interior to create the legal basis.

The previously respected army not only lost trust in politics and the population, but also among the soldiers. However, trust is an absolute prerequisite for military obedience in the sense of the above-mentioned oath and discipline. Therefore, "purges" in the army and legal reappraisal are of great importance in order to regain inner stability.

In Turkey's view, the internal and external situation did and does not allow for a period of weakness in the army, whereas additional peaceful military missions have to be fulfilled. E.g. on 30.09.2017 Turkey opened a military training base, the largest overseas military facility in Somalia, evidently to contain the terror organisation “Al Shabab” and thus contributing to the pacification of the country. It concerns the training of approximately 10,000 Somali soldiers and policemen in an established military base near Mogadishu. Even though only about 300 Turkish soldiers are probably deployed, the effort involved should not be underestimated. It ranges from secure strategic telecommunications to adequate medical care.[2]

A further order for the Turkish military results from 12 agreements with Sudan dated December 2017 concerning the island of Suakin/Sawakin on the Red Sea coast. Sultan Selim I had occupied this Sunni-oriented territory in 1517, which had a chequered history. Now the dilapidated port and dock is being rebuilt there and the repair of military and civilian ships is made possible besides the main port in Port Sudan. Even if this mission will only tie up a few soldiers, it will open up an important support base for the Turkish Navy at the Horn of Africa.[3]

Since 2019 another place of deployment for the Turkish army is Libya, which also belonged to the Ottoman Empire until 1912. After the overthrow of Muammar al Gaddafi in 2011, civil war is raging there. The two states have agreed on a “Security and military agreement” in November 1919 that Turkish soldiers and soldiers of the above-mentioned pro-Turkey Syrian FSA should be present in Libya and train pro-government Libyan soldiers. Not surprising, an intervention in the fighting against General Chalifa Haftar, supported by Russia,

1 Law 926 *"Türk Silahlı Kuvvetleri Personel Kanunu"* § 3 footnote (1) with reference to the State of Emergency Law 681 KHK *(Kanun Hükmünde Kararname)* § 12 from 02.01.2017. See Law 1111 *Askerlik Kanunu* (Soldier Law) §13. Law 4566 (*Harp okulları kanunu* - Law on Military Schools). A new conscription law (*Askeralma Kanunu*) No. 7179 - for men - followed on 20.06.1919.

2 Neue Züricher Zeitung dtd. 29.01.2015. Hannoversche Allgemeine Zeitung dtd. 24.08.2017. Wikipedia org. „Turkish Military Base in Somalia“.

3 Wikipedia. org „Suakin“. Ankara Anadolu Agency dtd. 28.04.2019.

started already;[1] Haftar does not feel bound by the agreement.[2] Turkey allegedly intervened in the north-western coastal area with rocket fire from the navy and the use of drones. In addition the IS is pursuing its own goals from the underground. The latter had announced an emirate in Sirte in 2014. A stable ceasefire agreement has not yet been reached, despite efforts by Russia and Turkey since early 2020.[3]

Parallel to the bilateral agreement, Turkey and Libya have created a new trouble spot by defining borders in the eastern Mediterranean for the purpose of exploiting gas deposits. Exploration by Turkey has already begun. Greece described the act as "contrary to international - and to maritime law". Naval forces of the two NATO states are threatened now in the Mediterranian sea with a further confrontation in addition to the long lasting one due to the disputed bilateral border in the Aegean Sea. The two parts of Cyprus are naturally also interested in economic exploitation. The oil reserves in Libya of course also arouse desires of everyone.[4]

The gas and oil-rich emirate of Qatar is another country with which Turkey has maintained close economic and military relations since at least 2014. The last Ottoman troops did not leave the country until 1915. A military agreement in Doha from 2014 and the stationing of about 80 soldiers was followed by a further agreement on June 8, 2017 with the now largely politically isolated country with a predominantly Sunni - Wahabi population. The military base in Qatar was to be increased to about 3000 soldiers, side by side with the US forces also stationed there. Here too, the Turkish military should primarily provide training support including joint exercises. Due to an embargo imposed on Qatar by Saudi Arabia and the United Arab Emirates, an arms cooperation is probably also involved.[5]

A survey along the Turkish border shows that there is currently almost no relaxed political atmosphere anywhere, which has an impact on the required operational readiness of the army.

A certain political stability in the Black Sea region stems from the "Black Sea Economic Cooperation" (BSEC), founded in 1992, which currently has 12 member states. In addition to the riparian states, other states have joined the agreement. Although the focus is on infrastructure projects such as electricity supply and road construction, cooperation in the field of counter-terrorism is also a topic. However, Turkey's existing tensions with Greece or Armenia and to some extent also with Russia cannot be resolved in this body, although they may be mitigated somewhat.[6]

Relations with Iran have recently eased somewhat. Economic interests play an important role, while Iran is suffering from the US boycott. The neighbouring states want to prevent a Kurdish state. However, there are still weighty aspects that rather divide the two states. The most important of these are the different positions on Syria, on its President Bashar al-Assad and the difference in religion, while at the same time Turkey is close to the Sunni Saudi Arabia as Iran's most important adversary. The different relations with Armenia and Israel are also a burden on mutual relations between Turkey and Iran.[7]

The relationship with Russia, traditionally tense in the context of Turkey's membership in NATO ("south-eastern pillar"), also due to hidden or indirect previous Russian arms deliveries to the PKK with SA-16 shoulder-fired anti-aircraft weapons, reached a further low point not only due to Russia's Syrian engagement, but especially after the shooting down of a Russian

1 FAZ dtd. 15.04.2020.
2 FAZ dtd. 29.04.2020.
3 FAZ dtd. 21.02.2020. DTJ Deutsch Türkisches Journal dtd. 19.12.2019.
4 Hurriyet Daily News dtd. 06 May 2019.
5 Die Zeit online and FAZ dtd. 08.06.2017. Also AFP and Reuters.
6 Wikipedia. org „BSEC“.
7 Wikipedia., org „Iranisch – türkische Beziehungen.

Suchoi Su-24 on 24.11.2015 by a Turkish F-16. In the meantime, however, despite existing boycott measures, bilateral relations with Russia have eased somewhat, parallel to Turkey's disgruntlement with partners in the West. Bilateral armaments cooperation has been intensified, e.g. with the procurement of the Russian S-400 air defence system, which has led to serious concerns by the USA. In response, the US initially stopped the delivery of modern aircraft to Turkey and the related technical cooperation. Erdoğan also saw the possibility of co-production and the acquisition of know-how from Russia. Although it cannot be assumed that the major powers will supply Turkey with weapons systems that allow deep insight into the most secret components, above all the "source code" or even “machine code” of their programmes, it is to be feared that, in addition to atmospheric disgruntlement with the USA and NATO, the interoperability of NATO systems will suffer or that the Russians will switch "their system" inactive if necessary. The danger of inactivation exists in principle for every system of complex technology, e.g. also for the satellite navigation systems GPS (US) and GLONASS (RUS). As a reminder, NATO had moved Patriot defence missiles near the Syrian border in 2012, whose procurement should have been an alternative from US-standpoint.

In the dispute over the enclave of Nagorny Karabakh, which has been occupied by Armenia since 1993, Turkey is on the side of Azerbaijan, which became independent in 1991. The disputed territory has declared itself independent under the name ARTSAKH, but has not yet been recognized by any other state. Officially there is an armistice. Turkey has basically good relations with Azerbaijan, which is now western-oriented, although the country has a predominantly Shiite population (85%), which is also subject to the principle of Laicism.

Since Georgia, after becoming also independent in 1991, broke with Russia and the CIS (Commonwealth of Independent States) in 2008, suffered from the results of a Russian intervention in the same year and is seeking membership of NATO and the EU. Relations with Turkey could have been intensified. Good examples are the common economic operation of the Baku-Tiflis-Ceyhan oil pipeline, the Baku-Tiflis- Erzurum gas pipeline and the Baku-Tiflis-Kars rail link via Georgia.

In the consideration of Turkey's neighbouring states, the relationship with NATO partner Greece must be addressed once again. As already mentioned, there has been a long period of antagonism, sometimes even enmity, between the two states, which has flared up time and again. Among the long-term problems are primarily Cyprus and the disputed border issues in the Aegean Sea and related airspace, combined with the question of the extension of territorial waters and economic interests. It was not until 1996 that the two small uninhabited islands Kardak and İkizce (Turkish names) and Imia and Limnia (Greek names) were the subject of a territorial dispute. In that year an armed conflict almost occurred. During a visit of these rocks by the Turkish chief of general staff Hulusi Akar on 29.01.2017 everything was brought back to mind, also the toleration of Öcalan by Greece until his capture in 1999. After the attempted coup in 2016, the military point of view is now also about the extradition of fled Turkish coupists, which was rejected by the Greek constitutional court. This Turkish demand, however, also affects other states, which have currently taken in these persons and have long been accused of giving shelter to PKK fighters or not pursuing them vigorously enough in court.

Turkey's relations with Egypt have also been tense since the military coup there on 3 July 2013 was successful and President Mohammed Mursi, a good friend of Erdoğan, with the Muslim Brotherhood was left behind. Erdoğan was and is on their side, which is why Muslim Brotherhoods are also seeking exile in Turkey. Egypt had prematurely celebrated the attempted military coup in Turkey in 2016. The current president and former General Fatah al Sisi, for his part, knows the rather secularly oriented military behind him. Turkey has currently lost with Egypt an important and powerful ally in that region.

Turkey already concluded a military cooperation agreement with Israel in 1996, despite fundamental political and ideological differences. since Turkey is actually on the side of the Muslim Palestinians, who have been in a bitter dispute with Israel for years. Turkey's relations with Israel had reached a low point with the incident on 31.05.2010 when the Turkish ship Mavi Marmara was boarded by the Israeli navy and 10 people were killed. Only with the apology of the Israeli Prime Minister Benjamin Netanjahu on 22.03.2013 and the payment of compensation bilateral relations have returned in June 2016 to some degree to normal. A new potential for conflict with Israel and the US emerged in 2019 with the decision of President Donald Trump to move the US Embassy to Jerusalem. In this context, President Erdoğan spoke of crossing a red line, because the interests of the Palestinians would then continue to fall far behind. After all, Turkey and Israel had been cooperating for a long time in the field of unmanned small aircraft/drones/RPV (Remotely Piloted Vehicles) of the Heron type. In the meantime, Turkey has nationally developed its own armed drone (İHA - *İnsansız Hava Aracı* - unmanned aerial vehicle) of the *Bayraktar* type (means "flag carrier"), procured it in 2014 and has thus once again entered another dimension of high technology. (Fig. 34).

As an interim conclusion, it can therefore be stated that Turkey not only remains militarily challenged as a result of ongoing operations at home and abroad, but is also confronted with military risks in the region, which could lead to military operations at any time. A strong, operational army is therefore indispensable under these political conditions. Its strength results first of all from the material-armament situation, which has already been mentioned in part and continues to develop well. In any case, government spending on security and defence, amounting to 3.1% of the gross domestic product for 2016, still appears to be sufficient for the armament requirements, although this amount also includes expenditures for the Ministry of Justice, the Ministry of the Interior, the police and the secret service organization (MIT). The Ministry of Defence is quoted at 26,451 billion Lira, which seems to be in line with the Stockholm SIPRI Institute's figure of 14.9 billion dollars at the exchange rate at that time.

Turkey is trying to acquire further know-how in the West e.g. in the joint development of a national missile defence system with France and Italy. But Turkey is also pursuing purely national paths in the arms industry to acquire technological independence. An example of this is the recent test of a missile with a range of 280 km, developed by the Turkish company Rocketsan, of the type "*Kaan*" (Kaan - Kağan - Leader) on the coast of the Black Sea on 11.05.2017.

Turkey already possesses the first national attack helicopter named "*Atak*" in its inventory, which is produced by the Turkish companies TAI and ASELSAN after a technology transfer from the Italian company Agusta Westland. (Fig. 30).

The new "Altay" heavy battle tank (Fig. 31) is also a prestige project. Following a technology transfer contract with the South Korean company "Hyundai Rotem", Turkey is developing a modern main battle tank, equipped e.g. with a gun from Rheinmetall, which enables the interchangeability of ammunition with Leopard II models. Since the end of 2017, 250 units have been under contract with the Turkish company BMC.

Another form of armaments cooperation is the production of systems with simpler technology and lower costs, thus additionally suitable for export. One example of this type is the Turkish-Indonesian co-production of a medium-weight main battle tank, the "Kaplan" (Tiger), by the Turkish company FNSS and the Indonesian company PT Pindad with British participation. Further Turkish armament projects for all branches of the armed forces, in the field of satellite technology, information technology (IT) and the ability to operate in cyberspace, backed up by sufficient and suitable personnel, give reason to expect that the Turkish Army will become even more modern in future, both conceptually and materially. The limits are primarily being determined by economic development and the availability of budgetary resources.

A further example of this development is the F-511 corvette (Fig. 32), which is recognisably modern and was built using stealth technology. It is a national product under the general designation MILGEM (*Milli Gemi* - national ship) and has been in service since 2011. Specialized in anti-submarine combat, the corvette is characterized by state-of-the-art armament and electronics. This includes the ability to master the electro-magnetic spectrum in the field of Electronic Warfare (EW). If necessary, it can take a helicopter on board.

One particular issue is being addressed by experts, which is related to the whereabouts of spent fuel rods from future Turkish nuclear reactors. As is well known, Turkey is developing a 4.8 GW nuclear power plant in Akkuyu on the south coast in the province of Mersin together with the Russian company ROSATOM. People are getting used to the idea that Turkey would not only gain access to nuclear weapons via the USA within the framework of the NATO concept of nuclear participation in war - it has its own means of transport, e.g. in the form of aircraft - but also wants to develop nuclear weapons itself. Cooperation with the nuclear power Pakistan[1] was conceivable. In any case, it is a fact that Russia and Israel already have nuclear weapons in the region that Ukraine formerly had, Iran is threatening to resume its nuclear weapons program[2] and its adversary Saudi Arabia also appears to be very interested. Saudi Arabia also maintains contacts with Pakistan in this regard. With the ban on the development, production, storage and use of chemical weapons, Turkey has already established clear regulations[3] for these weapons of mass destruction in Law 5564. With Laws 4083[4] and 5202[5], Turkey has also obliged the arms industry to maintain operations in case of need (during operations and war).

Apart from the material equipment, the fighting power of the army is mainly determined by its soldiers, quantitatively and qualitatively. As of April 2017, the total number of active (*etkin*) Turkish armed forces (including civilian personnel) was still estimated at 612,862, this figure still included the Jandarma and coast guard forces. The proportion of conscripts is still over 50 % with a compulsory military service of 1-12 months.[6] There are also considerable personnel reserves. Military service is only compulsory for men; women can enlist voluntarily. According to these figures, the Turkish army is still the second strongest in NATO and the eighth strongest in the world. Despite the ongoing provision of troops for the above mentioned countries the number of personnel appears to be sufficient.[7]

Turkey allows conscripts to be exempted from military service under certain conditions for remarkable payment. The state thereby is able to collect some billion lira when granting e.g. 70.000 permits. The Turkish General Staff insists on at least a short basic training, but basically does not really support this long-established practice, probably also for reasons of fairness of conscription, but recognises the primacy of politics.[8] On the other hand, the

1 http://www.deutsch tuerkische nachrichten dtd 10.04.2015 – Deutscher Militärexperte: Türkei entwickelt heimlich Atombombe. http://www.huffingtonpost.de. dtd 08.08.2017 Erdogan will eine Atombombe. https://de.wikipedia.org. Atommacht. https://de.sputniknews.com. dtd 14.08.2017 ukraine atommacht traum.

2 http://www.t-online.de. vom 15.08.2017 Iran droht mit Wiederaufnahme von Atomprogramm.

3 *Kimyasal silahların geliştirilmesi, üretimi, stoklanması ve kullanımının yasaklanması hakkında kanun.*

4 *Seferberlik ve savaş haline ilişkin harp sanayii faaliyetinin hakkında kanun.*

5 *Savunma sanayii güvenliği kanunu.*

6 *https://tr.wikipedia.org. – Askerlik hizmeti.* Law 7179 as of 25.03.1920 on recruitment of males : *Asker alama kanunu.*

7 https://tr.wikipedia.org. – Türk Silahlı Kuvvetleri.

8 http://www.hurriyetdailynews.com. dtd 17.10.2014 and 10.12.2014 „Turkish Parliament approves paid

proportion of female volunteers in the army still seems to have room for improvement, which was only 3.1 % in 2007.

The quality of the soldiers, including their attitude towards the state and their motivation on duty, is a direct consequence of their education and training at home, in childcare facilities, schools, universities and in the army. It is difficult to correct possible previous wrong early impressions later in the army, whereas compulsory military service offers the chance to appeal to many young people and influence their attitude towards the state. A modern leadership style of the superiors and a comprehensive varied training contribute to strengthening the recruits' understanding of military service and also help to attract young volunteers for serving a longer period.

A major concern of the state must remain the social security of the soldier in the event of wounding and disability, including support for surviving dependents in the event of death. The relevant institutions are therefore of great importance. For example, the OYAK *(Ordu Yardımlaşma Kurumu* - Organisation for the Support of the Armed Forces), anchored in Law 205,[1] has existed under the responsibility of the Minister of Defence since 1961. With Law 5715, the state takes care of the treatment of sick soldiers,[2] with Law 4109 it takes care of the support of their needy families,[3] with Law 4341 it takes care of the treatment of needy families of team ranks and non-commissioned officers[4] free of charge. For the general population, the Civil Defence Law No. 7126 [5] applies.

Another social institution is the foundation "*Mehmetçik Vakfi*", established in 1982, i.e. the Foundation for the Turkish Soldier. The term probably refers to a soldier by the name of Mehmet, who is said to have fallen in Libya in 1912 and was then honored as *Şehit* (fallen religious fighter); his name was then generalized. The last lines of this book are supposed to be dedicated to him, especially to the conscript loyal Turkish soldier who had the least say in his fate and who sacrificed himself. A building of his own in the Anıtkabir mausoleum in Ankara, the Mehmetçik Tower/*Mehmetçik Kulesi*, is also dedicated to him. May posterity remember him, learn the necessary lessons from history and that the Turkish proverb dedicated to him remains true:

"At ölür meydan kalır Yiğit ölür şan kalır".	**"When a horse dies, a void remains When a hero dies, his honour remains".**

military service bill".

1 https://tr.wikipedia.org. – *Ordu Yardımlaşma Kurumu.* https://de.wikipedia.org OYAK.

2 *Türk Silahlı Kuvvetleri hasta besleme kanunu.*

3 *Asker ailerinden muhtaç olanlara yardım hakkında kanun.*

4 *Muhtaç erbaş ve er ailelerinin ücretsiz tedavisi hakkında kanun.*

5 *Sivil Savunma kanunu..*

BIBLIOGRAPHY

Primary sources

British Parliament. *Dardanelles Commission, First and Final Report,(* London: 1917/1919)
Bundesamt für Verfassungsschutz, *Die Arbeiterpartei Kurdistans – PKK* (Köln: 1996)
Cazgır. Yavuz *Lise Tarih 2* (Ankara: 2005)
Turkish General Staff *Canakkale Savaşı, Anıtları ve Şehitlikleri* (Ankara: 2007)

Secondary sources

Addül Hamid (II), Sultan *Sayaşı Hatıratım* (Istanbul: 1987)
Atatürk, Mustafa Kemal *Nutuk* speech 1927 *Der Weg zur Freiheit* und *Die nationale Revolution1919 – 1927; Band II Söylev 1920 – 1927* (Leipzig: 2003. and Ankara, 1989)
Cakmak, Fevzi *Birinci Dünya Savaşında Doğu Cephesi* (Ankara: 2005)
Callwell, C.E. *Die Tagebücher des Foreign Minister Sir Henry Wilson* (Stuttgart: Union Deutsche Verlagsanstalt, 1930)
Cebesoy, Ali Fuat *Milli Mücadele Hatıraları* (Istanbul: 2010)
Churchill, Winston *Die Weltkrise 1911 – 1918* (Zürich: Amstutz,1947)
Diyanet *Kur-ân-ı Kerîm Açıklamalı Meâli* (Ankara:2002)
Dönitz, Karl *Die Kreuzfahrten der Goeben und Breslau* Berlin: Ullstein, 1936)
Dunsterville, Lionel *The Adventures of Dunsterforce* (London: Edward Arnold, 1920)
Guepratte, P.E. *L'Expédition des Dardanelles 1914 – 1915* (Paris: Bayot, 1935)
Goltz,Colmar Freiherr von *Denkwürdigkeiten* (Berlin: Mittler, 1929)
Harington, Charles *Tim Harington looks back* (London: Murray, 1940)
Hedin, Sven *Bagdad, Babylon, Ninive* (Leipzig: Brockhaus, 1918)
Inönü, Ismet *Hatıralar 1864 – 1973* (Yenişehir:Ankara Bilgi, 1992)
Izzet *Denkwürdigkeiten des Marschaalls Izzet Pascha* (Leipzig: Koehler, 1927)
Jones & Raleigh *The War in the Air,* 7 vol. (Oxford: University, 1922 – 1937)
Kannengiesser, Hans *Gallipoli* (Wolfenbüttel: Melchior, 2012)
Karabekir, Kâzım *Türkiye'de ve Türk Ordusunda Almanlar* (Istanbul: Emre, 2001)
Kiesling, Hans von *Mit Feldmarschall von der Goltz in Mesopotamien und Persien* (Leipzig: Dieterich, 1922)
Kressenstein, Friedrich Kress von *Mit den Türken zum Suezkanal* (Berlin: Vorhut, 1938)
Lawrence, Thomas Edward *Die sieben Säulen der Weisheit* (Stuttgart : Europäischer Buchklub, 2005)
Lloyd George, David *War Memoirs* (London: Odhams, 1938)
Mackenzie, Compton *Gallipoli Memories (*London: Cassell, 1929)
Moberly, Frederick James *History of the Great War* 4 Vol. (London: His Majesty's Stat. Office, 1923 – 1927)
Moltke, Helmuth von *Briefe über Zustände und Begebenheiten in der Türkei aus den Jahren 1835 – 1839* (Heidelberg: Arndt, 2000)
Morgenthau, Henry *Ambassador Morgenthai's Story* (New York : Double Day, 1918)
Mukhtar, Mahmud Pascha *Meine Führung im Balkankriege 1912* (Berlin; Mittler, 1913)

NATO HQ Istanbul (NRDC-T) *Official Turkish Briefing on the History of Turkish Landforces* (Istanbul: 2005)
Official Turkish Briefing on the History of Turkish Armed Forces (Istanbul: 2005)
Nunn, Wilfred *Tigris Gunboats* (London: Melrose, 1932)
Orbay, Rauf *Cehennem Değirmeni* (Istanbul: Truva, 2004)
Papen, Franz *Der Wahrheit eine Gasse* (München: List, 1952)
Reinhardt, Klaus *KFOR – Streitkräfte für den Frieden* (Frankfurt am Main: Blazek & Bergmann, 2002)
Sanders, Liman von *Fünf Jahre Türkei* (London: Dalton House, 2015)
Serno, Erich *Ausbau, Organisation und Tätigkeit der Türkischen Luftstreitkräfte im 1. Welt-krieg* (Deutsches Bundesarchiv Koblenz, Msg. 1/231)
T.C. Genelkurmay Başkanlığı *Çanakkale Savaşı* (Ankara)
Townshend, Charles *My Campaign in Mesopotamia* (London: 1920)
Desert Hell (Cambridge: 2911)
Toynbee, Arnold Joseph *The Western Question in Greece and Turkey* (New York: 1970)
Tröbst, Hans *Soldatenblut* (Leipzig: 1925)
Tröndle, Dirk *Mustafa Kemal Atatürk* (Zürich: 2012)
Trumpener, Ulrich *Germany and the Ottoman Empire 1914 – 1918* (Princeton: Legacy Library,1968)
Tuncay, Deniz *Türk uçak üretimi* (2004)

Secondary literature

A

Akçam, Taner *A Shameful Act* (London: Constable, 1999)
Alp, Tekin *Türkismus und Pantürkismus* (Weimar: Kiepenheuer1915)
Arfa, Hassan *The Kurds* (London: Oxford university, 1966)
Armstrong, Herold *Turkey in travail* (London: John Lane, 1925)

B

Babinger, Franz *Mehmed der Eroberer und seine Zeit* (München: Bruckmann, 1953)
Baron d'Armagnac *Nezib et Beyrout 1833 – 1841* (Paris : Laisné, 1844)
Bayar, Celal *Atatürk'ten Hatıralar (*Istanbul: 1995)
Baykara, Tuncer *Milli Mücadele* (Ankara : Kültür ve Turizm Bakanlığı, 1985)
Bekaroğlu, Mehmet *Siyasetin Sonu* (Ankara: Elips Kitap, 2007)
Benedikt, Heinrich *Der Pascha – Graf Alexander von Bonneval 1675 – 1747* (Graz:Bohlaus, 1959)
Birand, Mehmet Ali *Shirts of Steel* (London: Tauris, 1991) *30 Heisse Tage* (Köln: Önel, 1999)
Böhm, Walter *IFOR – Das Schwert der NATO in Bosnien* (Illertissen: Flugzeug GmbH, 1997)
Brauns & Kiechle *PKK* (Stuttgart: Schmetterling, 2010)
Bruinessen, Martin *Agha, Scheich und Staat* (Berlin: Parabolis, 2003)

C

Cadalvene, Edourd de *Deux Années de l'histoire d'Orient 1839 – 1840* (Paris : 1840)
Chack, Paul *On se bat sur mer* (Paris : 1928)
Clausewitz, Carl von *Vom Kriege* (Bonn: Dümmlers,1980)

D

Diyanet *Kur'ân-ı Kerîm Açıklamalı Meâli* (Ankara: 2002)
Demirhan, Pertev *Generalfeldmarschall Colmar Freiherr von der Goltz* (Göttingen: Göttinger Verlagsanstalt,1960)

E

EADS *Askeri Havacılıkta 100 Yıllık Türk/Alman Işbırlığı – 100 Jahre Deutsch/Türkische Zusammenarbeit in der Militärischen Luftfahrt* (Ankara: Mönch, 2011)
Erickson, Edward *Ottoman Army Effectiveness in World War I* (London: Routledge,2007)
Ordered to die (Westport: Greenwood Press, 2001)
- *Gallipoli* (Bamsley: Pen & Sword Military,2010)

F

Faroqhi, Suraiya *Geschichte des Osmanischen Reiches* (München: Beck, 2006)
Firuz, Ahmad *The Turkish Experiment in Democracy* (London: Hurst, 1977)
Foerster, Wolfgang *General Feldmarschall Colmar Freiherr von der Goltz* (Berlin: Mittler,1929)

G

Gehrke, Ulrich *Persien in der deutschen Orientpolitik während des ersten Weltkrieges* (Stuttgart:Kohlhammer, 1960)
Göyünç, Nejat *Atatürk ve Milli Mücadele* (Konya: 1984)
Goltz, Colmar Freiherr von *Der Thessalische Krieg und die Türkische Armee* (Berlin: Mittler, 1898)
Griehl, Manfred *Zeppelin- The German Airship Story* (London: Arms and Armour, 1990)
Gottschlich, Jürgen *Beihilfe zum Völkermord (*Berlin: Links, 2015)
Gülbeyaz, Halil *Mustafa Kemal Atatürk* (Berlin:Porthaus, 2003)
Gust, Wolfgang *Das Imperium der Sultane* (Hamburg: Nikol. 2007)

H

Hassenstein, Wilhelm *Das Feuerwerkerbuch von 1429, Erstdruck 1529* (München, Verlag Der deutschen Technik, 1941)
Hostler, Charles *The Turks of Central Asia* (London: WestportConnecticut1991)
Hummelberger, Walter *Wiens erste Belagerung durch die Türken 1929* (Wien; Österreichischer Bundesverlag, 1983)
Huntington, Samuel *Kampf der Kulturen* (Hamburg: Spiegel, 2007)

I

Imhoff, Karl *Die türkische Heeresmacht und ihre Entwicklung* (Halle: Gebauer – Schwetschke, 1916)
Inalcik, Halil *The Ottoman Empire* (London: Variorum, 1978)

J

Jordan, Karl *Der ägyptisch – türkische Krieg* (Zürich: Börsig, 1923)
Jorga, Nicolae *Geschichte des Osmanischen Reiches,* 7 vol. (Gotha: F.A. Perthes. 1997)
Jung & Mötz *Die KuK Streitkräfte im Ersten Weltkrieg 1914 – 1918* (Wien: Stöhr. 1995)

K

Kedourie, Sylvia *75 Years of the Turkish Republik* (London: Portland, 2000)
Keten, Ismet *The Ottoman Monograms – Tughra* (Ankara:2002)
Kieser, Hans Lukas *Die Armenische Frage und die Schweiz 1896 .- 1923* (Zürich: Chronos, 1999)
Kinross, Lord *The Ottoman Centuries* (London: Cape, 1977)
Atatürk (London: Weidenfeld & Nicolson, 1964)
Klever, Ulrich *Sultane, Janitscharen und Wesire* (Bayreth: Hestia, 1990)
Korn, Wolfgang *Schienen für den Sultan* (Köln: 2009)
Krämer, Gudrun *Geschichte des Islam)* (München: Beck, 2005)
Kraus *Die Fahrten der Goeben* Berlin: Ullstein, 1917)
Kreiser, Klaus *Kleine Geschichte der Türkei* (Stuttgart: Reclam, 2009)
- *Atatürk* (München: Beck, 2008)
- *Der Osmanische Staat 1300 – 1922* (München: Oldenbourg, 2008)
Kurter, Ajun *Türk Hava Kuvvetleri Cilt I – V (*Ankara: Air Force Command 2006)
Kreutel, Richard *Kara Mustafa vor Wien 1683* (Graz: Styria, 1982)
Kritobulos von Imbros *Mehmet II erobert Konstantinopel* (Graz: Styria, 1986)

L

Larcher, Maurice *La guerre turque dans la guerre mondiale* (Paris ; Berger – Levrault. 1926)
Lewis, Bernard *The Emergence of modern Turkey* (London: Oxford University, 1961)
Lisec, Eckhard *Der Unabhängigkeitskrieg und die Gründung der Türkei* (Berlin: Miles, 2016)
- *Der Völkermord an den Armeniern* (Berlin: Miles, 2017)
- *Die Türkische Armee* (Berlin: Miles,2018)
Lodemann & Pohl *Die Bagdadbahn* (Mainz: Hase & Koehler, 1988)
Lorey, Hermann *Der Krieg in den türkischen Gewässern I, II* (Berlin: Mittler, 1928, 1938)
Luther, Martin *Vom Kriege widder die Türcken* (Wittenberg: Hans Weiss, 1529)

M

Mc Munn &Falls *Military Operations* (London: Majesty's Stationary Office,1928)
Manstein, Erich von *Verlorene Siege* (Bonn: Bernard & Graefe, 2011)
Mantran, Robert *Osmanlı Imperatorluğu Tarihi I, II* (Istanbul: Say, 1992)
Matschke, Klaus Peter *Das Kreuz und der Halbmond* (Darmstadt: Wissenschaftliche Buchgesellschaft, 2004)
Meier Welcker, Hans *Seeckt* (Frankfurt Main: Bernard & Graefe, 1967)
Mohr, Anton *Der Kampf um Türkisch – Asien – Die Bagdadbahn* (Meißen: Klinkicht, 1919)
Moltke, Helmuth von *Der russisch – türkische Feldzug in der europäischen Türkei 1828 – 1829* (Berlin: Reimer, 1877)
Moukbil, Bey *La campagne de l'Irak 1914 – 1918* (Paris : Berger –Levrault, 1933)
Mühlmann, Carl *Das deutsch – türkische Waffenbündnis im Weltkriege* (Leipzig: Koehler, 1940)
Deutschland und die Türkei 1913 – 1914 (Berlin: Rothschild, 1929)
Murphey, Rhoads *Ottoman Warfare 1500 – 1700* (London: Routledge, 2005)

N

Naso, Eckart von *Moltke* (Berlin: Krüger, 1937)
Neulen, Hans Werner *Feldgrau in Jerusalem* (München: Universitas, 2002)
Neumann, Adrian *Die Türkei* (München: List, 1990)

Nicolle, David *Die Osmanen – 600 Jahre Islamisches Weltreich* (Wien: Tosa, 2008)
NN *Der Griechisch – türkische Krieg des Jahres 1897* (Berlin: Schall & Grund, 1897)
NN *Islam* (Köln: Honos)
Norwich, John *Byzanz* (Berlin: Ullstein, 2006)
Nowarra, Heinz *50 Jahre deutsche Luftwaffe* (Berlin: Verfasser, 1961)
Nutku, Emullah *Alte Kameraden* (Frankfurt am Main: Özkan, 1970)
Nye, Roger P. *The Military in Turkish Politics 1960 – 1973* (Ann Arbor: 1974)

O

Özakman, Turgut *Şu Çılgın Türkler* (Ankara: BILGI YAYINEVI, 2008)
Özbudun, Ergun *The role of the Military in recent Turkish politics* (Harvard University: 1966)
Okyar, Fethi *Üç Devirde bir adam* (Istanbul: Tercünan, 1980)

P

Palmer, J.A.B. *The origin of the Janissaries* (Manchester: John Rylands, 1953)
Paret, Rudi *Der Koran* (Stuttgart: Kohlhammer, 2010)
Patton, George (Jr.) *The Defense of Gallipoli* , Mil. Staff Study (Fort Shafter: 1936)
Pears, Edwin *The destruction of the Greek Empire and the story of the capture of Constantinople by the Turks* (New York: Greenwood, 1968)
Piri Reis *Kitab-ı Bahriye 1521* (Istanbul: Historical Research Foundation)
Poenicke, Herbert *Die Hedschas- und Bagdadbahn* (Düsseldorf: Vodi, 1958)
Pomiankowski, Joseph *Der Zusammenbruch des Osmanischen Reiches* (Graz: Akademischer Dr. & Verlagsanstalt. 1969)
Pope, Dudley *Feuerwaffen* (Bern: Scherz, 1965)
Poulton, Hugh *Top Hat, Grey Wulf and Crescent* (New York: University, 1997)

R

Rabenau, Friedrich *Seeckt* (Leipzig: Hase, 1941)
Raschid, El Harun alias Hintersatz, Wilhelm *Marschall Liman von Sanders Pascha* (Berlin: Eisenschmidt, 1932)
Richter, Heinz *Die Griechen im Osmanischen Reich 1913 – 1923* (Wiesbaden: , Harrassowitz 2018)
- *Die türkischen Meerengen in der internationalen Politik* Wiesbaden: Harrassowitz 2018)
- *Gallipoli 1915* (Mainz: Rutzen, 2013)

Robins, Philip *Suits and Uniforms* (Seattle: University, 2013)
Robinson, Richard *The first Turkish Republic* (Harvard: University, 1963)
Rohrbach, Paul *Die Bagdadbahn* (Berlin: Wiegandt & Grieben, 1911)
Runciman, Steven *Die Eroberung von Konstantinopel 1453* (München: Beck, 1990)
Ruşen, Eşref *Anafartalar Kumandanı Mustafa Kemal ile Mülâkat* (Istanbul: Devlet Matbaası, 1930)

S

Sabis, Ali Ihsan *Birinci Dünya Harbi* (Istanbul: Nehir Yayınları, 1991)
Sauer, Wilhelm *Admiral Souchon auf großer Fahrt* (Reutlingen: Enßlin & Laiblin, 1940)
Scharlipp, Wolfgang Ekkehard *Die frühen Türken in Zentralasien* (Darmstadt: WBG,2011)
Scherer, Friedrich *Adler und Halbmond* (Paderborn: Schöningh, 2000)

Scherff, Mauricio *Auf Kriegspfaden im Lande des Halbmonds* (in Hundertmark „Die Flieger“) (1914)
Schimmel, Annemarie *Die Religion des Islam* (Stuttgart: Reclam, 1990)
Schmauder, Michael *Die Hunnen* (Darmstadt: WBG, 2009)
Schmitterlöw, Bernhard von *Aus dem Leben des Gdeneralfeldmarschalls Freiherr von der Goltz Pascha* (Berlin: R. S. Rehler1926)
Schramm, Wilhelm von *Clausewitz – Leben und Werk* (Dießen: Huber, 1981)
Schulze, Carl *IFOR: Allied Forces in Bosnia* (in Europe Militaria No. 22) (London: 1996)
Shaw, Stanford, J. The Ottoman Empire in World War 1, Vol. 2 (Ankara: 2008)
Sık, Ahmet *000 Kitap – Dokunan Yanar* (Istanbul: 2011)
Sorgun, M. *Taylan Bitmeyen Savaş* (Ankara: 1972)
Sphrantzes, Georgius *Die letzten Tage von Konstantinopel* (Graz: Styria, 1973)
Steel, Nigel *Gallipoli* (London: Pen & Sword. 1999)
Steinbach, Udo *Geschichte der Türkei* (München: Beck, 2003)
Steuber, Werner *Jıldırım* (Oldenburg: Stalling, 1926)
Supf, Peter *Das Buch der deutschen Fluggeschichte, Vol. II* (Stuttgart: Drei Brunnen Verlag, 1958)

T

Tayareci. com INTERNET files on Turkish air force
Thomas, Lowell *Ritter der Tiefe* (Gütersloh: Bertelsmann, 1932)

U

Ünal, Mustaf Coşar *Counterterrorism in Turkey* (London: Taylor & Francis, 2012)
Uyar & Erickson *A military history of the Ottomans* (Santa Barbara: Praeger, 2009)

W

Wallach, Jehuda *Anatomie einer Militärhilfe 1835 – 1919* (Düsseldorf: Droste, 1976)
Germany and the Middle East (München: Saur, 1975)
Wagner, Reinhold *Moltke und Mühlbach zusammen unter dem Halbmond 1837 – 1839)* (Berlin: Lulu PR, 1893)
Weiher, Gerhard *Militär und Entwicklung in der Türkei 1945 – 1973* (Opladen: VS Verlag, 1978)
Wiegand & Wiegand *Halbmond im letzten Viertel* (München: Bruckmann, 1970)
Wolf, Klaus *Gallipoli* (Bonn: Reort, 2008)

Y

Yalman, Ahmet Emin *Kurtuluş Savaşında Anadolu Ekonomisi 1919 – 1922* (Ankara: 1998)
\- *Turkey in the World War* (New Haven: Forgotten Books1930)
Yavuz, M. Hakarı *The Emergence of a new Turkey* (Salt Lake City: 2010)
Yılmazata, Mehmet *Die Bagdadbahn* (Marburg: Tectum, 2013)

Z

Zimmerer, Heinrich *Die neue Türkei in ihrer Entwicklung 1908 – 1915* (Leipzig: 1915)
Zwehl, Hans von *Falkenhayn* (Berlin: Mittler, 1926)
Zürcher, Erik *Turkey – A modern History* (London: Tauris, 2005).

INDEX OF NAMES

S, Ş

T

U-Z

Band 60 **Heinz A. Richter,**
Griechenland 1950-1974. Zwischen Demokratie und Diktatur (2013) 600 Seiten, 125 Fotos, Hardcover, gebunden, € 49, ISBN 978-3-447-06908-3

Band 61 **Mihailo Popovic,**
Historische Geographie und Digital Humanities. Eine Fallstudie zum spätbyzantinischen und osmanischen Makedonien (2013) ca. 300 Seiten, 33 Abbildungen, 44 Karten, 8°, hard cover, ISBN 978-3-938646-49-6, € 32.-

Band 62 **Joachim Franz, Rosmarie Günther und Reinhard Stupperich (Hrsg.)**
„Ein Wald von Statuen“ Kolloquium zum 20jährigen Bestehen der Antikensaal-Galerie in Mannheim und zur Begründung der Kurpfälzer Abguss-Sammlung vor 300 Jahren 300 Seiten, zahlreiche Abbildungen, Hardcover, gebunden, ISBN 978-3-447-10302-2, € 37.-

Band 63 **Harald Gilbert,**
Das besetzte Kreta 1941-1945 (2015) 404 Seiten, 47 sw und 8 farbige Abbildungen, 1 Landkarte, Hardcover, gebunden, € 49, ISBN 978-3-447-10186-8

Band 64 **Harry Cliadakis** (ed. Heinz Richter)
Fascism in Greece (2014) 147 pages, 34 photos, hard cover, threadbound, ISBN 978-3-447-10188-2, € 39.-

Band 65,1 **Heinz A. Richter**
Krieg im Südosten I, Gallipoli 1915 (2014) 340 Seiten, 120 Fotos, 17 Karten, 1 Faltkarte, gebunden, € 42, ISBN 978-3-447-10118-9

Band 65,2 ***Krieg im Südosten II, Makedonien 1915-1918*** (2014) 250 Seiten, 91 Fotos, 4 Karten, gebunden, € 35, ISBN 978-3-447-10249-0

Band 66 ***Von Mainz nach Kreta im Winter 1942-43. Das Reisetagebuch des "Künstlersoldaten" Rudo Schwarz.*** (2015) 150 Seiten, 91 Seiten mit Reproduktionen des Tagebuchs und von Skizzen, 51 Fotos, Hardcover, gebunden, ISBN 978-3-447-10304-6, € 32.- (ed. Heinz Richter)

Band 67,1 **Heinz A. Richter, *Geschichte Griechenlands im 20. Jahrhundert,*** *Band 1: 1900-1939*, (2015) 350 Seiten, 4 Karten, Hardcover, gebunden, 40 Euro, ISBN 978-3-447-10396-5

Band 67,2 **Heinz A. Richter, *Geschichte Griechenlands im 20. Jahrhundert,*** *Band 2: 1939-2004*, (2015) 467 Seiten, 9 Karten, Hardcover, gebunden, 49Euro, ISBN 978-3-447-10398-5

Band 68 **Heinz A. Richter *Griechenland 1915-1917 im Spiegel russischer Akten*** (2016) 118 Seiten, Hardcover, 28 Euro, 2015 ISBN 978-3-447-10612-2

Band 69 **Heinz A. Richter *Griechenland 1945-46. Die britische Intervention*** (2016) 456 Seiten, 39 Fotos, gebunden, 49 Euro, ISBN 978-3-447-10533-0

Band 70 **Heinz A. Richter** (ed.), *Griechenland 1942-43. Erinnerungen von Elisabeth und Konstantinos Logothetopoulos* (2015) 320 Seiten, 3 Abbildungen, Hardcover, 28 Euro, ISBN 978-3-447-10460-9

Band 71 **Johannes Fouquet** und **Lydia Gaitanou**, ***Im Schatten der Alten? Ideal und Lebenswirklichkeit im römischen Griechenland*** (2016) 193 Seiten, zahlreiche Karten und Fotos, gebunden, 40 Euro, ISBN 978-3-447-10450-0

Band 72 **Heinz A. Richter *Der griechisch-türkische Krieg 1919-1922*** (2016) 222 Seiten, 132 Fotos, 18 Karten, 1 Faltkarte, gebunden, 30 Euro, ISBN 978-3-447-10656-6

Band 73 **Heinz A. Richter *The Greek-Turkish War 1919-1922*** (2016) 211 pages, 132 photos, 18 maps, 1 folded map, hardcover, 30 Euro, ISBN 978-3-447-10671-9

Band 74 **Heinz A. Richter, *Mythen und Legenden in der griechischen Zeitgeschichte*** (2016) 116 Seiten, 19,80 Euro, ISBN 978-3-447-10703-7

Band 76 **Heinz A. Richter**, ***Hellas und Zypern in meinem Leben. Erinnerungen eines Zeithistorikers*** (2017), 236 Seiten, 56 Tafeln mit 128 Fotos, 30 Euro, ISBN 978-3-447-10846-1

Band 77 **Heinz A. Richter**, ***Geschichte der griechischen Linken***, 560 Seiten, 99 Fotos, gebunden, 50 Euro, 2017; ISBN 978-3-447-10846-1

Band 78 **Harald Gilbert**, ***Der Krieg in der Ägäis 1943-1944***, 340 Seiten Text, 32 Seiten Fotos, 16-24 Seiten Karten im Text, Hardcover, xx Euro, (2017); ISBN 978-3-447-10913-0

Band 79 **Heinz A. Richter**, ***Geschichte der zypriotischen Linken,*** 248 Seiten, 16 Tafeln mit 47 Fotos, gebunden, 30 Euro, ISBN 978-3-447-10867-6

Band 80 **Heinz A. Richter**, ***Die türkischen Meerengen in der internationalen Politik 1900-1917***, 300 Seiten, 32 Tafeln mit 77 Fotos, 7 Karten, 1 herausnehmbare Faltkarte, gebunden, 40 Euro, ISBN 978-3--447-10915-4

Band 81 **Vaios Kalogrias**, ***Die Sicherheitsbataillone 1943/44. Hitlers griechische Armee***. xxx Seiten, xx Tafeln mit xx Fotos, xx Karten, gebunden, ca. xx Euro, erscheint im Herbst 2019; ISBN 978-3-447-10917-8

Band 82 **Caroline M. Fischer, *Das Land der Griechen ... gefunden. Mein Leben im griechischen Alltag seit 1979. Erinnerungen,*** *Gedanken, Impressionen.* xxx Seiten, xx Tafeln mit xx Fotos, xx Karten, gebunden, ca. xx Euro, ISBN 978-3-447-10951-2

Band 83 **H. Richter - S. Dordanas - V. Kalogrias**, ***Ernst von Falkenhausen. Tagebuch des deutschen Militärattachés in Athen 1914 - 1916*** xxx Seiten, xx Tafeln mit xx Fotos, xx Karten, gebunden, ca. xx Euro,; ISBN 978-3-447-10952-9

Band 84 **Heinz A. Richter,** ***Das Osmanische Reich im Ersten Weltkrieg bis zum Friedensschluss 1924,*** 274 Seiten, 32 Tafeln mit 103 Fotos, 32 Karten, 1 herausnehmbare Faltkarte, gebunden, 40 Euro, ISBN 978-3-447-11038-9

Band 85 **Heinz A. Richter,** ***The Ottoman Empire in WWI until the Peace in 1923*** 256 pages, 32 plates with over 100 photos, 32 maps, 1 folded map, hard cover, 40 Euro, ISBN 978-3-447-11045-7

Band 86 **Heinz A. Richter,** ***Die Griechen im Osmanischen Reich 1913-1923. Ihre Verfolgung und Vertreibung*** **198** Seiten, 32 Tafeln mit über 60 Fotos, 6 Karten, 1 herausnehmbar Faltkarte, hard cover, 40 Euro, ISBN 978-3-447-11131-7

Band 87 **Heinz A. Richter**, ***The Greeks in the Ottoman Empire 1913-1923. Their Persecution and Expulsion*** 188 pages, 32 plates with over 60 photos, 6 maps, one folded map in the back, hard cover, 40 Euro, ISBN 978-3-447-11150-8

Band 88 **Heinz A. Richter** (ed.), *Aspekte neugriechischer Geschichte* 132 Seiten, viele Fotos, hard cover, 30 Euro, ISBN 978-3-447-11132-4

Band 89 **Heinz A. Richter,** ***Modern Greek Myths*** 120 pages, hard cover, 19,80 Euro, ISBN 978-3-447--11165-2

Band 90 **Heinz A. Richter**, ***German-Greek Relation 1940-1960 and the Merten Affair*** 108 pages text, 28 photos on 12 pages, hard cover, 20; ISBN 978-3-447-11177-5

Band 91 **Heinz A. Richter,** ***Greece 1936-1946 Events and People*** 192 pages, numerous photos in the text, hard cover, 35 Euro, ISBN 978-3-447-11241-3

Band 92 **Heinz A. Richter**, **Greece 1947-1967 From Civil War to the Putsch on April 21, 1967** 190 pages, hard cover, 30 Euro,ISBN 978-3-447-11255-0

Band 93 **Heinz A. Richter**, **Operation Mercury the Occupation of Crete in May 1961** ca. 400 pages, hard cover, 45 Euro,ISBN 978-3-447-11323-6

Band 94 **Heinz A. Richter, Griechische Verteidigungsanlagen 1941. Die Metaxas-Linie**, 100 Seiten, 51 Fotos. 19 Karten, gebunden, 30 Euro ISBN 978-3-447-11378-6

Band 95 **Heinz A. Richter, Gallipoli 1915. The War in the Southeast 1** about 270 pages, 121 photos, 17 maps, 1 folded map, hard cover, 45 Euro ISBN 978-3-447-11393-9

Band 96 **Heinz A. Richter, Macedonia 1914-1918. The War in the Southeast 2** about 240 pages, 98 photos, 4 maps, hard cover, 39 Euro ISBN 978-3-447-11422-6

Band 97 **Heinz A. Richter, Greece in World War II** about 440 pages, 45 photos, 17 maps, hard cover, 45 Euro ISBN 978-3-447-11443-3

Band 98 **Eckhard Lisec, Tukish Armed Forces from Early History to Modern Times** about 120 pages, 45 photos, 17 maps, hard cover, 30 Euro ISBN 978-3-447-11443-3